SOVIET SELF-HATRED

SOVIET SELF-HATRED

The Secret Identities of Postsocialism
in Contemporary Russia

Eliot Borenstein

CORNELL UNIVERSITY PRESS   ITHACA AND LONDON

Copyright © 2023 by Cornell University

All rights reserved. Except for brief quotations in a review, this book, or parts thereof, must not be reproduced in any form without permission in writing from the publisher. For information, address Cornell University Press, Sage House, 512 East State Street, Ithaca, New York 14850. Visit our website at cornellpress.cornell.edu.

First published 2023 by Cornell University Press

Library of Congress Cataloging-in-Publication Data

Names: Borenstein, Eliot, 1966– author.
Title: Soviet self-hatred : the secret identities of postsocialism in contemporary Russia / Eliot Borenstein.
Description: Ithaca : Cornell University Press, 2023. | Includes bibliographical references and index.
Identifiers: LCCN 2022034393 (print) | LCCN 2022034394 (ebook) | ISBN 9781501769870 (hardcover) | ISBN 9781501769887 (paperback) | ISBN 9781501769900 (pdf) | ISBN 9781501769894 (epub)
Subjects: LCSH: National characteristics, Russian. | Russians—Attitudes. | Post-communism—Russia (Federation) | Russia (Federation)—Social conditions—1991–
Classification: LCC DK510.34 .B665 2023 (print) | LCC DK510.34 (ebook) | DDC 947.086—dc23/eng/20220816
LC record available at https://lccn.loc.gov/2022034393
LC ebook record available at https://lccn.loc.gov/2022034394

For Joan
The mother I never knew I needed

"What does it feel like . . . to end up in what's essentially another country?"
"It feels as if there are new complications."

Eugene Vodolazkin, *The Aviator*

Contents

Acknowledgments	ix
Introduction: Postsocialism and the Legacy of Shame	1
1. Zombie Sovieticus: The Descent of Soviet Man	24
2. The Rise and Fall of Sovok	40
3. Just a Guy Named Vasya	60
4. Whatever Happened to the New Russians?	80
5. Rich Man's Burden	96
6. Russian Orc: The Evil Empire Strikes Back	121
Conclusion: Russian Self-Hatred	154
Notes	163
Works Cited	171
Index	183

Acknowledgments

In recent years, I've had the obnoxious good fortune of writing several books at once, which has many advantages: it keeps me from getting too bored, frustrated, or overly invested in a single project. But it also makes keeping track of whom to thank all the more complicated: didn't I already express my gratitude to that friend in the front matter to Project A? Were they really involved in my thought process for Project B? As I try to reconstruct my emotional and intellectual debts, I start to wish I'd used one of those programs that helps lawyers keep track of billable hours.

Still, I can't say this makes me long for a world in which we punch the clock for emotional labor. So, with a few exceptions, I'm going to round up the usual suspects: my colleagues in the Russian and Slavic Studies Department and the Jordan Center for the Advanced Study of Russia (Irina Belodedova, Rossen Djagalov, Bruce Grant, Boris Groys, Mikhail Iampolski, Ilya Kliger, Katya Korsounskaya, Yanni Kotsonis, Anne Lounsbery, Evelina Mendelevich, Anne O'Donnell, Leydi Rothman, Sasha Shpitalnik, Josh Tucker, Maya Vinokour) and in the Office of Global Programs (Janet Alperstein, Zvi Ben-Dor Benite, Peter Holm, Linda Mills, Nancy Morrison, Marianne Petit, William Pruitt) at New York University.

Once again, Deborah Martinsen caught more typos than I could ever imagine making, and I am sorry she is not around to see the final product.

I'd also like to thank the participants in the 2016 "Radiant Futures: Russian Fantasy and Science Fiction" conference at the Jordan Center, where I presented a version of the Russian Orcs chapter: Tony Anemone, Anindita Banerjee, Jacob Emery, Sibelan Forrester, Helena Goscilo, Yvonne Howell, Amanda Lerner, Mark Lipovetsky, and Maya Vinokour.

A portion of chapter 1 appeared, in different form, as "Our Borats, Our Selves: Yokels and Cosmopolitans on the Global Stage," *Slavic Review* 67, no. 1 (2008): 1–7. A version of part of this chapter was presented at the Mid-Atlantic Slavic Conference in 2008. The first draft of the entire manuscript was serialized on the Jordan Center blog and on eliotborenstein.net.

I never cease to marvel at my good fortune in working with Cornell University Press, now for the fourth time. My editor, Mahinder Kingra, has shepherded this manuscript though more drafts than I care to recall and has yet to make a suggestion that was not an improvement. I also had the great pleasure of once again working with Carolyn J. Pouncy, queen of all proofreaders.

My always supportive family was around for the revisions of this book in ways that I had not expected. During the long months of the early COVID-19 pandemic, we spent much more time than usual in the same room, albeit left to our own (digital) devices. Franny, Lev, and Louie, I apologize for all the times I didn't hear you when my headphones were drowning you out with white noise. Next time, you should probably text me.

All translations are my own, except when indicated otherwise.

SOVIET SELF-HATRED

Introduction

POSTSOCIALISM AND THE LEGACY OF SHAME

Whatever motivations one might ascribe to the leaders in the Kremlin, it is safe to say that Moscow is unlikely to launch an attack on Voronezh. Voronezh, an urban provincial capital in Central Russia, is the thirteenth most populous city in the Russian Federation, with no significant ethnic tensions or separatist movements. Why, then, has the notion of bombing Voronezh been a perennial Russian meme since 2008?

Urban folklore points back to Russia's brief war with Georgia that year, in support of the breakaway region of South Ossetia. At the time, an unnamed Voronezh city councilman supposedly complained that the money allocated by the federal government for the reconstruction of bomb-ravaged South Ossetia was three times the sum given to the Voronezh region for three years: "Why don't they bomb Voronezh instead? At least then we could build decent roads." The fact that no one has ever verified the quotation hardly matters; it took on a life of its own, popping up whenever conditions seemed right (Dudukina). When the United States imposed sanctions on the Russian Federation in 2013, the Duma responded with a ban on US adoptions of Russian orphans, thereby reviving the meme's use. More recently, "bombing Voronezh" has been invoked to describe the government's moves to isolate Russia from the global Internet. Whenever it looks like the Russian government is punishing its own people for perceived foreign slights, the skies over Voronezh are filled with metaphorical munitions.

"Bombing Voronezh" would sound pathological if it weren't so obviously satirical. The point is not about a mythical eternal Russian masochism or even about the state's hostility toward its own people. Rather, the target is a state apparatus that is so preoccupied with postimperial overreach and lost great-power status that it blithely wastes resources on projects that prop up national prestige on the country's (former) borders rather than address the more pressing (and more boring) demands of day-to-day governing. "Bombing Voronezh" points in the direction of a compensatory project—namely, the reconstruction of a communal identity in the aftermath of Soviet state socialism.

"Bombing Voronezh" combines the two central themes of this study: the reconfiguration of a collective selfhood for a postsocialist world and the legacy of self-hatred. The collapse of the Soviet Union left its former constituent republics with multiple identity crises. In its last years, the USSR was losing its very reason for being (communist ideology); what did it mean to build a new country on the Union's ruins? As the legal successor to the Soviet Union, not to mention the de facto first among fifteen equals, the newly constituted Russian Federation did not have the luxury of casting the USSR as an occupying force that had finally been cast out. Instead, the Soviet legacy was a source of both pride and shame. The emerging discourses of Russianness spent the first three Soviet decades oscillating between a rhetoric of inferiority and an aggressive response verging on self-aggrandizement.

Many of the more salient geopolitical aspects of this question have been widely explored in the scholarly literature. These include the tensions between a blood-and-soil-based nationalism and a multinational, resurgent imperialism; the relationship between Russia and the other former Soviet republics (the Near Abroad); the emphasis on Russian Orthodoxy as a "state-forming" institution; and the search for a new Russian "national idea."[1] The present study shifts the emphasis from politics to affect by focusing attention on the development of identity discourses around emotionally charged imaginary categories.

Most of the identity constructs examined here are not meant to describe the entire nation, population, or commonwealth (at least, not always) but constitute the imaginary identities that Russians have been trying on for the past few decades, often by projecting them onto discrete, sometimes despised, segments of the population. In response to the profound sense of displacement associated with the Soviet collapse, identities are continually contested and renegotiated, whether on the level of state television and media, speculative fiction about Russia's history and its missed alternatives, online communities, or urban folklore. This is a process of imaginative identity formation—alienating one subgroup from the general population as a means of exploring the larger question of Russian communal selfhood—whose frequent result is the identification of Russian subgroups that distill a sense of pride or shame, or even both at the same time.[2]

This identity crisis is clearly linked to the destruction of the USSR, which is experienced as the decline and fall of Russia as a great power. Russian discourses surrounding the loss of great-power status have been treated quite productively in terms of aphasia and despair, trauma, and nostalgia, while the various attempts to process and reinscribe the Soviet cultural legacy fit well within Mark Lipovetsky's notion of the "post-sots."[3] But for my purposes, contested Russian identities in the wake of the Soviet collapse are best balanced on a simple axis of pride and shame. Pride rested on the country's cultural, industrial, and scientific accomplishments; its defeat of Nazi Germany; and the strength of Soviet Union's role as one of the two great superpowers. Shame came from the recognition of the USSR's crimes against its own people, its weakness as a guarantor of consumer comforts, its suppression of dissent, and, for lack of a better word, the "uncoolness" of its mass culture, consumer culture, and fashion when compared to the West. This shame would only be exacerbated by the miserable state of the Russian Federation in the 1990s: crime-ridden, impoverished, and dependent on its former rivals for assistance that, often as not, seemed to only make things worse.

The Roots of Self-Hatred

My search for a framework to understand these phenomena led me to studies on minority identities, this despite the fact that, whatever the iteration of Russian statehood, "Russians" are clearly a majority. But, as is the case with Serbs in the former Yugoslavia, numerical majority (or, failing that, plurality) is not a guarantor of the comforts usually associated with majority identity—that is, the ability to think of one's own identity as unmarked or neutral, as white people tend to do in the United States (Jovic). As explanations for why confidence in the Soviet Union eroded in the 1980s, replaced by despair in the 1990s, two ethnic studies models suggest themselves: self-hatred and melancholia.

As a concept, self-hatred has been most clearly elaborated as a phenomenon within the Jewish community. Sander Gilman's landmark 1990 study, *Jewish Self-Hatred*, argues that the phenomenon is the result of "outsiders' acceptance of the mirage of themselves generated by their reference group—that group in society which they see as defining them—as a reality" (2).

Gilman identifies a key mechanism in self-hatred in the isolation of a particular subgroup within the community of outsiders that can bear the entire burden of "otherness," allowing, in this case, the "good" Jews to feel unsullied by ethnic slander: "the quality ascribed to them as the Other is then transferred to the new Other found within the group that those in power have designated as Other" (4).

Jewish self-hatred is a controversial notion, most notably because of its use by some in the Jewish community against fellow Jews who criticize Israel.

Paul Reitter, in *On the Origins of Jewish Self-Hatred*, notes the "sense that today the phrase 'Jewish self-hatred' can serve only as a smear" (121). But even beyond the phrase's political afterlife, Reitter, in his critical genealogy of the phenomenon, shows both its productivity and its limits. Polemicizing with Shulamit Volkov, he finds both her and Gilman to be too restrictive in their understanding of the term: "Why shouldn't the 'hatred' in 'Jewish self-hatred' refer also to an animus that played itself out more fruitfully and incisively?" (123). And why must Volkov insist on the purity of this singular emotion: "The 'more typical' mix of 'shame,' 'disgust,' and 'despair' shouldn't count, according to Volkov" (124). Though Reitter does not approach the question from this vantage point, his book is a reminder that discussions of Jewish self-hatred usually treat emotions in general, and hatred in particular, as settled questions. What happens when we bring affect theory into the mix?

In her 2004 book, *The Cultural Politics of Emotions*, Sara Ahmed investigates the "sociality of emotions," the way in which emotions constitute and are constituted by collective bodies such as the nation (8). Among the many affective states she discusses are two that are particularly important for reconsidering the concept of self-hatred, as well as its potential relevance to the post-Soviet context: hatred and shame.

According to Ahmed, conventional understandings of hatred are inadequate when it comes to understanding the relationship between self and other: "Rather than assuming that hate involves pushing what is undesirable within the self onto others, we could ask: *Why is it that hate feels like it comes from inside and is directed towards others who have an independent existence?*" (50). Hatred, she writes, is both ambivalent and a "form of intimacy," an "investment in an object [that] becomes part of the life of the subject even though (or perhaps because) its threat is perceived as coming from outside" (50). In effect, the connection between the subject (that does the hating) and the object (that is hated) becomes symbiotic: "hate sustains the object through its mode of attachment, in a way that has a similar dynamic to love, but with a different orientation" (51).

Ahmed recasts hate as a form of intimacy that necessarily complicates the relationship between self and other, implicitly revealing that hatred is, by nature, *perverse*. It is perverse in the etymological sense of "turning away or turning back," but also in terms of Freudian desire: hatred is a libidinal attachment. Strangely (or, perhaps, perversely), this understanding of hatred has the potential to free self-hatred from its familiar taint of the perverse. By projecting negative characteristics onto a particular subset of one's own stigmatized group, those who experience self-hatred are taking the libidinal logical of love and hatred to its logical conclusion. The feelings for the other are always about the self.

Like hatred, shame also involves a complicated dynamic between self and other, even if it is more apparent. Shame is different from guilt. Where guilt is simply culpability for a bad action, shame is attached to the very selfhood of the transgressor. It is not just a matter of doing something bad, Ahmed argues, but of being bad for having done the bad act: "*the badness of my action is transferred to me*, such that I feel myself to be bad and to have been 'found' or 'found out' as bad by others" (105). In its framework, shame, like hatred, is intersubjective, requiring at least the possibility of an other in order to function. The classic sense of shame involves the culprit's public exposure to the community's disdain, as exemplified by one of the Russian words for shame: *pozor*, whose morphology contains a root for "seeing" or "vision." This, however, is the deep structure of shame; shame can be felt even when there is no one else to see it: "Shame as an emotion requires a witness: even if a subject feels shame when she or he is alone, it is the imagined view of the other that is taken on by a subject in relation to herself or himself" (105).

In keeping with the overall themes of her book, Ahmed is particularly interested in the way in which emotions can be both individual and collective; when they are collective, they help constitute the notion of a particular body politic of community (for better or for worse). So Ahmed's greatest concern in discussing shame involves the individual and collective sense of having committed injustice against others (as in, for example, the case of slavery in the United States): "What is striking is how shame becomes not only a mode of recognition of injustices committed against others, but also a form of nation building. It is shame that allows us 'to assert our identity as a nation'" (102).

Applying Ahmed's insights to self-hatred yields multiple benefits. First, her treatment of hatred and shame help depathologize self-hatred. This is important, because, as Reitter's critique of the term's use in political debate shows, there is nothing more hateful to a given group than signs of self-hatred. In the Jewish context, "self-hatred" turns traits that could be either neutral or positive into symptoms of degeneration: self-deprecating irony is therefore displayed by people who wish desperately to be different, and individual rejection of a mainstream Jewish practice or political point of view can only be rooted in an unhealthy rejection of one's identity (rather than, say, a genuine disagreement or desire to do something in one's own way). And if an element of self-hatred is actually present, is it entirely destructive?

Second, Ahmed's complication of the relationship between self and other pushes Gilman's work further away from the empirical and into the symbolic. Her model of intersubjectivity does not require self and other to be entirely distinct (or even entirely real) entities. In itself, this insight is not new; it is a truism of psychotherapy that the patient's conflicts with a parent are ultimately as much about the internalized version of the parent as the actual mother or father, who need be neither present nor even alive for the therapy to have value. This, in turn, calls into question the relationship between "real life" and the frameworks used to understand it. If the subject is a particular collectivity (group, country, nation) and the stories it tells itself about both itself and a given object of comparison, we can see that the relationship between empirical data selected as evidence and the narrative framework the evidence justifies is just as multidirectional as Ahmed's approach to hatred: the narrative, once it exists, supports itself through examples that legitimize it.

In the post-Soviet context, this dynamic plays itself out in the sociologist Lev Gudkov's brilliant and confounding 2004 book, *Negativnaia identichnost'* (Negative identity). Gudkov argues that Russians after the Soviet collapse construct a "negative identity" based on hostility toward a Western (often American) other. Their envy of their more successful international rivals inculcates what Gudkov calls a "social asthenic syndrome," a passive, apathetic outlook on the world. Social asthenia appears to be a kind of lazy person's *ressentiment*, the hostility toward a perceived superior enemy that somehow doesn't quite coalesce into a program of action. As Vladislav Zubok argues, "Gudkov sets the bar very high for Russia and Russians. He makes no effort to hide that his ideal prototype of the society that Russians failed to emulate is the United States, with its long tradition of voluntary associations and local initiative" (192). How much of Gudkov's approach is informed by his own disappointment in his country's perceived failure to meet this standard?

In the American context, recent scholars of (non-Jewish) ethnic identity have more and more turned to a new framework: racial melancholia. Eventually taken up as a heuristic for African Americans in Joseph R. Winters' *Hope Draped in Black: Race, Melancholy, and the Agony of Progress*, the concept was initially elaborated in an article by David L. Eng and Shinhee Han as a "depathologized structure of everyday group experience for Asian Americans" (667).[4] Asian Americans, they write, find themselves mourning an original, preimmigration "home" while experiencing melancholy over the endless deferral of eventual acceptance within the American "melting pot":

> Mourning describes a finite process that might be reasonably aligned with the popular American myth of immigration, assimilation, and the melting pot for dominant white ethnic groups. In contrast, melancholia describes an unresolved process that might usefully describe the unstable immigration and suspended assimilation of Asian Americans into the national fabric. This suspended assimilation—this inability to blend

into the "melting pot" of America—suggests that, for Asian Americans, ideals of whiteness are continually estranged. They remain at an unattainable distance, at once a compelling fantasy and a lost ideal. (671)

Obviously, the Russian context is different. Assimilation is not the issue for Russians; what is "suspended, conflicted, and unresolved" is the relationship with the lost USSR. In our case, racial melancholia suggests a structure of feeling rather than a model to follow or impose. Both self-hatred and (racial) melancholia offer productive ways to address post-Soviet Russia. As categories, they overlap in time and space, but each focuses on a specific aspect of contemporary Russian identity. Self-hatred most clearly operates when intellectuals and media figures adapt stereotypes about Russian backwardness in order to project them onto an at times imaginary Russian subgroup, shifting the burden of stigma from "good" Russians to "bad" Russians. Melancholy, a category examined in the conclusion of Alexander Etkind's *Warped Mourning*, underlies a more complex reaction formation, an obsession with lost great-power status that exceeds the bounds of mere nostalgia (Eng and Han's "compelling fantasy and lost ideal"). Rather than mourn a past greatness and move on, post-Soviet melancholia will not let go of the USSR's imperial grandeur; this does not have to translate directly into a desire to rebuild the Soviet Union itself (a motivation often attributed to Vladimir Putin) but lends an appeal to an imagined recreated great-power structure that can finally compensate for the loss.

That appeal is part of the focus of Gulnaz Sharafutdinova's magisterial study, *The Red Mirror: Putin's Leadership and Russia's Insecure Identity* (2020), which, as the subtitle suggests, is devoted to the post-Soviet identity crisis I have begun to describe. While Sharafutdinova is careful not to paint a picture of Russia as a country where everything is masterminded by a Svengali in the Kremlin, her primary focus is on the ways in which Russia's leadership exploits the ambient anxieties about the country's identity and destiny in order to create a narrative that legitimizes the Putinist system. She writes:

> Vladimir Putin's politics of collective identity reclamation has rested on the following important objectives and mechanisms: (1) making sense of the experience that Russian society went through in the 1990s in a way that resonated with ordinary Russians; (2) reconstructing the Russian national identity by emphasizing the positive aspects of the Soviet and pre-Soviet experience and by playing into the core cognitive structures that made up the Soviet collective identity; and (3) working to instill a sense of pride and positive distinction associated with belonging to the Russian nation. (19)

Her analysis is spot-on, as are her objections to some of the reigning sociological paradigms in post-Soviet Russia, which I discuss later. Like Sharafutdinova, I am concerned with the idea of collective identities in Russia, but where *Soviet Self-Hatred* differs is in focusing on the manifestations of the problem rather than the Putinist solutions. The identity formations discussed in the following chapters are not part of a state-sponsored response but rather the result of popular desires to reconceive group identities on the fly. *Soviet Self-Hatred* is about identity as a mask, an image, or a performance. It is about shame, but also about the defiant pride that uses shame as a point of departure.

But what is (or was) postsocialism? For that matter, what does it mean to be "post-Soviet"? And how do Soviet self-hatred and post-Soviet shame haunt the scholarly and political debates about the boundaries of postsocialism?

Tethered to the Post

On December 27, 2019, the radical Russian poet Roman Osminkin made a humorous early New Year's pronouncement on Facebook: "The proverbial 'post-Soviet' will be over when the last viewer of *Irony of Fate* chokes on the last spoonful of Olivier salad." His friends and followers immediately understood, but explaining the references to the broader, non-post-Soviet world highlights the post's recursive nature. The post-Soviet exists as a community of people who share a set of Soviet references; getting the joke requires at least a tenuous membership in the club. Ergo, the post-Soviet will be over when there is no one left to find Osminkin's words immediately funny.

There is no shame in not getting the joke; to the contrary, the joke works by exploiting a shared feeling of light, amused shame. For decades, (post-)Soviet families have rung in the new year by watching Eldar Ryazanov's 1976 film, an accidental love story and farce premised on the unrelenting sameness of Soviet domestic structures. After a drunken celebration, Zhenya, the male lead, is mistakenly put on a plane from Moscow to Leningrad after passing out. When he wakes up, he gives the taxi driver his address (3 Builders' Street), where there turns out to be a building exactly like Zhenya's on the Builders' Street in Moscow. Somehow, his key opens the door, and he collapses on what he thinks is his bed. The apartment's actual tenant, a young woman named Nadya, is shocked by this turn of the events, but by the time the movie finishes up its third hour, the two of them have, of course, fallen in love. The film remains a beloved classic, simultaneously encouraging nostalgia for a simpler time while highlighting the sheer visual monotony of the Soviet built environment. Learning that your apartment key opens any number of identical doors is a meta-utopian discovery. In the nostalgic/

utopian reading, everyone belongs to the almost fractally homologous socialist construction, thereby living in a world that encourages random but heartfelt horizontal ties between strangers (who are never really strangers but friends or comrades you have yet to meet). The dystopian reading, in which the interchangeable residents of interchangeable buildings represent humanity at its most faceless and fungible, practically writes itself, even if it is never the focus of the film proper. In any case, the post-Soviet afterlife of *Irony of Fate* is an annually recurring celebration of alienation's opposite: wherever you go, you are already at home. Now that so many Russian speakers live in the diaspora, such a message has a visceral appeal.

As for the Olivier salad, this is a holiday staple whose visual aesthetic (a pile of gray mush interspersed with flecks of orange and green) is not for the faint of heart. It is, of course, a Russian dish traditionally served on New Year's Eve. Made of potatoes, pickles, peas, carrots, and meat smothered in mayonnaise, the salad seems to spark both nostalgia and revulsion at the same time.[5] This is the perfect recipe for the post-Soviet condition.

Of necessity, this book uses the terms "post-Soviet" and "postsocialist" as liberally as a post-Soviet cook scoops the mayo into the Oliver salad. They are not quite interchangeable, nor are they uncontroversial. Throughout most of its three-decade lifespan, "postsocialism" has been a theoretical framework and term of convenience whose premises are frequently called into question by the very scholars who work in the postsocialist field. "Post-Soviet" has clearer geographic boundaries but raises the same concerns about temporality posed by postsocialism: when will it ever end?

The terms "postsocialist" and "post-Soviet" have a built-in limitation, in that the "post" suggests an expiration date that comes sooner rather than later. It took only a few years after 1989/1991 for people to start claiming that the terms were passé. The haste with which the terms were declared invalid is rather suspicious. While I would not wish to deny that conditions have changed significantly since 1991, there is something symptomatic about the desire to declare the phenomenon to be almost over.

Postsocialism is the broader term—one that, unlike post-Soviet, suggests a subfield with an intellectual and theoretical foundation more than simply a time and place. The problems with the term rest on both of its constituent parts: "post" and "socialism." Socialism points to a framework that could, theoretically, extend beyond the former Soviet Union and Central and Eastern Europe to include, say, Cuba, China, and Vietnam, and yet the study of postsocialism tends to replicate Cold War political geography. There was also the possibility of understanding postsocialism as referring not only to countries that used to be socialist, but to the state of existence in a world that has apparently rejected state socialism as a viable alternative to capitalism. In that case, the only thing not possible after socialism is . . . socialism.[6] From such a vantage point, we are all postsocialist, no matter where we make our home. Yet this, too, has not come to pass. One of the drawbacks of postsocialism, then, is that it may simply be another name for a familiar set of area studies.

While there is more to postsocialism than mere academic rebranding, the issue is still worth considering; paradoxically, it might be through the recognition of this geographic shell game that the field could begin to view postsocialism as a condition that affects the entire world. That the collapse of the Soviet Union and the fall of the Berlin Wall represented a huge upheaval for the citizens of the (now former) USSR and of Central and Eastern Europe is a given. But the repercussions were quickly felt by Western academics who either had or were working toward credentials to study a world that had suddenly vanished. Some political scientists and economists recast their area of specialization as the transition from communism to capitalism and from dictatorship to democracy. Humanists (including anthropologists) were generally reluctant to follow their social science counterparts; "transition" encoded a teleology that assumed not just a particular outcome but a settled view of the recent past (communism). Moreover, transitology had inadvertently replicated the very flaw that doomed Soviet Studies: it tied its fate to an object that promised permanence but proved to be fleeting. One need not be an anti-neoliberal skeptic to see that, thirty years after the Berlin Wall, the notion of a transition to democracy (and even to free markets) is now suffused with its own wistful nostalgia.

The failure of transitology is a reminder that the stakes surrounding postsocialism (and, to a lesser extent, the post-Soviet) include the disciplinary and the institutional. The US State Department's choice of "Eurasia" and even "Central Eurasia" was a way to preserve intellectual resources and funding; the selective embrace of Eurasia by academia is accompanied by a serious scholarly apparatus but is also one more way of giving a name to something that threatens to be nameless. The field(s) affected were trapped in a truly odd situation: the fields existed, but their object did not.

Postsocialism, as both object and field, is haunted by shame and inadequacy. The inadequacy is clear enough; like so many "posts," it is a hard term to define and an even harder one to love. Indeed, the scholars of postsocialism, the people who presumably have a stake in the term, are among the first to declare their discomfort. Isn't it just another form of orientalism? Is it a truly broad and comparative intellectual paradigm or just a term of convenience? Elizabeth Dunn and Katherine Verdery provide a concise and coherent definition of postsocialism in an online reference volume meant to explain key terms in the social sciences:

> Postsocialism is not just the study of the period after the end of Communism. Like postcolonialism, it is an analytic, a way of looking at

societies in both East and West that were shaped by state socialism and the Cold War. Focusing on capitalism's alter ego, postsocialism looks at how production, consumption, identity and sovereignty were shaped by the experience of one-party rule and central planning, and it reflects critically on the enduring effects of socialist ideas about the role of state and market in social life.

As a mission statement, this paragraph is excellent, but it runs into a problem common to ex post facto definitions: it is not quite capacious enough to include all the scholarly work that colloquially falls under the postsocialist rubric. After all, the claim to clear parameters is meant to ward off the possibility that postsocialism might just be a period term masking as a conceptual framework. They continue: "If postsocialism is no more than a chronological designation referring to what comes after socialism, then we can only usher it toward the exit. After all, no one now refers to western Europe as 'post-feudal'" (Dunn and Verdery).

Rhetorically, this is an excellent move. But there is a reason we do not refer to Western Europe as post-feudal: we have better terms available. Moreover, it is a safe bet that people in feudal times did not refer to their time as feudal, nor did early capitalists know that they were capitalists. We are stuck with postsocialism until we come up with something better, and by the time we do, the term will most likely be retrospective.[7]

All of the phenomena treated in this book implicitly address the postsocialist experience—more specifically, the post-Soviet experience. For the former USSR, the terms can function interchangeably, but the post-Soviet contains an important feature that the postsocialist lacks: the nagging reminders of past imperial glory. The countries of postsocialist Eastern Europe can cast the last three decades in terms of national liberation, as can the fourteen non-Russian successor states of the USSR (even if some of them do not). Russia was not "liberated" from a foreign power; indeed, if we believe any number of conspiracy theories about the collapse of the USSR, the dismantling of the Soviet Union was the moment when foreigners took over.[8]

For all its flaws, "postsocialism" retains a few key virtues: first, it emphasizes the economic system over the political system, thus avoiding the trap of equating capitalism with democracy; second, it is sufficiently elastic to be potentially viable for as long as necessary; and third, it discourages the lazy habit of naming each Russian era after the man in charge (the Yeltsin Era vs. the Putin Era). The term "post-Soviet" has all those virtues and more, precisely because the term is so empty: it covers whatever has happened since the Soviet collapse, remaining neutral about economics, government, culture, or foreign policy. After nearly three decades, though, one can sympathize with the aggravation that accompanies the constant reference to the old regime. In 2012, Putin even went so far as declaring the post-Soviet period to be over.⁹ This statement has a virtue of its own: reminding a Putin-obsessed West that just because the Russian president says something, that does not mean he has the power to make it actually happen. It is simply too early to tell if Putin's third and fourth terms truly represent a "new era" for Russia.

There is, however, one definitive event that we have yet to reckon with, because reckoning with it at this point remains impossible: Russia's criminal, bloody invasion of Ukraine in 2022. The book you are reading now was written well before February 24, 2022; in fact, it was just a few weeks away from going to press. At the time I write this (less than two months later), the invasion does seem to mark the end of an era. But whether or not that is true, and to what extent, will be much clearer by the time this book is in print. Academic publishing cannot keep pace with current events, and attempting to make a definitive statement about the war as a turning point would be folly. Nonetheless, even if 2022 truly does mark the end of both the post-Soviet and postsocialism, the concepts are still crucial for understanding what comes next. If this book, which took shape as an examination of contemporary Russia, turns out to be about a discrete historical period, then so be it.

But I do think it is important, at least at this early stage, to resist the temptation to reevaluate every aspect of Putin-era Russian culture in light of the president's brutal war of choice. To do so would be to impute an unwarranted teleology to the past two decades, as though everything in Russia were developing according to a sinister master plan. Before February 24, the invasion was close to unthinkable; the main reason for immediately reclassifying is simply that it happened. However, this is not the first time the Russian Federation has invaded Ukraine; since the 2014 annexation of Crimea and Russian-backed separatist rebellions in the Donbas, the hostilities never ceased. Thus Ukraine comes into this book at the points where it makes the most logical sense: chapter 6 and the conclusion.

The Virtues of a Weak Theory

Why are we in such a hurry to move on from postsocialism and the post-Soviet? Kevin Platt declared an end to the post-Soviet back in 2009, partly in response to the Russian invasion of Georgia. Five years later, the Russian annexation of Crimea makes Platt look either prophetic or premature.¹⁰ Integral to both Platt's and Putin's declarations of the end of an era is an understanding of the post-Soviet to be about state power, as well as the strength that the country projects to the broader world. Not that there are no differences in their approach; Putin quotes Russophile, quasi-fascist philosophers, while Platt quotes the poet Timur

Kibirov. Also, Putin has an army and, last I checked, Platt does not. One argument is built on sheer strength, the other on nuance.

In his essay "The Post-Soviet Is Over," Platt references Serguei Oushakine's important article, "In the State of Post-Soviet Aphasia," which argues that the sheer "in-betweenness" of the post-Soviet "does not provide any cues about the direction to follow, it does not channel one's identificatory process; instead it outlines the paths that should *not* be taken" (995). Oushakine writes further:

> I have suggested that one of the most striking aspects of this discursive behaviour ... was the loss of a metalanguage and thus the loss of ability to "dissect" the metaphor of the "post-Soviet." This lack of knowledge about one's own location and being, I proposed, is closely connected with absence of the post-Soviet field of cultural production that could have provided the post-Soviet subject with adequate post-Soviet discursive possibilities/signifiers. Such absence of an adequate post-Soviet interpellation capable of "naming" the subject undermines the very foundation of the existing discursive field and its institutions. The "post-Soviet" remains an empty space, a non-existence, devoid of its subjectifying force, its own signifier, and its own meaning effect. (1010)

One of the things that stands out about this paragraph, besides its insights into the post-Soviet condition, is how many times a set of sentences talking about the emptiness of the post-Soviet finds itself using the phrase "post-Soviet." This is not a strike against Oushakine's thesis about the discursive void left by the Soviet collapse; there is a good reason that it is so influential. But, admittedly with the benefit of nearly two decades' hindsight since the essay's publication, I would suggest that we look for the meaning of the post-Soviet in other places. Oushakine's work is that of an anthropologist, while Platt (in 2010's "Zachem izuchat' antropologiiu?" [Why study anthropology?]) has proclaimed an "anthropological turn" in literary studies; I propose pushing a bit further into anthropology in order to find our way out of it.

The collapse of the Soviet Union was the culmination of a decades-long process that was about not just political ideology but fundamental belief systems. It is instructive to look at the language that older, antiliberal post-Soviet citizens often use to describe perestroika and the subsequent undermining of Soviet values: *koshchunstvo* (sacrilege), *sviatotatstvo* (also sacrilege), even *bogokhul'stvo* (blasphemy). Whether we talk of the lack of "morality" or a "national idea," what is lost is the sense of something sacred.

But how long can that loss last? "Post-Soviet" is, initially, meaningless, but so was "Soviet" (from the Russian word for "council," it was appropriated by the Bolsheviks out of naked opportunism). "Post-Soviet" eventually means something from the sheer accumulation of instances of its use. We cannot expect people to provide a coherent definition of the post-Soviet in a set of ethnographic interviews. Again and again, attempts to address the post-Soviet ideological vacuum head-on end in frustration (as Yeltsin's state commission to develop a new national idea demonstrates).[11] Asking for a coherent formulation of the post-Soviet on demand is like expecting native speakers to explain the fine points of a grammar that they have internalized without consciously learning (just ask the average Russian to elucidate verbal aspect or verbs of motion, or native English speakers to provide rules for using the definite article). I submit that these discursive issues resolve themselves indirectly.

It is easy (and even correct) to claim that "post-Soviet" and especially "postsocialism" are murky, poorly defined concepts whose meaning shifts from speaker to speaker (Gordon). But perhaps this is also a virtue. The flaws of postsocialism are the opposite of those to be found in transitology; not only is the term not teleological, but it threatens to be *anti-teleological*. There is no clear road map out of postsocialism because the topography of postsocialism consists of circles, cul-de-sacs, blind alleys, dead ends, and roads to nowhere. Postsocialism is *messy*, which is both a key part of its unattractiveness and a justification for its retention. The first postsocialist decade in particular was tumultuous, if not downright chaotic. Why should the framework for its analysis be any different?

In addition to the obvious economic, social, and political dislocations brought on by the end of socialism, the years following 1989/1991 were (and perhaps remain) a crisis of naming. Names mattered intensely; one of my favorite headlines of 1990, which I unfortunately did not save, was paired with a picture of an unhappy crowd that took to the streets: "Slovaks protest lack of hyphen." This was the so-called hyphen war over the proper name for Czechoslovakia after 1989, a conflict resolved by obviating the need for punctuation when the country dissolved into the Czech Republic and Slovakia. Four of the constituent republics of the USSR changed their names after the breakup (to Belarus, Kyrgyzstan, Moldova, and Turkmenistan), while cities, streets, and subway stations through the former USSR were restored to their pre-Soviet nomenclature. Meanwhile, a whole set of new alliances and political structures arose whose names never quite stuck, such as the Commonwealth of Independent States, while old terms such as *rossiianin* (Russian, but not necessarily ethnic Russian) were awkwardly resurrected.[12]

Many of the twenty-first-century governments of postsocialist countries are keen on putting the chaos of the 1990s behind them, and Russia seems to be taking the lead. But the desire to cordon off the early, freewheeling postsocialist years from the more stable (and more authoritarian) world now being built is a hygienic impulse that must be distrusted, if not outright rejected. At this particular point in time, when the Nineties are demonized and Putinism trumpets the glories of the Soviet past, we cannot allow the Nineties to become a self-contained period against which the "post-post-Soviet" can be defined. Electing to view the Nineties and the Putin years together (as Irina Souch insists on doing in her masterful 2017 study, *Popular Tropes of Identity in Post-Soviet Russia*), is a political statement as well as an intellectual one.[13]

Any demarcation of one time from another is vulnerable to complaints of arbitrariness, a charge Martin Muller levies at a postsocialism that extends from 1989/1991 to the present but is equally applicable to a version of postsocialism that ended years ago. Temporal frameworks always risk overemphasizing rupture. Certainly, this is true of the revolution of 1917, and it is also the case for 1991, and possibly for 2000. When we choose our moment of rupture, we are endorsing a narrative whose ramifications might not be immediately clear. Postsocialism may commit the sin of turning 1991 into a definitive rupture, but, at least in the Russian case, it has the virtue of not assenting to the Putinist salvational myth of a New Russia in the twenty-first century.

Postsocialism as a theory is weak, a feature that also constitutes postsocialism's strength. For it is weakness that makes the postsocialist condition in general and its post-Soviet variant in particular so threatening to the political and cultural figures who would prefer to talk about it in the past tense. My argument is not that Russia, Russian culture, the Russian state, or any other Russian institution was or is inherently weak, but rather that a preoccupation with, and subsequent rejection of, weakness is part of the Russian postsocialist/post-Soviet experience. The compensatory demand for the projection of strength does not constitute the death of postsocialism; ruminating over weakness and rejecting it are both forms of engagement.

Multiple definitions of the post-Soviet and postsocialist can be teased out by examining the various answers to two sets of questions. First, the interrogative "Who are we?" or "Who is this subset of us?"—which is the focus of the present study. What are the identity formations that have some purchase in the wake of the Soviet collapse? The second set of questions is inherently conditional-subjunctive: we find out who we are by looking at who we could have been or by compulsively traveling to the key historical moments that led us to this day.

The Cast of Characters

Most of this book is devoted to an examination of these identities, from their roots in shame and self-hatred to their occasional assimilation into narratives of national pride. Chapters 1–5 deal specifically with Soviet self-hatred, starting with the late-Soviet phenomenon known as *sovok*. When referring to a person rather than to the whole country, the term *sovok* projected Soviet insecurities about culture and sophistication onto a particular kind of yokel who was the source of embarrassment, humor, and even, occasionally, pride. As the USSR faded into history, the sovok was succeeded by a figure who would seem to be his opposite: the New Russian. Where the sovok was poor, the New Russian was rich. Where the sovok had difficulty navigating the world of much-desired consumer goods, the New Russian reveled in it (but still managed to get things wrong). Where the sovok was obsessed with his own particular notion of culture, the New Russian wouldn't know culture if it hit him in the face with a thousand-dollar handbag. What they have in common is their capacity to shame, by embodying the embarrassing yokel whom more sophisticated Russians would prefer either to forget or, if necessary, keep alive as a cathartic figure of ridicule.

More recently, similar anxieties manifest themselves in the elites' disdain for the common "herd" (*bydlo*) and liberals' disgust with the Crimea-obsessed, pro-Putin, nationalist *vatniki* (named for the cheap, puffy coats they are said to wear). Both the bydlo and the vatniki continue the process of alienation that had already accelerated with the figure of the New Russian, for the speaking subject who uses these words is denying all kinship with their targets (though *vatnik* has the complication of being an ethnic slur when deployed by Ukrainians). These chapters will have a more historical (and even philological) scope, since I trace the development of the term *sovok* back to the 1980s, its rise in the discourse of the late 1980s and 1990s, its manifestations in film and mass culture, and the near disappearance of the term in the past ten years as a reference to people (but not as a reference to the Soviet Union or Soviet system, which was always one of the word's two primary meanings). I also chart a similar history of the term "New Russian" and discuss the conditions that have made this term less relevant than it was at the turn of the century.

The vatniki and the rest of the post-Soviet bestiary are different ways of framing the problem of the Russian Federation's new public sphere. As we shall see, Dmitrii Bykov, in his novel *Living Souls* (*ZhD*, 2006), invents a category of mentally deficient wandering urban shamans called Vasyas (Vaski), a fantastic extrapolation on the crisis of homelessness that has beset the country since the Soviet collapse. But danger lurks indoors as well; the Russian couch potato is also easily construed as a threat to a healthy body politic. Both the hyperpatriotic Vatnik and the unwashed masses of bydlo can be encountered on the street, but their natural habitat places them in front of the television set, occasionally shouting their agreement with whatever the state channels tell them.

These imaginary identities map themselves across four axes: culture, wealth, effectiveness, and criminality. In addition, some will be framed in terms of heredity or pseudobiologism, while others will not. The sovok, for example, is alternately proficient or deficient in high culture, depending on who defines him, but is always a failure when it comes to mass culture and civilized behavior under the conditions of the marketplace. He is ineffectual by definition, does not engage in organized crime, and has little connection to money (unless one counts its lack). Heredity and faux biological discourse do come up, but more as a matter of rhetorical flare than as the basis for an argument about sovok speciation. Even Zinoviev's Homosos (see chapter 1), the sovok's most immediate precursor, uses the language of biological type for satirical rather than persuasive ends.

When we turn to the New Russian in chapters 4 and 5, we will find the sovok's mirror image. The New Russian has no culture and is defined instead by his wealth, effectiveness, and criminality. As he evolves into a more domesticated type (the rich Russian), he attempts to cut his criminal ties, cultivate a new role as a patron of high culture, and engage in a self-justifying discourse of "good genes" and innate nobility. As repulsive as the New Russian might be, he still has a path forward toward respectability.

The Russian Orc of chapter 6 has a complicated connection to culture (proclaiming the virtue of high culture but from a stance of aggressive pseudosavagery), sees himself as effective but finds the categories of both crime and wealth not particularly relevant to his place in the world. Genes, heredity, and degeneration, in contrast, are all part of the Orc's Manichaean worldview.

This chapter, "Russian Orc: The Evil Empire Strikes Back," examines an attempt by members of online science fiction and gaming communities to reclaim negative stereotypes of Russia as a point of pride. Insisting that the Western world sees Moscow as "Mordor" and Russians as "Orcs" (even though all evidence suggests that this framework is entirely internally generated), these people take on the mantle of "Orc-dom" voluntarily, a self-orientalizing gesture that amounts to appreciating Russians for their "savage vitality." Self-proclaimed Orcs have reappropriated not just Tolkien but the simplistic, pop-culture-inspired metaphysics of American exceptionalism as articulated by Ronald Reagan and extended by George W. Bush. Fine, they say, we'll be your evil empire. But we'll do it with an irony and pride that you will never entirely comprehend. The Orc identity has its roots in self-hatred, in that it is based on an identification with archetypal villains. But it also points to the simplest way self-hatred is overcome, or at least gives the appearance of being overcome: by reversing the valences and turning shame into pride.

By now, the reader may have noticed one thing that these characters have in common: they are all men. One might chalk this up to one of sexism's more benign forms (the unexamined assumption that everyone is male unless otherwise specified). But even if that were the case, the lack of even a minimal effort to imagine them as women (or even to come up with their female counterparts) is significant—especially given the long-standing tradition of representing Russia itself as a woman (Rodina-mat', Mother Russia), a practice that is consistent with national symbolism throughout Europe. The country is a woman, while its inhabits or defenders are her "sons." As I discussed in *Overkill*, when Russian women are forced to bear symbolic weight, sometimes as individuals but more often as representatives of particular types, their function is not to round out the picture of Russia by acknowledging that women make up roughly half of the country's population. Rather, women embody the country's success or failure in husbanding its resources. In the first post-Soviet decade, Russian women's emigration, sexual involvement with foreigners, or prostitution all mapped onto Russian (male) shame over the country's transformation into an exporter of oil and minerals to the more "developed" world. If we even briefly entertain the common assertion that "our women are the most beautiful in the world," we should also consider who the "we" is that is speaking, and what is their gender.

Part of the early post-Soviet mass cultural project was the reassertion of a supposedly primal or natural masculinity as a remedy for decades of socialism thought to have infantilized Soviet men. The new worlds of crime, business, and politics were men's playground, and action heroes began to proliferate on the screen and page. Some of these heroes managed to be briefly popular, if not iconic, though in the most prominent cases (such as the characters played by Sergei Bodrov, Jr.), it is difficult to disentangle the hero's cult following from that of the actor who played him. Yet none of these characters rose to the level of national archetype; they were admired or disdained as individual personalities, even if critics and fans found no shortage of symbolic meaning in their stories.

Despite his popularity, the action hero is a poor candidate for representing the aspirations or anxieties of the nation, in that his adventures are too far from anything like people's lived experience. He may be admirable, but in terms of relevance, he may as well be a starship captain. Granted, actual Orcs are thin on the ground as well, but they are available in a way that Russian Rambos and starship troopers are not. Orcs, though imaginary, are a part of an existing mass culture that has real purchase in the popular imagination. The Russian Orc is as much an interpretive strategy as he is a character, the reclamation of a misreading that is, in itself, exclusively a Russian product (the identification of Orcs with Russia and the Soviet Union).

Unlike the Orcs, the other identities in this book are a response to the emergence of specific Russian real or imaginary types in reaction to a changing world. They maintain men's primacy as the subject of nearly any given story, but they also hint at masculine inadequacy. Both the sovok and the New Russian are defined in terms of consumption rather than production, style rather than substance. To the extent that the New Russian overlaps with organized crime, he does have one quality that the other identity formations lack: power that can be understood in traditionally masculine terms. The sovok is hapless; the vatnik is a belligerent, impotent drunk; and the Vasya is either a hick (in popular usage) or a cross between a hobo and a holy fool (in Bykov's novel); these are men whose tragic flaws include a near-total lack of agency. There is ample room for a feminist critique of post-Soviet women's own lack of agency, but the broader culture since the late 1980s has emphasized women's secondary, supportive role as a precondition for the restoration of a post-Soviet order that returns men to their "natural" dominant role (previously stripped from them by an infantilizing, supposedly gender-neutral Soviet state).

Even those identity formations most closely identified with masculine abjection are still functioning within the framework of the thinkable and permissible, and therefore still subject to inclusion in the category of "Russianness." By contrast, the demonization of the LGBTQI community that crystallized in the passage of the "gay propaganda" law in 2013 excludes an entire subset of the population from the Russian world. Queerness is continually defined as a disorder brought into Russia by the West, sometimes as part of a plot to weaken the national character and exacerbate demographic difficulties. Queers, by definition a challenge to conventional notions of masculinity, are troped as foreign elements that must be purged from the body politic. One of the implicit aims of the homophobic campaigns of the past fifteen years has been to make queerness an identity that is incompatible with the Russian.

The Fandom Menace

The chapter on the Russian appropriation of the Orc identity is the culmination of the trends examined in this volume for a number of reasons. First, there is the important pivot from shame to pride. Second, the Orc identity, far more than that of the sovok or the New Russian, is a response to imagined perceptions of Russians from outside of Russia. Third, the Russian Orc combines two important meanings of the word "fantasy," in that the identity is entirely a matter of the imagination, while also rooted in fantasy as a genre of literature and entertainment. The Russian Orc is a response to an imagined external (Western) alienating gaze: not the eye of Sauron, but the face of Medusa, solidifying Russia into something monstrous and unchanging.

This immediately raises the question of scale: whatever value judgments one might make about Russian nationalism, it is obviously a significant phenomenon—look no farther than the separatist movement in Ukraine and the mobilization of support in the Russian Federation. By comparison, the Russian Orc is not just a niche category but one that looks positively lightweight. What possible significance could arguments about fantasy characters have?

By now, my readers will not be surprised at my assertion that such imaginary characters do have real meaning and weight. Starting with *Plots against Russia*, I have been using the materials I study in service of a broader thesis that I believe can be proved only by example: mass culture is worthy of study not just because it reveals something about "real" culture and politics, but because the categories of mass culture have so colonized the popular consciousness that they themselves have a value as an interpretive framework. We should not just study pop culture using "proper" intellectual and theoretical categories; we should see what happens when we look at politics and ideology using pop cultural narratives as our model.

The Orc phenomenon can be a case study of the role of nationalism in fandom. The connection between the two concepts is not original; Hailong Liu speaks convincingly of "the emergence of fandom nationalism," using an aggressive Chinese social media campaign and cyberattack as a key example (125–47 v.). What I propose goes a few steps further. While fandom can certainly be understood in terms of nationalism, we have much to gain by considering nationalism as a variety of fandom.

What, after all, is "fandom"? Lori Hitchcock Morimoto and Bertha Chin note that Benedict Anderson's notion of the "imagined community" (used to define a nation) has long been applied to fandom: "A central truism of English-language media fan studies is that modern fandoms are 'imagined communities' fostered by technologies that enable geographically dispersed people to overcome time and distance in forging virtual communities of affect" (174).

Morimoto and Chin are more concerned with fandom's ability to transcend the national, which is consistent with the general critical attention to transnationalism and alternatives to sovereignty. The kind of fandom I have in mind is an imagined community that, on the contrary, is devoted to national borders and the idea of sovereignty. Consider the definition of "participatory culture" (a variation on fandom) offered by Henry Jenkins and his colleagues in 2009:

> For the moment, let's define participatory culture as one with
> 1. relatively low barriers to artistic expression and civic engagement, strong support for creating and sharing creations with others,
> 2. strong support for creating and sharing creations with others,
> 3. some type of informal mentorship whereby what is known by the most experienced is passed along to novices,

4. members who believe that their contributions matter, and
5. members who feel some degree of social connection with one another (at the least, they care what other people think about what they have created). (5–6)

In other words, a fandom arises from the common interest and engagement of a group of people united by their commitment to a beloved object. The object, however, is not a clearly defined, finite "thing"; more often than not, it is a storyworld, one that—even if it has a beginning, middle, and an end—can still be approached as open-ended. That storyworld could be Tolkien; it could be *Star Trek*. It could also be France—or Russia. Nationalism is fandom, and nationalists are fans of their nation.

Yes, this is an oversimplification, and even an offensive one. That is precisely the point. From the inside, nationalism is a locus of power and meaning, a metanarrative that explains and justifies the world in which the nationalist lives. From the outside, it can look ridiculous.

Consider the problem with studying fan cultures from the outside: even as we try to resist the temptation to look down on them, to the outsider the concerns of, say, anime fan culture appear silly or unimportant. Is *Avatar: The Last Airbender* really anime? Which ending of *Neon Genesis Evangelion* is the "right" one, the last episodes of the television series or *The End of Evangelion*? Then recall how easy it is to satirize the nationalist. Jonathan Swift mocks the conflict between France and England (and the two churches that each represent) as a fight between Big-Endians, who break the bigger parts of their eggs before eating them, and Small-Endians, who do the opposite.

Or, for that matter, recall Freud's dismissal of conflicts between ethnicities or nations as the "narcissism of small differences." His point is that, from a distance, the feuding sides look nearly identical, and the issues that divide them appear petty and absurd. He is not wrong, but he is also not entirely right: this assessment works only when one assumes an imagined privileged position that is somehow "above all that." This is the position of someone who is unmoved—that is, someone who is not a fan. From this standpoint, the nationalist and the fan are always wrong by definition.

Just as there is obviously more than one way to be a nationalist, there is more than one way to be a fan. One of the central distinctions among fan communities has real explanatory potential when applied to the Russian Orc, and perhaps to nationalism more broadly. On one side we have the fan as he is generally pictured by the outside world: the fan who is obsessed with the minutiae of his beloved storyworld, and who polices its boundaries with zeal that can appropriately be termed "fanatical."[14] This is Comic Book Guy from *The Simpsons*, who will gladly correct anyone who cannot remember exactly when Rogue joined the X-Men.[15] In a 2009 *LiveJournal* post, a user dubbing herself "obsession_inc" called this "affirmational fandom"; six years later, LordByronic on Reddit proposed the term "curative fandom," which has also come to be known as "curatorial fandom." Whatever the name, this is a kind of fandom that prizes storyworld knowledge as lore, the fan equivalent of biblical literalism in Christian circles and strict constructionism among legal scholars.

By contrast to what she sees as the male-dominated affirmational fandom, obsession_inc proposes "transformational fandom," a primarily female community "all about laying hands upon the source and twisting it to the fans' own purposes, whether that is to fix a disappointing issue (a distinct lack of sex-having between two characters, of course, is a favorite issue to fix) in the source material, or using the source material to illustrate a point, or just to have a whale of a good time." Transformational (or transformative) fandom prizes the creative activity of the fans themselves, whether that be fan fiction, critique, or art. For the transformational fan, fandom is about making meaning rather than simply parsing received wisdom.

The transformation/affirmational binary in fandom is inherently political, in ways that become even more obvious when we transpose it to the realm of the nation and ideology. Conservative nationalists the world over insist on their own particular narrative of the nation, built on key moments of triumph or martyrdom, but rarely guilt or shame. When liberals point out the mistakes or crimes that are part of the nation's history (such as slavery in the US past and caging migrant children in the US present), they are accused of being unpatriotic, or even of hating their own country.

For the nationalist as affirmational fan, the country's history consists of canonical events that cannot be questioned, only celebrated. In twenty-first century Russia, we see this approach most clearly when the narrative is challenged, as when the independent news channel Dozhd TV dared in 2014 to ask its viewers if Leningrad should not have surrendered to the Nazis and was nearly shut down as a result (Englund). Another example is the outrage in 2015 when the director of Russia's state archive, Sergei Mironenko, asserted that the story of Panfilov's twenty-eight guardsmen who died heroically defending Moscow in World War II was a myth. Culture Minister Vladimir Medinsky's response was especially revealing: "It's my deep conviction that even if this story was invented from the start to the finish, even if Panfilov never existed, even if there was nothing at all, it's a sacred legend which it's simply impossible to besmirch. And people who try to do that are total scumbags" (Walker 2016).

Medinsky's slur is typical of affirmational nationalist fans the world over: to them, loving one's country means subscribing to a canonical narrative and never deviating from it. Liberals are saddled with a more complicated story of patriotism, one that allows for history to be opened up, expanded, and questioned. This is a history that includes a country's mistakes and crimes and makes room for previously neglected voices. Patriotic liberals are transformational fans.

The affirmational/transformational fan dynamic proves enlightening when we turn to the Donbas. In *Plots against Russia*, I expanded on the idea expressed most notably by Dmitrii Bykov, that the war in Ukraine was a "writers' war," one in which authors of bad military science fiction moved from fantasy to reality.[16] But at least on the separatist side, it is also the violent, real-life expression of extreme affirmational fandom. After all, the separatist generals included men who had previously made a name for themselves in military reenactments. Donbas is a giant live-action role-playing game (LARP) with real-life casualties.

If there is one lesson we should take from the imposition of fantastic categories onto real-world situations, it is that we underestimate the power of the imaginary at our own peril. The stories we tell can become the stories that we are forced to live.

1

ZOMBIE SOVIETICUS
The Descent of Soviet Man

Barely two decades old, the twenty-first century has proven itself a huge disappointment, at least from the point of view of prognostication. By now, according to a plethora of utopian schemes dating back to the nineteenth century, the world was supposed to be united, even homogenous. Edward Bellamy's 1888 utopian novel, *Looking Backward*, casually predicted global unity, an assumption later confirmed in countless popular science fictional representations of Earth's future. Socialists of all stripes disdained the nation-state and the empire when the twentieth century began, only to throw themselves wholeheartedly into the pointless slaughter of World War I. The United Nations gave hints of a future unity that would erase the failure of the League of Nations from memory. Space flights provided external photographs of the planet earth (the "big blue marble") that inspired a sense of common destiny. Rock stars sang "We Are the World," Francis Fukuyama predicted the end of history, and game theory made local knowledge look quaint.

To see just how the local has taken its revenge (and to get a hint as to what this might have to do with the former Soviet Union), we need look no further than the embarrassing yokel who conquered the entertainment world: Borat Sagdiyev. Created by Sacha Baron Cohen in the mid-1990s, the Borat character was featured on his *Da Ali G Show* (1999–2004) before spinning off into his own movie, *Borat: Cultural Learnings of American to Make Benefit Glorious Nation of Kazakhstan* (2006). Based on a doctor Baron Cohen met while vacationing in Astrakhan (a phrase that sounds as unlikely as anything else to come out of the British comedian's mouth), Borat is supposed to be a journalist from Kazakhstan traveling in Britain (and, eventually, the United States) in order to report to his audience back home (Strauss).

Americans lined up to see the film, which was number one at the box office during its first weekend (Rich). Kazakhstan's government had to tone down its initial outrage at the Central Asian nation's portrayal as the homeland of joyfully clueless urine-drinking, Jew-hating, sister-shtupping rapists.[1] The film board of the Russian Federation recommended against the movie's distribution on Russian territory, citing the potential for inciting nationalist hatred. And, inevitably, Baron Cohen and his studio were threatened with lawsuits from a veritable rainbow coalition of offended parties: American frat boys, New York feminists, Romanian Roma, and, at least at first, the aforementioned government of Kazakhstan. Such strange international bedfellows provide a glimpse of Borat's globalist scope, uniting disparate cultures through his brash violation of the norms of multicultural etiquette, thereby, ironically enough, bringing his enemies together in an angry and offended variation on "It's a Small World after All."

For Americans, Borat is a familiar type, the usually (but not always) Second World yokel who has been a figure of fun since the days of the Cold War. Steve Martin's and Dan Ackroyd's crass, Czechoslovakian "Wild and Crazy Guys" from *Saturday Night Live* in the 1970s, Andy Kaufman's Latka Gravas from *Taxi* in the 1980s, the linguistically challenged narrator of Jonathan Safran Foer's relentlessly annoying *Everything Is Illuminated* (later portrayed by Liev Schreiber in the film of the same name), the hapless refugee in Stephen Spielberg's *Terminal*, the hopelessly backward natives of mud-ravaged Elbonia in the comic strip *Dilbert*, and the pornography-loving adolescent on *That '70s Show*, whose unpronounceable name is replaced by the acronym "Fez" for "foreign exchange student" (although we do learn that the first five k's in his last name are silent). Combining good-hearted buffoonery with the slightest threat of aggression, the yokel is almost always male (the women from their countries are usually portrayed as peasant mothers, shrews, and whores from central casting). Most of these yokels fit a particular type: they are sexually preoccupied, prone to ostensibly hilarious malapropisms, and strangely lovable despite—or perhaps because of—their utter inappropriateness. Suddenly, the title of Edward Bellamy's *Looking Backward* takes on a whole new meaning.

None of this is, of course, Russian or from Russia, but Slavists quickly accepted this material as their own. In 2008, *Slavic Review* came out with a special cluster on Borat—including my own article, "Our Borats, Our Selves: Yokels and Cosmopolitans on the Global Stage," on which the present text heavily draws. Robert A. Saunders, a political scientist specializing in Russian and Central Asia, published a monograph the following year, *The Many Faces of Sacha Baron Cohen: Politics, Parody, and the Battle over Borat*. More than a decade later, and even before Baron Cohen revived the character for 2020's *Borat Subsequent Moviefilm*, this caricature still haunted the region, with Kazakh athletes at international sporting events continuing to be humiliated when, instead of their country's actual national anthem, their hosts play "O, Kazakhstan," the song penned by Baron Cohen for the end credits of the movie ("Kazakhstan, Kazakhstan, you very nice place/From plains of Tarashek to northern fence of Jewtown/Come grasp mighty penis of our leader/From junction with the testes to tip of its face!")

Borat resonates because, despite Baron Cohen's presumably limited knowledge of the former Soviet Union and complete mischaracterization of Kazakhstan, the character exemplifies a particular kind of Soviet and post-Soviet shame usually designated by the word *sovok*: the sense that the (former) country, which once prided itself on its modernity and a utopian ideal of internationalism, had degenerated into a nest of embarrassing yokels. Borat is the ex-Soviet idiot abroad, the embarrassing reminder of Old Country backwardness, an unassimilable alien. One of the telltale moments in the film comes when Borat's Southern dinner party hostess optimistically assesses the faux Kazakh's potential: "You could be Americanized someday." Two minutes later, Borat returns from the bathroom with a plastic bag containing his own feces. Where can I put it, he asks her, in an exchange that is truly emblematic. With his body and its unsightly products, Borat has issued her a challenge: assimilate that!

As a figure in popular culture, the yokel is a reminder of everything the cosmopolitan wishes to leave behind: the painfully ethnic, localized, and uncivilized set of customs that used to define him and that unsympathetic onlookers can still deploy against him at will. Despite the fact that the postwar Stalinist anti-Jewish campaign turned "cosmopolitan" into a dirty word, the citizens of the Soviet Union were supposed to represent the best of the multinational cross-fertilization that modernity facilitated. The Soviet or post-Soviet yokel turned an optimistic anthropological imagination into a site of degeneration.

It's Raining New Men

Borat is an underinformed Western fantasy about a phenomenon whose roots go far deeper than anything Baron Cohen could have learned during his Astrakhan beach getaway. Nor did he need to know all that much, because the local yokel is, paradoxically, a common global phenomenon. What culture does not have yokels of its very own as reliable fodder for embarrassing, self-deprecating laughter? It is most visible as a reflection of the immigrant experience. Elsewhere I've argued that Borat is a variation on a familiar Jewish anxiety about backward relatives from the Old Country; Gene Yang's 2006 graphic novel,

American Born Chinese, explores a Chinese-American version of roughly the same anxieties. This does not mean that the yokel is just for immigrants. White, unhyphenated Americans have looked down on "white trash" since the country was young.[2]

But the USSR and its successor states provide a unique setting for such fantasies of national abjection because of the Soviet Union's role as an unprecedented sustained, self-conscious experiment in synthetic, ideological, and utopian identity formation. As is so often the case, one could argue that the United States was the country's rival when it came to such matters, but the American circumstances were significantly different, involving transoceanic colonization, the genocide of the indigenous population, race-based slavery, massive immigration, and an ideology that, while no doubt present, was soft-peddled by comparison to the Soviet project.[3] Moreover, the Soviet experiment with identity cannot be separated from its remarkable, simultaneous project of rapid modernization. Before we can talk about the degeneration of Soviet identity, we need to look at its development, from Marxist, prerevolutionary utopianism through the first revolutionary decade's rhetoric of the New Man, and on to the Stalinist development of the New Soviet Man.

First, let us address the terminological elephant in the room: should we really be saying "New Man" rather than "New Person"? After all, the Russian term is *novyi chelovek*, not *novyi muzhchina* (a phrase that would explicitly be about an adult male's way of being in the world). The English phrase connotes a sexism that the Russian would seem to lack, although it is certainly worth remembering that the Russian word for "person" is masculine in gender. But I would argue that it is more in keeping with a feminist framework to use the word "man" rather than "person," following the example of Lynn Atwood, who, in *The New Soviet Man and Woman: Sex Role Socialization in the USSR* (1990), used masculine nouns and pronouns in her translations from the Russian because attempting "to rectify the male bias in the Russian language ... would be totally misleading" (14). I choose to say "new man" rather than "new person" not despite the term's sexism but because of it.

The new person included women, but it included them as an afterthought or as a variation on the male prototype, who would always be discussed first.[4] One could, for example, talk about the "new woman" or "new Soviet woman" in reference or contradistinction to the "new *chelovek* [person]," but there was never any reason to do the same for the "new man" (adult male) and the "new person." The new person was a man, unless otherwise specified. This should not come as a surprise, since it is in keeping with general usage in Russian (and, for that matter, English) at the time. It is also ideologically consistent, a homology to the Bolshevik approach to feminism: yes, women must be liberated from patriarchal servitude, but as a corollary to the overall liberation of the proletariat rather than as a goal unto itself.

The idea of the New Man is fundamentally utopian (despite Marx's explicit denials of anything utopian about Marxism), based on the common utopian anthropology of human malleability. Belief in an unchanging human nature is intrinsically conservative and definitely incompatible with utopias, since, if people never change, there's little point in trying to create a perfect system. Instead, appeals to human nature are a prominent dystopian or antiutopian trope, going back to Dostoevsky's underground man.

Scholars have long treated the "New Man" and the "New Soviet Man" as interchangeable, but Anna Krylova persuasively argues for maintaining a distinction between the two. The New Man, she writes, is a creature of the pre-Stalin era, inspired by a "collectivist ethos of the Bolshevism of the 1910–1920s that rejected the ontological differentiation between the individual and his or her social milieu" (341). The New Man was not just collectivist but proletarian through and through, while the New Soviet Man of the 1930s would gradually phase out both of these values.[5]

One of the reasons this distinction has remained obscure has to do with the differences between public discourse in the 1920s and the 1930s. In the 1920s, the New Man was an idea to be debated and developed, a concept that was, as it were, up for grabs. When the New Soviet Man evolved in the 1930s, the shift in emphasis from, among other things, collectivism to innate talent, was developed in pedagogical journals and Stalin's edits of Komsomol decrees. The public representation of the New (Soviet) Man started to change, but the processes that led to these changes were not, in themselves, public or even necessarily the result of a set of conscious decisions about the New Man per se.

Whoever the New Man would be, his coming was heralded long before his arrival, and his character was the subject of spirited polemics by people who could make no claim to be his peer. Despite its optimism, utopian anthropology is haunted by a version of the same problem that plagues the very idea of the utopian system: an inability to imagine a convincing path from here (imperfection) to the utopian promised land. It is a problem of cause and effect: the ideal system will produce the ideal people, but the ideal people are not yet available to implement the ideal system, which must inevitably be constructed by men and women who are the flawed product of an imperfect world. The makers of the new world cannot be New Men; at best, they view the new world from the outside, like Moses in Moab.

The point is that whatever he would be, it was not simply "Russian." New Russians would take decades more to appear and mean something entirely different (although Boris Akunin has Erast Fandorin's now elderly son, an émigré in the

United Kingdom, casually and disdainfully refer to the Soviets as "new Russians' in 2000's *Altyn-Tolobas*). The New Man was supposed to transcend the false consciousness of nationality in favor of his aggressively proletarian identity. Unfortunately for him, the New Man shared yet another flaw with his utopian roots: it was far easier to describe him satirically, in the negative light of dystopia, than to make a convincing, detailed portrait of this yet-to-be-seen paragon.

Old Dogs and New Ticks

Mikhail Bulgakov transformed the fable of the New Man into a cautionary tale about the dangers of social engineering in his 1925 short novel, *Heart of a Dog*. When Professor Preobrazhensky (Professor Transfiguration) transplants human glands to a common mutt named Sharik, the result is a crude, sloganeering self-identified proletarian who starts making a career in the new Soviet bureaucracy. Bulgakov attacks the ideology of the New Man on two fronts simultaneously: nature (what do you expect when your raw material is a dog?) and nurture (much of what the newly renamed Sharikov says and does results from the unselfconscious adoption of official discourse).

With the institution of the New Economic Policy (NEP) after the Russian Civil War, the New Man was haunted by a disturbing rival, who was both a holdover from the old world and potentially a harbinger of something even more crass: the NEPman, who was preoccupied with creature comforts and status rather than proletarian virtues and the building of communism. It is telling that Vladimir Mayakovsky's famous satirical play on the subject, *The Bedbug* (1929), explicitly compares Prisypkin, its protagonist, to a blood-sucking parasite after scenes in which his grotesque materialism has been explicitly highlighted. The play jumps to the far future, when Prisypkin is on display in a zoo as *Philistinius vulgaris*, which is even worse than the bedbug found with him: "There are two parasites, differing in size but the same in essence: the famous *Bedbugus normalis* and—and the *Philistinius vulgaris*. Both have their habitat in the moldy mattresses of time. *Bedbugus normalis*, when it has guzzled and gorged on the body of a single human being, falls under the bed. *Philistinius vulgaris*, when it has guzzled and gorged on the body of all mankind, falls on top of the bed. That's the only difference!"

Though the play's critique of its own audience is devastating (Prisypkin looks out from the stage and addresses his viewers as "My people! My own people!"), it provides an implicitly optimistic frame that simultaneously emphasizes what is at stake. We know from the final scene that the NEPman has died out, but we are also reminded that, as a phenomenon, he is of historic importance because of the revolutionary context: he is an atavism that must be wiped out if the new men of the future are to come into being.

The discourse of the age of NEP (essentially, the 1920s) made it continually clear that the character of the new world was still in formation, lending to otherwise trivial questions the weight of history in the making. Moreover, the question of the new world's character was rarely separate from concerns of the New Man who was to inhabit it. Just ten years into the postrevolutionary era, this problem would provide the ideological underpinnings of an emotional family drama: Yuri Olesha's *Envy*.

Bulgakov satirized the New Man by imagining him as a kind of Frankenstein's monster: with no real biological parentage, the New Man was a New Mutt resulting from the dubious social/scientific experiments of the class that conceived the Russian Revolution: the intelligentsia. Mayakovsky projects the genealogical problem forward, with Prisypkin's prospective father-in-law imagining him as the guarantor of the next generation's social status and well-being, while the denizens of the far future look at him as a terrifying missing link. In *Envy*, Olesha sticks firmly within the ten-year postrevolutionary frame of his 1927 publication in order to ponder just how New Men are made and who they actually are.

Olesha's New Man is only briefly given his own words and his own point of view, and even then it is in a letter accidentally stolen by his rival. Instead, he remains something of an anthropological curiosity to those who are unable to share in his Newness—an object of desire, admiration, and, of course, envy. The first half of the novel is narrated by Nikolai Kavalerov, a twenty-seven-year-old man who, despite his youth, is anything but new. An outsider quite literally looking in (into windows, into mirrors, onto soccer fields), Kavalerov has recently been taken in by Andrei Babichev, an older, overweight Food Trust functionary who found him lying drunk on the street. Andrei is working toward the complete transformation of everyday life, from the construction of superkitchens that will turn the family kitchen into a historical relic to the recipe for the perfect sausage to feed the laboring masses.

Structurally, *Envy* is a family drama, even a melodrama: Andrei Babichev has a brother, Ivan, his ideological opposite (or as opposite as one gets in the absence of actual political counterrevolution). Appalled by his brother's "New World" and its assault on sentimentality and the domestic sphere, Ivan proposes a "conspiracy of feelings" to counter drab revolutionary rationalism. Ivan's daughter, Valya, runs away from him and his mad ideas, to be protected by her uncle Andrei (who puts her up in an apartment). Andrei had also taken in another stray: the prototypical New Man Volodya Makarov, an accomplished athlete and would-be "Edison of the New World," who clearly has a bright future. It is only when Volodya is out of town that Andrei happens upon the drunken, homeless

Kavalerov, offering him the couch that he neglects to mention is normally occupied by Volodya. Envious of Andrei's success, Kavalerov is driven to fury by the prospect of eviction upon Volodya's return. After storming out, Kavalerov meets Ivan, joins Ivan's "cause"—on which, more below—and is encouraged to kill the man who wronged him. (Ivan doesn't know that the man in question is his own brother.) Ivan and Kavalerov soon encounter Valya, and Ivan drops to his knees and abandons his crusade. Kavalerov goes to the soccer match between the Soviets and the Germans, in which Volodya is the home team's star player. Utterly discouraged, he leaves the game before it is over, gets drunk, and sleeps with his slatternly landlady, Annushka, only to find Ivan is there with them, offering a toast to indifference and proposing that the two men now get to take turns having sex with Annushka. The end.

What makes this tawdry plot so compelling—indeed, what actually drives it—is the explicit understanding on the part of all the men involved—Kavalerov, both Babichevs, and Volodya—that everything about their domestic arrangements can be interpreted only in light of the conflict between the Old World and the New, waged between the New Men and their Neanderthal-like presocialist precursors.[6] At twenty-seven, Kavalerov seems to think of himself as roughly the right age to be the New Man (although, technically, he's a bit too old) but blames his miserable existence on a world that has no room for his aesthetic insights and his personal point of view. He is as he says, "as old as the century," in comparison to Volodya and Valya, whose exact ages are not specified, but who are coded as young in way that Kavalerov is not. By contrast, Andrei Babichev, indisputably too old be the New Man, is nevertheless part of the movement that gave him life.[7] After a brief crisis of doubt, when Andrei wonders how he can have paternal feelings in this new, postfamilial world, he doubles down on this connection across male generations, allowing himself a typically parental pride in his "offspring."

Ivan, though belonging to the same generation as Andrei, looks backward rather than forward, paradoxically projecting onto his daughter (a member of the younger generation) all the romantic qualities of a bygone era. But Valya chooses Andrei and Volodya over her own father—and, in Kavalerov's mind, over Kavalerov himself, even if she doesn't know of his existence. Volodya and Valya's qualities as New People are frustratingly generic: their physical health, optimism, athleticism, and Volodya's focus on the practical sciences. In fact, despite the number of ways in which Volodya is held up as a model of the new masculinity, both he and Valya suffer from a socialist version of the "terrible perfection" Barbara Heldt identified in her 1987 book of that title as the defining flaw of nineteenth-century Russian heroines: they are chronically underdescribed paragons of virtue.

Olesha's most important contribution to the idea of the New Man was not his depiction, a task at which the author repeatedly proved unfit, but his discursive framing. In the absence of a fully fleshed-out New Man, Olesha gives us unparalleled access into the minds of the people who are obsessed with the New Man ideal. In *Envy*, despite how much the New Man is meant to be desirable, that desire is always tainted (i.e., turned into envy) by the anxieties that the very phenomenon instills in those around him. Olesha's New Man exists not as a person but as an ambulatory reality distortion effect, given power by the libidinal energy invested in him by others.

The New Soviet Man and His Gerontologist

One of the problems with using "new" as part of a term of art is that "new" should, in all fairness, have a short shelf life. This is not always the case, as any surviving elderly founders of the New Criticism can attest. But the term has much more obvious limitations when attached to human beings or entire generations—some of the men who populated Brezhnev's famously geriatric Politburo may have been New Men or even New Soviet Men in their youth, but applying the term to them in 1980 would have seemed like the punch line to one of the many Brezhnev jokes that circulated in late Soviet urban folklore.

As mentioned above, Anna Krylova shows that the New Man was quietly replaced by the New Soviet Man beginning in the mid-1930s, with a shift in emphasis from proletarian and collective values to something much more vague. This vagueness was an appropriate attribute to go along with the nearly empty signifier "Soviet," allowing it to stand for whatever values emerged at a given time. Strikingly, she notes that at the Tenth Komsomol Congress, Stalin chose the word "Soviet" to describe the youth organization's members rather than "proletarian": "foreshadowing the kind of revisions to be applied gradually to the Soviet state's founding documents over the next thirty years, the Komsomol organization was to remake itself in the image of the 'New Soviet Person.'" Note that this was in 1936, when future General Secretary Yuri Andropov, who would take office in 1982 at the age of sixty-eight, was twenty-two years old.

Fortunately for future old people throughout the Soviet Union, the New Soviet Man would, like his predecessor the New Man, discreetly change his name, in a move that presumably reflected the passage of time more than any actual ideological innovation. In the postwar years, he was simply the Soviet Man. What is important at this stage, and up until the point when the Soviet Man becomes the object of satire and contempt, is not the ideological or ethical content that attaches to the term (whether it involves collectivism, optimism, technocratic practicality, or dedication to an ideal) but the mere fact of the "Soviet Man" as a set phrase and immediately legible notion of something particularly *Soviet*.

After World War II, that "Soviet-ness" might often be based on pride in the victory over fascism, an indisputably worthy accomplishment that is difficult to assimilate to an ongoing character trait (aside from the pride itself). While every country probably has its own ideas about a national type, they are more often ethnic or religious or, in the case of the United States, the basis of more than a century of national mythmaking. The Soviet Man, like the Soviet citizen, is not national in this sense; he is supranational, based on an idea that is supposed to be more progressive than the mere fact of empire. When Serguei Oushakine notes in "In the State of Post-Soviet Aphasia" that young people have difficulty defining the "post-Soviet," should we really be surprised? It took decades for any sense of a Soviet Man to come together, decades that involved the intellectual labor of party officials, pedagogues, journalists, and writers, and even then, the Soviet Man was something of a moving target. The Russian Federation is, like the Soviet Union, multinational, but it is so far unwilling to be either an empire or a thoroughly ideological state, while dismissing the simple goal of the general welfare of the population as somehow too boring. Post-Soviet Man's lack of a fixed identity is as stable an image as we are likely to get for some time.

All of this is further complicated by the issue with which this chapter began: the movement from the positive Soviet Man to his abject double. What eventually would become the sovok first had to endure an intermediate stage of degradation, when Soviet Man was cast as Homo Sovieticus.

In theory, "Homo Sovieticus" could have been a neutral term, or even a positive one if it had been adopted voluntarily by the people it purported to describe. Mikhail Geller claimed that he encountered the phrase in a 1974 book titled *Sovetskie liudi* (Soviet people), which called the USSR the "fatherland of a new, more advanced type of Homo sapiens: Homo sovieticus." Moreover, he claims that the term was used in the Soviet Union as part of a Latin instruction for future doctors, *Homo sovieticus sum* (Heller, 43, as quoted in Bogdanov).

Even if this is the case, it is a rather obscure example. According to Geller, it was the first Latin phrase the medical students learned. That's all well and good, but it is also Latin: under what circumstance were they actually supposed to use these words? As a rare reference to the contemporary world in the instruction of a dead language for people who need to be able to understand their profession's specialized vocabulary, it holds little promise as a transmissible meme, let alone as a term of art for pedagogy or propaganda.

Instead, the phrase makes much more sense historically as a diagnosis from afar and therefore as a phenomenon that is nearly always presented as negative.

With one perestroika-era exception, it would never really catch on in the Soviet Union; Latin words were more likely to seem pretentious than anything else. But the very failure of "Homo Sovieticus" to spread *internally* among the Soviet population only sets in relief the eventual success of *sovok*, a much catchier (and native Russian) word whose meaning would overlap with its Latin counterpart quite significantly.

Konstantin Bogdanov and Maja Soboleva, among many others, trace the term back to a 1962 study by Joseph Novak (*Homo sowjeticus*). Even in early scholarly works that used the phrase to describe a phenomenon that the authors considered negative, the words themselves had yet to become a term of abuse, nor were they on any reasonable path to becoming part of the Russian vocabulary. All that would change with the publication of Alexander Zinoviev's novel, *Homo Sovieticus*.

Zinoviev is one of the more vexing figures of the late Soviet emigration. Though immensely prolific and quite well-known throughout his life, he has faded into obscurity since his death in 2006. This is probably because of the highly tendentious nature of his work and the impossibility of pigeonholing him into any particular category. The head of Moscow State University's Logic Department, he was a dissident throughout the 1970s. When his first two satirical novels were published in the West, Zinoviev became persona non grata, and he emigrated to Munich in 1978. He continued to write scathing anti-Soviet fiction and nonfiction through the 1980s but was appalled by Gorbachev and perestroika. In his later writings, he praised Stalin and collectivization while raging against the West.

Before this ideological shift, Zinoviev wrote *Homo Sovieticus* (published in Russian in 1982 and in English in 1985). The book is an example of Zinoviev's favorite genre, the combination novel/satire/political tract, with characters identified according to type ("Critic," "Cynic") rather than actual names. Though technically a work of fiction (with the premise that the narrator is a KGB agent in the Western émigré community, writing back to his superiors), *Homo Sovieticus* is more concerned with taxonomy than character or plot. As Zinoviev writes in his preface: "This book is about Soviet Man. He is a new type of man, Homo Sovieticus. We will shorten him to Homosos. I have a dual relationship with this new being: I love him and at the same time I hate him; I respect him and I despise him. I am delighted with him and I am appalled by him. I myself am a Homosos. Therefore, I am merciless and cruel when I describe him. Judge us, because you yourselves will be judged by us" (5).

Zinoviev, in telling us his attitude toward his chosen subject, is both prefiguring the manner in which the sovok, Homo Sovieticus's next iteration, will be handled by his compatriots, and instructing the reader. I have titled this book *Soviet Self-Hatred*, a term I stand by, but self-hatred does not have to mean the complete absence of self-love. Homo Sovieticus is meant to prompt both groans of embarrassments and smiles of recognition.

Yet even in this preface, the terminology proves to be fraught with meanings intended and unintended. The move from "Soviet Man" to "New Man" to "Homo Sovieticus" is not just a matter of listing synonyms but rather of switching both semantic registers and discursive categories. "Soviet Man" could still be a mere placeholder, while "New Man" evokes the socialist/utopian traditions discussed earlier in this chapter. "Homo Sovieticus" is not just Latin; it is a biological term that suggests both an evolutionary process and the rise of a separate species. Given the Marxist emphasis on nurture over nature, this is deeply ironic, but considering the Stalin-era conflation of the sociological with the biological (as in the idea of the "hereditary proletarian"), it is also appropriate in its inappropriateness. The scientism implied by "Homo Sovieticus" is the logical conclusion of the quasi-biological, quasi-anthropological approach to the inhabitants of socialism that is inherent in the phrase "New Man." No wonder Zinoviev is so happy to appropriate the term as the title of his novel. Literalizing the metaphor of utopian socialist anthropology, it recasts the discourse of social progress as one of speciation.

Homo Sucker

But is Homo Sovieticus the next step in human (social) evolution, or a cautionary tale of Lombrosian degeneration? Homo Sovieticus becomes that much harder to take seriously as an evolutionary advance by the third sentence of the book, when Zinoviev offers his Russian abbreviation for the cumbersome Latin: Homosos (Gomosos). The word is undeniably polemical, particularly since "Homosov" would be a more obvious contraction.

In Russian, "Homosos" cannot be pronounced with a straight face. *Gomosos* sounds dangerously similar to *Gomosek*, a common Russian slur for "homosexual" (not the worst one, certainly, but not exactly a compliment). *Sos* is the Russian root for "suck," and can be found in another word that is similar to *Gomosos*: *pylesos*—vacuum cleaner, literally dust-sucker. And, not to put to find a point on it *khuesos* (cocksucker). So *Gomosos* sounds like "Man sucker" or "Homo sucker" (but not Agamben's "Homo sacer").

So who is the Homosos, according to Zinoviev? We can extract a catalogue of often contradictory characteristics from the author's quirky and nonlinear book.

Homosos is a collectivist:

> Our involvement in the life of a collective in almost all the important and unimportant areas of our life: that is the foundation of our psychology. The soul of the Homosos lies in his participation in collective life. Even the ideological processing which we protest about so often looks different from over here. It looks like a means of involving the individual in collective life. Ideology unifies the individual consciousness and unites millions of little "I"s into one huge "We." (84)

Homosos is a spiteful internationalist:

> I am a healthy Homosos: that is, a supranational creature. And a healthy Homosos is glad whenever any nation comes to grief. (37–38)

Homosos is patient and resilient:

> Food prices have gone up. Will the Homosos arrange a protest demonstration? Of course not. The Homosos has been trained to live in pretty dreadful conditions. (197)

Homosos is deferential to authority:

> The Homosos always tries to put a spoke in the wheels of anyone disrupting the customary forms of behaviour; he toadies to the powers-that-be; he is on the side of the majority of his fellow-citizens who are approved by the authorities. (197)

Homosos is a creature of ideology rather than morality:

> If one looks at the behaviour of the Homosos from the viewpoint of some abstract morality, he seems to be a completely immoral being. The Homosos isn't a moral being, that's true, but it isn't true to say that he is positively immoral. In the first instance he is an ideological being. And on that basis, he can be either moral or immoral, according to circumstances. Homososes are not villains. Among them there are many good people. But the good Homosos is a man who either doesn't have the opportunity to cause other people harm or who finds no special need to do so. But if he has the opportunity, or is compelled, to do evil, he will do it not less but even more thoroughly than the most inveterate villain. (198)

Homosos is not all bad:

> The Homosos is not only an agglomeration of shortcomings. He also possesses numerous valuable traits. Or, to be more precise, he possesses

> qualities which are either good or bad according to the circumstances and depending on the criteria of evaluation applied. One and the same quality will manifest itself as good in some circumstances and as bad in others. For some people the quality will be, or seem to be, a good one; for others, bad. Among the mass of Homososes one can discover all the characteristics known to humanity, but in specifically Socialist (Communist) forms and proportions. While the Homosos reflects in himself the properties of his social entity, he is at the same time only a partial function of that entity. (198)

Homosos is the future:

> Evolution-wise the Homosos is not decadent. On the contrary, he is the highest product of civilization. He is superman. He is universal. If need be, he can commit any frightfulness. Where it is possible, he can possess every virtue. There are no secrets which he cannot explain. There are no problems which he cannot solve. He is naive and simple. He is vacuous. He is omniscient and all-pervasive. He is replete with wisdom. He is a particle of the universe that bears the whole universe within itself. He is ready for anything and anyone. He is even ready for the best. He awaits it, although he doesn't believe in it. He hopes for the worst. He is Nothing; that is to say, Everything. He is God, pretending to be the Devil. He is the Devil, pretending to be God. He is in every man. Gentle reader, look into yourself and you will see there at least the embryo of this crown of creation. For you yourself are human. You yourself are Homosos. (198–99)

Homosos, then, approaches what would come to be called the sovok, but with much less emphasis on culture, decorum, manners, and taste. Instead, what the two have in common is their ambiguous status as a category that is obviously disdained as a negative other, but at the same time accepted as a ruefully accurate description of the self.

Perhaps my earlier dismissal of the phonetic similarity between "homo sucker" and "homo sacer" was too hasty. Homo sacer, as elaborated by Giorgio Agamben, is the man who has been excluded from all social and legal life as a citizen; he can be killed, but he cannot be used as a ritual sacrifice. Homo sucker (Homosos) exists entirely as a social phenomenon—he is constructed by the political/ideological system into which he is born. His is only *bios* ("qualified life," political life); no wonder so much late- and post-Soviet postmodernism focuses on the physiological, the life of the unmediated body (Vladimir Sorokin, Viktor Erofeyev, Valeria Narbikova, Yuri Mamleev): as an alternative to Homosos, *zoe* (bare life, the life of the animal, nonpolitical body) starts to look positively attractive.

The opposite of Homo sacer, Homosos is the sacrifice demanded of the late-/post-Soviet subject as the price of entry into a post-Homosos world. At times as charming as he is embarrassing, he anchors the subject in a network of connections from which extrication is essential. But wherever Homosos goes, he remains Homosos, bringing along with him the system that produced him. Sacrifice is impossible; indeed, as we shall see when we get to the sovok, the more one attempts to abandon the stigmatized identity, the more one proves just how good a fit that identity is.

Homo Sovieticus's more neutral-sounding precursor, Soviet Man, had one important last gasp in the final years of the Soviet Union. Yuri Levada, the preeminent Soviet/Russian sociologist of his time, led a five-year research project between 1989 and 1994 using opinion surveys to understand the "simple Soviet man." Levada and his team had assumed that they were writing the epitaph for a dying breed but would conclude that Soviet Man still walked among the living.

This was a strange twist for Homo Sovieticus, who began his life as a political aspiration (the New Soviet Man), was cleverly reframed as political satire by Zinoviev, but had never been a good fit with actual sociological research. In an article in *Slavic Review* as well as a blog post with the Wilson Center (both published in 2019), Gulnaz Sharafutdinova argues that the project was undermined by the tensions between empirical research and a clear political agenda:

> Empirically grounded and methodologically robust, it was a scientific project that claimed to explain social reality. Like any scientific endeavor conceived in a positivist tradition, it sought to be ideologically neutral, and derived its authority and legitimacy from that alleged neutrality.
>
> But it was not neutral. It combined a specific view of what human beings were about with a historically contingent theory of how the communist system operated and a vision of how the two, the individual and the system, were interconnected. ("R.I.P. 'Soviet Man'")

Levada's efforts yielded a great deal of data and were integral to the subsequent work of Boris Dubin and Lev Gudkov. But in taking "Soviet Man" seriously as something real rather than discursive, the Levada group ended up reifying an ideological construct. As Sharafutdinova writes, "essentialist and deterministic views of individual personality underpinning the Levada project that guide the current use of the Soviet man category are more politically and ideologically driven rather than being based on the state of the art in social psychology" ("Was There a 'Simple Soviet' Person?," 173). In a 2001 article, Levada defined the Soviet person as "isolated," "simplified," easily "mobilized," and subject to "doublethink" (*dvoemyslie*) (8–12).

Levada himself did not call his subject "Homo Sovieticus," but the term repeatedly crops up in the literature *about* Levada, most notably by Sharafutdinova herself. As a social scientist, Levada avoided the inflammatory terminology in which Zinoviev reveled yet came to similar, depressing, and essentialist conclusions about his people's capacity for democratic politics and independent thought. Sharafutdinova takes issue with the Levada Center's work on methodological grounds but in her "R.I.P. 'Soviet Man'" blogpost is at least as troubled by Soviet Man's political ramifications in an era of increasing authoritarianism: "Such interpretations engage a circular logic of codetermination of Russia's authoritarian regime and the human material that allows the system to exist in the first place. The circular method of argumentation absolves Russia's political and economic elites of any responsibility for the condition of Russia's state institutions, society, or economy."

Both her complaint and her critique are valid, but in her objection to Levada's and the Levada Center's Soviet Man research, she focuses on the flaws in the Soviet Man as sociological model. I would argue that the problem is not with the Soviet Man as a category but with the attempt to deploy him outside of his natural habitat. Like the sovok who came after him, both the neutral-sounding Soviet Man and the obviously polemical Homo Sovieticus make sense only in the realms of the imaginary and the symbolic. They function as ideology, not as meaningful sociological categories, and their import lies in their deployment (ranging from acceptance to rejection), and not in any capacity to describe living people or populations.

As Soviet identities moved from glory to stigma, the terms involved faced a serious memetic obstacle. On the positive side, the nomenclature is simple, immediately legible, and, most important, linguistically productive: the variations on "new man" simply follow the phraseological model established by the New Man himself: New Man, New Soviet Man, Soviet Man. "Homo Sovieticus" was a jarring linguistic intervention. Not only was it Latin (a language that has shallow roots in Russian culture) and phonetically unappealing; it was an import, and not a particularly sexy import at that. "Homosos" was definitely a step forward, but the source of its attraction was also an obstacle to its widespread adoption: it manages to be ideologically anti-Soviet and an implied dirty joke at the same time. By the mid-1980s, all these terms would be swept into the dustbin of history, or rather, history's dustpan. For it is the dustpan (*sovok*) that became the most widespread term for deriding the Soviet person as the Soviet project was on its way out.

2
THE RISE AND FALL OF SOVOK

When it came to catchiness, the word *sovok* had every advantage. First, it involved the repurposing of an already existing word (dustpan). Second, it phonetically resembles the object of derision (the Soviet). Third, and most important, it circulated the same way as the best critical or anti-Soviet cultural phenomena did during Soviet times, as folklore. "Homosos" was the product of a single author, whose tendentious work could not have been all that widely available as samizdat and who, in any case, has neither the moral urgency of Solzhenitsyn nor the inspired whimsy of Vladimir Voinovich (falling uncomfortably, and unproductively, somewhere between the two). *Sovok*, in contrast, belonged to everyone who used it.

This does not mean that no one has claimed authorship. On the contrary, there are at least four people who are often credited with inventing the term.[1] The Soviet singer-songwriter Alexander Gradsky (1949–2021) recalled in a 2009 interview that, at some point in the mid-1970s, he and his friends went looking for a place to drink (his mother and Yuri Shakhnazarov's grandmother wouldn't let them drink at home). So they all sat down in a sandbox but didn't have any cups or glasses. Rather than drink straight from the bottle, they gathered up the sandbox toys that someone had left behind and used them instead: a toy shaped like a bunch of grapes, a little house, a pear. . . . Gradsky ended up using a toy dustpan with the words "Dustpan. 23 kopecks" on it, which was "the most Soviet possible situation." Gradsky admits that he cannot prove this story, and in any case, he is not happy with how the word has developed: "It was supposed to be an affectionate nickname. Like an explanation of the hopelessness and senseless of struggling, an attempt, as it were, to invite people to raise their hands and shrug: 'What are you gonna do? We're all like that.' Then some idiots made it an insult. But that's not what it was."[2]

The critics Pyotr Vail' and Alexander Genis are frequently credited with coining the term, something that Genis categorically denies. Instead, he claims that he first heard the term on Brighton Beach, as an insult describing visitors from the USSR who bought everything they could find, "like vacuum cleaners" (*pylesosy*), which somehow got shortened to *sovki*. This explanation makes little phonological sense (how do you get from *pylesos* to *sovok*, which have only two letters and no syllables in common?), but at least we can cross Vail' and Genis off the list of potential authors.

The third potential author (or fourth, if Vail' and Genis count as two) has the weight of philological authority behind him: the philosopher Mikhail Epstein. After all, inventing words is part of his stock in trade, and he (like Vail' and Genis) has written a great deal about Soviet culture, which would suggest that unlike in Gradsky's case, the word *sovok* would have arisen as part of a larger philosophical or analytical framework. And, indeed, this is what Epstein himself has claimed in numerous interviews and essays. The clearest elaboration of his case can be found in a 2008 online essay, "Sovki i drugie." He rejects the connection between *sovok* and its literal meaning (dustpan) at the heart of Gradsky's explanation: "If we replace it with 'shovel' (*lopata* or *lopatka*), also used in children's games, we see that calling people who are Soviet through-and-through 'shovels' would be strange and inappropriate." In other words, the term is based entirely on phonetic resemblance.

According to Epstein, he came up with the term in 1984, when he began work on his book, *The Great Sov'*—*Sov'* being a made-up term for a nation, analogous to Kievan Rus'. Of course, *Sov'* was meant to be a stand-in for the Soviet Union, in this case inhabited by *sovichi*, who were divided into various castes, including the passive, ordinary working people called *sovki* (the plural of *sovok*). The book was published in 1988, and in 1989 Epstein read parts of it aloud over the BBC's Russian service, which he assumes is how the word spread.

All the same, Epstein is not happy with how the word ended up being used; he intended it to be "lyrically ironic," even mildly affectionate. Because of the mockery and scorn that he feels usually accompanies the word, and quoting Lev Anninsky's opinion on the subject, Epstein states, "I've come to hate this term, and have said so publicly and in print, and would never use the word on my own" ("Sovki i drugie").

With all due respect to Epstein, it seems more likely that he facilitated the word's spread rather than definitively coining it; given the number of claims of the word's earlier use, we are probably faced with a word that arose independently more than once. Epstein's own explanation of his authorship would support the likelihood that the word *sovok* could have been invented more than once, since its memetic success appears to be predicated on how much it sounds like the word "Soviet." The fact that it also means "dustpan" may well be a happy accident. But who, or what, is a sovok?

A Sovok Is a Person, Place, or Thing

The first problem with defining a sovok is that it is actually three things at once: an object (a dustpan), a person, and an entire country. The object is the easiest part, but it is worth noting that there is something appropriate about the fact that a largely derogatory term pertaining to the Soviet Union conjures up images of trash and abandonment, particularly once the Soviet Union was no longer a going concern.

Nowadays *sovok* as slang for "Soviet" is probably used most often to describe the Soviet Union and the Soviet way of life. When I searched the Universal Database of Russian Newspapers, the term unsurprisingly declined in use in the past decade or so, and when it did appear, it was almost always in relation to the country and system, and not as a description of a person. This makes a great deal of sense when you consider that one of the more prominent concerns of late Putinism is whether or not the Russian Federation, out of nostalgia or geopolitical scheming, is sliding back to Soviet ways (and whether or not that is a good thing). In other words, are the leaders of Russia trying to "drag us back to sovok" or "revive sovok"? Posing the question in this way encodes an attitude toward the outcome; if asked unironically, it assumes that going back to sovok is a bad thing. The object of anxiety, then, is the country, not individual people.

But before we get to people, we should acknowledge an intermediate use for the term, somewhere between people and place. In the 1990s, sovok could be used as an explanatory shorthand for why something is poorly run, or why a person behaves badly. Here sovok describes an ongoing, systemic condition that has an impact on daily life. Detached from a specific object, sovok becomes a diagnosis of a familiar, lamentable condition.

In all these cases (sovok as dustpan, as USSR, and as referent to systemic dysfunction), the word requires little by way of specification. People may argue vehemently about how appropriate it is to call the Soviet Union a sovok, as the writer Zakhar Prilepin did in a 2016 Facebook post generating hundreds of comments. When conservatives and nationalists rage against using the term *sovok*, it is only a matter of a very short time before the victory over the Nazis is deployed as a rhetorical cudgel against those who would dare be dismissive of Soviet accomplishments.

But the rejection of the word is about pride and moral one-upmanship, not about the definition of the term itself. Prilepin (and the numerous *Zavtra* columnists who make the same point) wants to cancel out the sovok, eclipsing it with the Great Victory and the very real sacrifices made by generations of Soviet citizens. These are competing narratives, but they are not arguments on substance. When the Soviet Union is called sovok, everyone knows what this means: economic deprivation, administrative incompetence, defective consumer technology, an intrusive public culture, bombastic rhetoric that is easily ignored, and widespread hypocrisy. Of course, this is not the entire story of the Soviet Union; neither is the Soviet victory in World War II.

Calling someone a sovok is another matter entirely. After all, one could theoretically live in a system one despises while rising above its flaws. But the polyvalence of sovok suggests the hegemonic power of the system, and its inseparability from the people who are its product. It is now a truism that, on the whole, Brezhnev-era dissidents were fundamentally Soviet in their anti-Soviet opposition (reliant on the same binary oppositions that operated in the Soviet system, and often just as categorical as the people they opposed). *Sovok* in its various definitions and manifestations did not describe dissidents per se, but it did recognize the difficulty of escaping Sovietness through simple rejection.

The paradox of the New Man was his dependence on the system to produce him: how could the Old Men create a world that would give rise to New Men? In the late Soviet era, that same paradox reproduced itself, but in reverse: how could the product of the Soviet system reject not only its values but the ways in which this system produced the very people who would oppose it? *Sovok* answers this question in the negative: it is simply not possible.

Singing a Declaration of War

The idea of the sovok spread throughout the Russian-speaking world largely as oral folklore, gaining greater notoriety when the bard Igor Tal'kov gave it a theme song. In the summer of 1998, he composed "Sovki," an anthem that he would sing in concerts over the next several years until his murder in the fall of 1991. The original Russian consists of rhymed couplets and quatrains, but my prosaic translation of these excerpts should convey the song's overall point:

> They don't think, don't feel, don't hear,
> They can't see a damned thing.

> They don't love, don't suffer, don't search,
> Don't strain their brains
> Their hands are shovels, their eyes are coins,
> And instead of faces they have square sovki [dustpans].
>
> Sovki, we won't give you our country!
> Sovki, we declare war on you! . . .
>
> They're not to blame for their creation.
> They were fostered by the authorities,
> Who benefit from breeding degenerates,
> So as not to accidentally collapse.
> What have we come to after twenty centuries,
> If all Russia is groaning because of the sovki?

Decades later, viewers watching clips of Tal'kov's performance of the song on YouTube (https://www.youtube.com/watch?v=J9hTXmJZR2o) are less likely to notice his political boldness than what now appears to be an awkwardly dated Eighties look, not to mention the fact that the instrumental accompaniment is shamelessly stolen from the 1983 Yes song, "Owner of a Lonely Heart," already five years old at the time of the song's composition.

Tal'kov's anthem declaring war on old-fashioned Soviets who were proud of their isolation from the West looks and sounds formally like the work of someone blindly copying Western models—the very phenomenon hard-liners condemned. The song is a vivid example of the sovok's inescapable double bind: how do you reject sovok values in a way that does not make you look even more like a sovok?

A Tribute to Sovok of the Week

Given the folkloric origins and unofficial dissemination of the term, it should come as no surprise that definitions of the sovok vary from person to person. What all the definitions have in common is that they focus on whatever qualities the speaker identifies as *specifically* Soviet and, more often than not, negative or embarrassing. A sovok does not exist in a vacuum; not only is his definition dependent on the attitude of the person using the term, but he is also defined almost entirely in terms of his interactions with the world around him. This is why, despite the word's apparent "anti-Soviet" flavor, it fits so poorly in terms of the Cold War paradigm that gave us Homo Sovieticus. A sovok is not brainwashed, nor is he a true believer who identifies entirely with the reigning ideology. Such ideas are not just simplistic; they are too focused on interiority.

The natural habitat of the sovok (person) was the sovok (country), formed by and interacting with sovok (the phenomena of the broken systems in which he operated). So let us first look at sovok in terms of consumer culture. Here sovok starts out at a distinct disadvantage, for it is not, technically, the individual sovki who are to blame for the drabness and poverty of Soviet consumer life. But sovki seem to be both entirely at home in their Soviet garb and Soviet decor while also embarrassingly envious of anything perceived as better or finer.

The sovok-as-bad-consumer is by no means the only version of the phenomenon, but it is certainly the one most conducive to relatively good-natured humor. Naturally, such humor made its way to the Internet. For a brief, glorious time in the 2000s, a website established by three post-Soviet émigrés devoted itself exclusively to the topic of sovok. Titled Sovok of the Week, it was located at the now-defunct sovokoftheweek.com domain, which at this point is accessible only through the Internet Archive's Wayback Machine. One of its creators, Vadim Jigoulov, self-published a book in 2014, *A Record of Interesting Choice: Tales of a Post-Soviet Man in the West*, which ended by reproducing a classic Sovok of the Week post: a Buzzfeed-style quiz to allow readers to assess their own levels of *sovkovost'* (sovok-ness). As a compendium of sovok clichés, it is invaluable, and so I reproduce it in its entirely:

> *Your wife's relatives are coming over for dinner this evening and there are no potatoes in the house. What do you do?*
>
> 1. Don your Turkish-made Adidas knockoffs and head down to the market to buy a kilo of potatoes.
> 2. Don your Turkish-made Adidas knockoffs and lecture your wife about the need to plan ahead for dinner guests before heading down to the market for a kilo of potatoes.
>
> *Once you're at the market, you see two rival potato-sellers whose booths are side-by-side. What do you do?*
>
> 1. Compare prices and quality of goods and then make your purchase accordingly.
> 2. Look to see which potato-seller will throw in a free onion to sweeten the deal.
>
> *As the potato-seller is weighing your purchase on a set of rusted scales, her neighbor starts her sales pitch: "Young man! Young man! You should buy my potatoes, not hers. Mine are from Orel!" What do you do?*
>
> 1. Smile and tell the old woman that next time you'll be sure to buy her potatoes.
> 2. Tell the woman bagging your potatoes to shove off and go buy the rival's potatoes. Potatoes from Orel always taste better. Everyone knows this.

CHAPTER 2

Your wife has also asked you to pick up a little something from the market so she can make a salad tonight. What do you buy?

1. Lettuce
2. What's lettuce?

On the walk home you bump into your friend Viktor Andreevich, who starts telling you about the hockey game he went to last night. What do you do?

1. Listen to his story and then ask polite follow-up questions about the score.
2. Interrupt him with an anecdote about the time you almost got tickets to see the Czech national team play Spartak.

On Saturday afternoons you like to visit the public library. Why?

1. To read current newspapers and keep up-to-date on politics and world events.
2. To read back issues of "Sovetskii Sport" [*Soviet Sport*] from the 1980s and enjoy the 27-ruble *kotlety* [cutlets] in the state-subsidized cafeteria.

After a long night of drinking vodka, you wake up with a furious hangover. What do you do?

1. Take a few aspirin, drink a glass of water, and take a hot shower.
2. Drink beer.

While walking through the park on a crisp fall afternoon you spot an attractive young woman sitting on a bench. What do you do?

1. Smile and strike up a conversation.
2. Warn her that sitting on a concrete bench will make her sterile.

Your friends are sharing photographs from their recent vacation to Bulgaria. What do you do?

1. Display interest in their stories and listen attentively.
2. Break out the old Soviet proverb: "A chicken is not a bird and Bulgaria is not abroad."

Your neighbor's car won't start and he's late for work. What do you do?

1. Offer to let him borrow your jumper cables.
2. Start telling an endless story about the time your car broke down when you were driving your sister-in-law's stepmother to the airport.

You're about to dig into a big plate of pasta. What do you put on top?

1. Grated cheese and marina sauce.
2. Ketchup

You're riding on the bus when a ticket-collector starts waddling down the aisle collecting tickets. You, of course, don't have one. What do you do?

1. Pay the 25-cent fine and continue to your final destination.
2. Get off at the next stop.

A legless war veteran is playing the accordion in a metro underpass. What do you do?

1. Give him some spare change.
2. Ask him if he knows "*Den' Pobedy*" [Victory day]

You are attending a free performance at the local House of Culture. When the piece concludes, what do you do?

1. Wait for the conductor to put down his baton and applaud politely while the orchestra takes its bow.
2. Immediately start shouting "Bravo! Bravo!" and rush down the aisle to throw flowers on stage pushing the innocents aside.

During the concert intermission, you and your date head to the buffet. What do you do?

1. Buy two glasses of champagne and two red caviar sandwiches.
2. Split a bottle of mineral water and take the *salo* [pork fat]-and-butter sandwiches out of your back pocket.

After the buffet, you and your date promenade around the foyer of the concert hall. What do you do?

1. Discuss the first half of the performance in a quiet, conversational tone of voice.
2. Loudly lecture your date on the architectural style of the concert hall.

While your date is powdering her nose, you wait for her in the smoking gallery near the restrooms. What do you do?

1. Smoke a filtered Davidoff and wait quietly.
2. Smoke a Belomor Canal [Soviet cigarette brand] and strike up a conversation about America with the foreigners standing nearby.

You need to go to the bathroom but your roommate is using it?

1. You patiently wait until he finishes.
2. You walk in the kitchen and utilize the sink according to your immediate needs.

In the context of sovok lore, the first thing that is striking about the Sovok of the Week test is that it is so clearly meant to be funny. This is not to imply that the sovok is never a laughingstock; quite the contrary. But even though the sovok is the product of Soviet/Russian urban folklore, he does not usually fit the traditional genres associated with it. As a compendium of foibles, the sovok could reasonably have been expected to join the large cast of characters that populate Russian jokes: the ethnic stereotypes (the Georgian, the Jew, the Chukchi), the trickster/scamps (Vovochka), and the repurposed heroes of Soviet mass culture and propaganda (Chapaev, Shtirlits).

Yet this is not the case. The jokes about the aforementioned characters are not just numerous but represent categories that are endlessly productive. Young Russians today tell and invent jokes about Chapaev while only having the vaguest sense of who Chapaev was supposed to be. But my search for jokes about the sovok yielded only one page with a significant list (http://www.vysokovskiy.ru/anekdot/sovok/). It contains fifty entries, but that number is deceiving; many of them are about the Soviet Union rather than the Soviet person, a few are about dustpans, while others, though meant to be funny, do not match the format of the Russian joke (*anekdot*) (there are several humorous poems, for instance).

Thus it is telling that this example, though produced by Russian speakers, was written in English and marketed to an English-speaking or bicultural audience, using a form (the quiz) that is widespread both in earnest and as parody. The Russian *anekdot* is quite different from contemporary American humor, and its resemblance to the joke telling of previous American generations makes it seem dated.[3] Since the 1960s, American stand-up comedy has become observational and is generally tied to the persona of the comedian. The Russian *anekdot* is impersonal and thus portable, continuing to circulate as oral folklore. Arguably, one feature of a sovok could be the insistence on telling and retelling *anekdoty*, whether the listener wants to hear them or not, while the sovok himself is ill-suited to the conventions of the *anekdot* genre.

Perhaps the sovok is not a distinct enough character type to sustain an *anekdot*, in that he is not entirely an other. Given how much of the humor centered on the sovok is about the sovok's ignorance about consumer culture and taste, and given the timing of the sovok's dissemination (the late 1980s–1990s), even someone sophisticated enough to recognize the absurdity of the sovok's reaction would also be perhaps painfully aware of how short a distance they have come from sovok status.

Dressing for Failure

On sovokoftheweek.com, the sovok is surrounded by a set of clear consumer signifiers. Not Adidas but Turkish knockoffs. Ketchup rather than marinara sauce. *Salo*-and-butter sandwiches brought from home rather than expensive caviar and champagne. Belomor Canal cigarettes rather than Davidoff. All of this could suggest snobbery, but the narrative stance is bemused embarrassment over the "bad" brands rather than crass pride in the "good" ones. In stark contrast to the New Russians, the point is *inconspicuous* rather than conspicuous consumption. The next step in evolution from the sovok is neutrality rather than garishness, since the sovok's own attachment to trashy consumer culture, against the backdrop of increasing consumer sophistication, ends up, in a perverse way, as ostentatious. The things that surround the New Russian are unavailable to the "neutral" narrator, while the accoutrements of the sovok are painfully familiar, because the narrator is only a few steps away from an existence that used to be unmarked, but now is unmistakably sovok.

This is why the sovok phenomenon is haunted by so much ambivalence. One wants to reject the sovok as tacky while also retaining an affection for the naive simplicity of a much more straightforward consumer lifestyle. Such simplicity is by no means value-neutral. The late Soviet media and educational system condemned what was called *veshchizm*; literally "thing-ism," the word is most commonly translated as materialism, but as a Russian linguistic invention it manages to completely avoid any association with the philosophical materialism so fundamental to Soviet thought (dialectical materialism) (Chernyshova, 53–55; Epstein 1995, 363–64).

Starting with the campaign against the *stiliagi* in the 1950s, it became important to condemn those who chased after nice clothes and cool gadgets. The rejection of *veshchizm* combined expedience (there was no way the Soviet Union was going to satisfy consumer demand) with moral superiority (why should mere material objects matter so much?). Though the vocabulary used in the Soviet struggle against *meshchanstvo* (petty-bourgeois preoccupations) had long gone stale, it did not conflict with an appealing romanticism that could be found in everything from spontaneous gatherings and camping trips to the antimaterialist ethos of Soviet hippies.[4] Condemning the sovok on the grounds of sheer consumer tackiness is a tacit admission that having nice material goods is good and that matter *matters*.

As the references to youth culture suggest, the sovok also had a role in intergenerational conflict; as perestroika wore on, young people were more open in their demands for nicer things, much to the consternation of many of their parents.

Moreover, the ambivalence about the sovok—that is, the way in which the sovok is simultaneously embarrassing and endearing—is far more legible in the West if we compare it to phenomena associated with immigration. The cheapness and tackiness of the sovok find echoes in the fiction and memoirs of first-generation immigrants writing about their parents. Of course, the post-Soviet story is, technically, not one of immigration—we are primarily concerned with the culture of people who remained in the Russian Federation after the fall of the USSR. But the experience of the Soviet collapse is comparable to that of emigration, in that the adult citizens of one country (the USSR) found themselves struggling to deal with the new realities of another (the Russian Federation).

When this displacement is confined to the literal, everyday world (that is, stories of once-Soviet people trying to make their way in a no longer Soviet world), mockery of the sovok can cut too close to the bone. Where is the pleasure in making fun of old people whom the world has passed by? A much safer and more reliable source of humor about the gap between sovok styles and the new consumer culture is found in tales of the sovok traveling to foreign lands. After all, one of the joys of travel literature is discovering not just the "natives" of another country but the strengths and foibles of one's own people that reveal themselves when one is abroad.

We will see our fair share of this at the end of this chapter, when we look at Yuri Mamin's 1993 film, *Window to Paris*. For now, the tropes of the traveling sovok are well catalogued in Gennady Belostotsky's 2009 review of the film *Kostya Gumankov's Paris Love*: "Around one-quarter of the film plays out (for the nth time) the arrangements for sending Soviet tourists abroad, with a large part taken up by variations on the theme 'sovok in Paris' (sausage and *salo* in suitcases, the immersion heater in the hotel, the shopping trips to stores that have everything you could want!)."

Though the term *sovok* was popularized only in the 1980s, the phenomena it named had all been around for quite some time. Mocking someone as sovok only makes sense in the face of an alternative. The Soviet-era traveler with his immersion heater and his canned "Tourist's Breakfasts" may look pathetic, but is he to blame? Stories like *Kostya Gumankov's Paris Love* can turn the sovok of old into an object of bittersweet nostalgia rather than derision. But the sovok rejected by a member of the late Soviet counterculture, a black marketeer/future entrepreneur, or the privileged scion of the well-connected Soviet elite is another thing entirely. That sovok is always backward, and always in danger of being left behind.

The sovok's plight becomes more pointed after 1991, when sovok-the-country is no more, but sovok-the-attitude and sovok-the-person could not have been expected to disappear as quickly as the system that created them. Now, in one of the many ironies that bracket the rise and fall of the USSR, the sovok would occupy a position homologous to the groups that, in the 1920s, were considered "holdovers of the past" (*perezhitki proshlogo*), largely people with petty bourgeois attitudes. The 1920s holdovers were bad subjects in part because they placed too much emphasis on wealth and creature comforts; the sovki-as-holdovers are bad subjects in part because they cannot master the codes of the new capitalist consumer culture. Marx defined class in terms of relation to capital, but the bad subjects of twentieth-century Russia are defined in relation to consumption.

This is why so much of the discourse around both the sovok and his subsequent offspring revolves around taste. As Pierre Bourdieu famously argued in *Distinction*, there is nothing natural about taste; rather, it is a function of cultural capital. The "correct" cultural capital is both signaled and constituted by the possession of "good" taste; while the scope of good taste may evolve over time, the possession of cultural capital allows individuals to develop their taste along with the rest of their class. But perestroika and the end of the Soviet Union, in addition to all of the material and political upheaval they entailed, provoked a crisis of taste. As the borders between Soviet culture and Western mass cultures fell, the values and behaviors of Soviet elites were inevitably challenged. Yesterday's good taste could be today's embarrassment.

The sovok is a problem of both value and values, particularly for those who are tempted to condemn him. Looking down on the sovok may appear to be simple snobbery, but it can verge on philistinism: how comfortable should we be when we laugh at people who are unwilling or unable to keep up with the demands of conspicuous consumption? In mocking the sovok, are we implicitly accepting consumer capitalism as the measure of all things?

Accepting the sovok is no less a trap. Does it mean aligning oneself with the self-righteous voices of Komsomol organizers lambasting a teenager for wanting to buy jeans? Or accepting the basic premises of Soviet economics, which neglected human comfort in favor of heavy industry, military buildups, and vague promises of a better future, all undermined by the obvious corruption of the well-connected elites? Or, even worse for members of the Last Soviet Generation, does accepting the sovok mean that their parents' generation, the "Sixties people" (*shestidesiatniki*), who talked endlessly about humanism and morality, might actually be right?

The most destabilizing thing about the sovok is that he may simply be a typical member of the late Soviet intelligentsia. This is more or less the case made by Victor Pelevin in his 1993 essay, "Dzhon Fauls i tragediia russkogo liberalizma" (John Fowles and the tragedy of Russian liberalism). Using the British author's 1963 novel, *The Collector*, as his point of departure, Pelevin compares the plight of the post-Soviet intelligentsia to that of Miranda, the novel's kidnapped heroine.

Miranda's complaints about the soulless, money-obsessed people surrounding her remind Pelevin of essays in the (then) contemporary Russian press by outraged and confused intellectuals, whom he also compares to the pathetic protagonists of Anton Chekhov's *The Cherry Orchard*. This last comparison, while not original to Pelevin, is particularly apt, since *The Cherry Orchard* is a play about the hapless members of a dying class forced to sacrifice what they thought they've always truly valued (the beautiful, the spiritual) for what turns out to be the only value recognized by the world around them—money.

Pelevin cites an essay by Genis, apparently from *Nezavisimaia gazeta*, but every reference I have found to it cites only Pelevin's own essay. Therefore, I will use it the same way Pelevin does: as a point of departure. According to Pelevin, Genis took a brief detour into the "metaphysical aspect of *sovkovost'*": "Freed from the laws of the market, members of the intelligentsia [*intelligenty*] lived in an imaginary, illusory world. External reality in the form of the beat cop only now and then would wander into their version lived according to the laws of *The Glass Bead Game*. Strange, blurry esoteric phenomena with no counterparts in the other, real world were born here."

Pelevin argues that the sovok is merely a recent name for an old phenomenon, one that in Russia is usually associated with the intelligentsia: a sovok "is quite simply a person who does not accept the struggle for money or social status as life's goal." As such, sovok can only be superfluous in the Russia of the 1990s: "Now this nonfunctional appendix of the Soviet soul turns out to be an unaffordable luxury." His conclusion inevitably leads us to the protagonists of chapter 4: the New Russians: "Of course, the sovok must be displaced [*potesnit'sia*], but the problem is that his replacement is not Homo faber but rather the dark, criminal guys who can be considered middle class only after a fifth shot of vodka. In addition, the majority of the ideological opponents of sovok can't seem to understand that being petit bourgeois—and especially being enthusiastic about it—hasn't gotten any less vulgar due to the collapse of Marxism."

On the battleground of market capitalism, then, the sovok is a metaphysical conscientious objector. Pelevin's approach was revived over a decade later (in 2005) by Dmitrii Bykov in an article for *Moskovskaia pravda*. Expanding on the idea that the sovok lives in an imaginary world, Bykov adds: "His country is imaginary, and that is why romanticism is possible there. Today's Russia, where there is no place at all for idealism, is a place that the sovok has nothing to do with: now it's hard to imagine that, for an entire generation, *The Master and Margarita* was a cultural event, and the Taganka [Theater] was a spiritual luminary."

All the different understandings of sovok-the-person share a sense of backwardness, of being left behind, but they vary according to the speaker's attitude toward the nature of the post-Soviet order, the Soviet past, and the extent to which "the Soviet" is identified with something lofty (defeating Hitler for conservatives; "high culture" for intellectuals). Yet framing the sovok as a member of the intelligentsia is at least as much a trap as simply looking down on him as a bad consuming subject. The *sovok-intelligent* depends entirely on accepting the opposition between market and culture that was so important to the intelligentsia itself. It requires an acceptance of a late-Soviet intelligentsia outlook, one that looks increasingly limited with the passage of time. Are our choices really between the Soviet-style intellectual and the thug? For an answer, we need look no further than the two men who appear to be making this argument. If anyone has had a career demonstrating that intellectuals and the market can come to an arrangement, it is Victor Pelevin and Dmitrii Bykov. Each is hugely popular, and their work is taken seriously in intellectual circles; even when a book by Pelevin or Bykov is raked over the coals, this only shows that ignoring them is not an option.

Neither Bykov nor Pelevin could be called "romantics," so their defense of the sovok as an outmoded intellectual is intriguing. They were young enough and flexible enough to bridge the gap between the Soviet and the post-Soviet, and to express highbrow concerns with the tropes of mass entertainment. Perhaps for them the sovok is a holdover of a different kind: for writers who have made it big in the post-Soviet world, the sovok is a poignant reminder of those who have been left behind. They never had to face the choice to sell the cherry orchard, but they were old enough at the time to recognize that something important was being lost.

"I'll Buy the Wife Some Boots"

Pelevin's invocation of Chekhov's *The Cherry Orchard* to explain the pathos of the sovok is apt for many reasons, not least of which is that it once again connects the sovok with geography. We have already seen that the sovok is forced to share a nickname with his country of origin, suggesting a synecdochal relationship: wherever sovok-the-person goes, he brings sovok-the-country with him. This, too, is a play on classic elements of the Russian national myth, which emphasize that the great-souled Russian is at home only in the wide-open spaces of his motherland. Reaffirming this myth in the 1990s is by no means neutral; it is one thing to trumpet the glories of home when you cannot leave, and another when the entire world is suddenly open to exploration. The post-Soviet traveler who visits exotic Europe or America, only to realize there's no place like home, is practically its own genre in the first post-Soviet years. Even commercials get into the act. When Lyonya Golubkov, the salt-of-the-earth protagonist of the serialized commercials for the MMM pyramid scheme, uses his newfound wealth to take his brother with him to California for the 1994 World Cup, they are impressed that everything there is not like at home (*vse ne po nashemu*). But his brother Ivan, in what amounts to their exit interview before leaving the states, declares, "American beer is good. But our vodka is better!"

The MMM ad campaign was a brilliant piece of marketing, exploiting the Russian viewing public's near-insatiable appetite for soap opera.[5] The campaign featured a cast of characters designed to appeal to every significant demographic targeted by the pyramid scheme: the single woman, Marina Sergeevna, who trusts no one; Lyonya Golubkov, the unemployed crane operator; Igor and Yuliya, a young married couple; and the seventy-year-old retiree Nikolai Fomich. The word *sovok* is never uttered, as is to be expected; it is, after all, a derogatory term. But the aesthetic of the MMM commercials is sovok from start to finish. Everyone wears typical Soviet-style clothes, from Lyonya's track suit to the pensioner's shabby coat, and all of them are established as models of audience identification who carefully keep derision away.

Lyonya the crane operator is accused of being a *khaliavshchik* (freeloader) and an *oboltus* (lazy, useless idiot); his profession evokes the tropes of Soviet honest labor, but the accusations point to their inverse: the shoddy hackwork of the exertion-avoidant sovok. Lyonya responses by appropriating the language of MMM itself: "I'm not a *khaliavshchik*. I'm a partner" (MMM's preferred term for investor). The pensioners unable to find their bearing in the harsh, capitalist 1990s are the epitome of the backward, pathetic holdovers of a bygone era. In the early days of the commercial campaign, all their desires are petty and materialistic, hence Lyonya's famous initial response to MMM's promise of a rapid return on investment. With a thoughtful look in his otherwise vacant eyes, Lyonya smiles and says, "I'll buy the wife some boots . . ."

Small wonder that the reaction in the mainstream press was so different from the testimonials of MMM's "partners" themselves. MMM purchased full-page advertisements in the national newspapers, chock-full of testimonials from satisfied investors (whether real or fake is impossible to determine). Op-ed writers had little but contempt for Lyonya and his ilk. The dreams of MMM's heroes were petty and embarrassing; everything about them was low-class. Presumably, that was exactly the point. Pelevin identifies the sovok with the intelligentsia, but that is by no means the primary understanding of the phenomenon. MMM's commercial soap opera reproduced the sovki as pure lumpenSovietariat, with gentle humor but little subtlety creating a simulacrum of its target audience as people deserving of both sympathy and success. MMM cast a wide demographic net, but the cultural representations it spread over the airwaves did not include the intelligentsia.

Rich Sovok, Poor Sovok

The most expansive artistic vision of sovok would appear one year before the MMM commercials: Yuri Mamin's 1993 comedy *Okno v Parizh* (Window to Paris). A joint Russian-French production (called *Salades russes* in France), *Window to Paris* retains some of the sympathy for its subjects shown by Ryazanov in *Nebesa obetovannye* (The promised heavens, 1991) but with a much stronger satirical bent. And, like *The Promised Heavens*, its subjects (nearly all sovki) range from crass proletarian slobs to refined otherworldly intellectuals, all while Mamin avails himself of what was already becoming a classic trope, the sovok abroad.

The hero of the film—Nikolai Chizhov, a teacher in a school that has transformed itself into a lycée—is a quirky, charismatic music instructor who wants to bring art and joy to the lives of his young charges (whom school officials seem determined to transform into the business leaders of the future). Wild-eyed and wilder-haired, Chizhov is played by Sergei Dontsov, who, under his birth name Sergei Dreiden, is best known to Western audiences as the Marquis de Custine in Alexander Sokurov's 2003 *Russian Ark*. There is an appealing symmetry to Dontsov/Dreiden's star turns in these two films, produced ten years apart. The title of Mamin's movie is an obvious reference to Pushkin's *The Bronze Horseman*, which describes the creation of St. Petersburg as the fulfillment of Peter the Great's desire to open a "window to Europe," while Sokurov's title suggests a Russia that must close itself off to weather a global catastrophe.

In *Window to Paris*, Dontsov gives us an intelligent, kind-hearted sovok who can embrace the beauty of the unfamiliar (Paris) while rejecting any suggestion that he abandon his Russian home. *Window to Paris* ends on a strong note of love for Russia, but it is a clear-eyed love that sees both charm and blight at the same time. In *Russian Ark*, Dreiden's Custine is a haughty, Russophobic Frenchman who can see the beauty of the Hermitage's Western treasures only while rejecting the possibility that Russia has anything of its own to offer. Sokurov's deployment of Custine is nakedly polemical; the love for Russia embodied in *Russian Ark* is defensive and reactionary. The best that the West has to offer is preserved in the "Russian ark" of the Hermitage Museum; it is the only "window to Europe" that Russia really needs.

The premise of Mamin's film is the discovery of a window in a St. Petersburg communal apartment that allows people to travel back and forth to Paris instantaneously, at least until the window closes again for another decade. The movie's own global distribution traveled a path that was equally magical, playing throughout Europe and the United States to positive reviews. And like the window in the film, Mamin's own window to international stardom was closed off abruptly. There had been talk of putting *Window to Paris* forward as the Russian Federation's nominee for the Best Foreign Language Film in the Academy Awards, but all such hopes were scuttled by the intense campaign of a much more powerful opponent: Nikita Mikhalkov. The chair of the nomination committee stepped down in frustration, to be replaced by Andrei Konchalovsky. Konchalovsky, also known as Mikhalkov-Konchalovsky, is, in addition to being a renowned filmmaker in his own right, Nikita Mikhalkov's brother. Mikhalkov's *Burnt by the Sun* was selected as Russia's Oscar entry and ended up winning the award.

The irony of Mikhalkov's triumph over Mamin starts with politics, since the nationalist, anti-Western Mikhalkov edged out a liberal director for an American award. But it does not end there. As we will see in the conclusion, Mikhalkov became obsessed with winning the Academy Award for best picture, producing a mostly English-language, aggressively nationalist melodrama that barely made a ripple abroad. He also made a sequel to *Burnt by the Sun*, a box office flop in Russia and an utter non-event in Europe and North America. Mamin, who articulated a premise in *Window to Paris* that naturally left the door (or window) open for a sequel ten or twenty years later, was reduced to unsuccessful attempts at crowdfunding a follow-up in 2014.

Mikhalkov's combined obsessions with Russian nationalist content and Western validation make him a fine example of a certain type of sovok, bringing together the tacky aesthetics of excess and stereotype with the privileges of post-Soviet wealth. By contrast, Mamin, at least when it comes to *Window to Paris*, looks like his own sovok hero: underpaid, with few possibilities to take advantage of the new economic and cultural nexus around him, he is obliged to try to crowdfund his sequel, like Chizhov and his students performing on the streets of Paris in the hopes of donations (Dazhunts). Sadly, Mamin was less successful at this sort of fundraising than his characters were.

Mamin's film never made it to the Oscars; perhaps looking for a window to Hollywood in addition to the *Window to Paris* is just asking for too much. And in any case, Mikhalkov and Hollywood are a much better fit. Mamin's film brings its hapless characters to what for Russians is the traditional capital of world culture, all the while embracing their essential tackiness as something almost lovable.[6] Mikhalkov's aesthetic is all about a tackiness that pervades his work while remaining unacknowledged. He wants to make his own *War and Peace*, but with all the stylistic restraint of *Moulin Rouge* and the moral nuance of *Battlefield Earth*. When Mamin's Russian communal apartment dwellers start hawking Russian chachkas on the streets of Paris while singing "Ochi chernye," he is inadvertently previewing Mikhalkov's own strategy for making it in Hollywood.

And this is part of what makes *Window to Paris* the great sovok text of the 1990s: Mamin's film is about products of the Soviet system trying, failing, and ultimately refusing to adapt to two different new worlds: post-Soviet St. Petersburg (which has replaced their natural habitat) and Paris (one of the most storied sites of Russian emigration). The window of the title is a magical object that allows for a new spin on an age-old Russian question: should I stay or should I go?[7]

Chizhov, the music instructor, is devoted to his country's future in the form of the young children he teaches. Unlike his superiors, Chizhov is more concerned with his pupils' souls than he is with their job prospects. He is otherworldly even before the window gives him access to another world. Witness his comical, but slightly creepy, ability to make his children follow him wherever he goes when, like the Pied Piper, he plays his flute. Like the Pied Piper, and like so many of the fairies of myth, he could rob his "village" of its future; indeed, when he brings the children to Paris, and they initially want to stay, he very nearly does just that. Instead, he uses both the power of persuasion and the power of his flute to bring them back home, all the while urging them to make their home a better place than it is now. Like the would-be builders of communism who would never actually be the ideal residents of the world they wanted to create, Chizhov knows that the only way he can improve the fallen world around him is to set its young natives on a better path.

Chizhov, then, is Pelevin's version of the sovok: the member of the intelligentsia who rejects the cash nexus as the be-all and end-all of his life. First, he declines a well-paying gig in Paris because it turns out that it is for nudists and would require him to conduct without wearing pants; then he passionately convinces his young charges that the material temptations of life in France do not outweigh their duty to improve their country. This positive spin on the sovok gives us a charmingly impractical man with an unfailing moral compass, appropriating for the intellectual one of the very qualities national folk mythology usually reserves for the "ordinary" Russian: unsophisticated by a set of standards that are perceived as inherently alien, he wins us over because he has a good heart.

The other adult Russian characters conform much more closely to the less idealized image of the sovok. These are the residents of the communal apartment that houses the mysterious window. Chizhov moves in with them after an elderly woman supposedly dies (she's actually just gone off for her regular, once-per-decade jaunt to the French capital), and they are as crass and coarse as Chizhov is refined. Rarely speaking in anything lower than a shout, they drink, fight, and, once they find the window, antagonize their French neighbor, who eventually learns a few choice Russian swearwords in order to communicate. Once in Paris, they become a walking, dancing, singing embarrassment: playing the hurdy-gurdy on the street for money, hawking souvenirs, and generally exploiting every

Russian stereotype that comes to mind. For them, Paris is not a place of beauty or wonder; it is a collection of easy marks.

They are not the only tourists in the history of art and literature to miss what is right in front of them. In E. M. Forster's *Room with a View*, one of the men remarks, "You know the American girl in *Punch* who says, 'Say, Poppa, what did we see in Rome?' And the father replies, 'Why, guess Rome was the place where we saw the yaller dog.' There's traveling for you." But the Russians in *Window to Paris* take Philistinism to new heights by combining it with a naked greed for consumer comforts. In the film's most memorable scene, they actually dismantle a Citroën in order to bring it back to St. Petersburg through the window, piece by piece. At another point, the drunken communal apartment dwellers have racked up an 8,500-franc taxi bill, but they manage to pay it by convincing the French Communist Party to lend assistance to this "Russian delegation." Meanwhile, when their French neighbor accidentally finds herself in St. Petersburg, she may as well have entered the ninth circle of hell: surrounded by drunks and boors, covered in the filth that the city seems determined to heap on her, she ends up in jail, weeping desperately until Chizhov finds and saves her.

Yet embarrassing as her Russian neighbors may be, the communal apartment dwellers manage not to cross the line into pure loathsomeness. On the contrary, they are warm, intermittently fun to be around, and, above all, resourceful. They are picaros, tricksters, and folk heroes. The sophisticated post-Soviet viewer might look down on their bad taste while still smiling at their familiarity.

Sovok without a Home

The protagonist of the 2019 science fiction novel, *Famous Men Who Never Lived* by K. Chess, is a survivor of an alternate timeline, one of the thousands who narrowly escaped a nuclear apocalypse. A New Yorker now living in a version of the city that is just familiar enough to feel like home and just alien enough to instill in all her fellow Universally Displaced Persons a sense of profound wrongness, she lives a funhouse version of the refugee experience. She speaks the language, but it is full of unfamiliar slang, and the political order of her new world (our world) is incomprehensible. She is always home, and she will never be home.

Window to Paris, with its own fantastic device of instantaneous travel, highlights a motif common to the sovok texts we have examined. When the sovok travels, he is made painfully aware that he is in the wrong place. He needs to be at home, even though his natural habitat no longer exists in its original form. The sovok is always nostalgic, but never entirely at home. For Chizhov, return home is a geographic imperative—he blithely brainwashes his students and hijacks a plane to make it happen. But it is also a question of temporal deferral. His old world is gone and, for Chizhov, that is not *entirely* a bad thing, but the new world will probably only be ready when he is no longer around to enjoy it. This makes him a parody of both the New Soviet Man and the Bolshevik dreamers who were trying to pave his way. The degraded offspring of the man of the future is stuck being a holdover from the past.

The sovok, like the "new" Soviet man, had a built-in limit on his life span. As the Soviet past began to recede, the culture found new ways to stigmatize categories of "backward" people without anchoring them to a specific, now vanished, moment in time.

3
JUST A GUY NAMED VASYA

If statisticians with time on their hands wanted to make a Venn diagram of the two devoted Russian musical fandoms that were likely to have the smallest area of overlap, they could do worse than selecting Bravo (1983–) and Kasta (1995–). Bravo, which began as a Moscow-based underground band in Soviet times, made a name for itself with its rockabilly stylings and retro rock vibe. Kasta emerged from the provincial town of Rostov-on-Don as one of the more interesting examples of post-Soviet rap/hip-hop. I would put their album covers side-by-side only if I were casting a post-Soviet remake of *West Side Story*.

The vast aesthetic chasm between Kasta and Bravo is also what ultimately connects them. The two groups are bound together by the magic of parody. In 1991, Bravo released an album that was retro even by its own standard: "Stiliagi iz Moskvy" (Hipsters from Moscow). One of its hits was a song, presumably set in the 1950s, about an impeccably dressed young man who could always be counted on to make an appearance at any event where celebrities could be found (a Sovremennik theater performance, a Spartak-Dinamo soccer game), usually with a beautiful woman on his arm:

> Ask anyone on Tverskoi Boulevard
> Who's the best at dancing the twist and rock-'n'-roll,
> Who's the best at playing Elvis on the guitar,
> All of them'll say, all of them'll say. . . .

And here is where the lyrics take a turn. The song's composer, Evgeny Khavtan, wanted a name that listeners would find pretentious, like Edik, but the lyricist,

Valery Siutkin, thought that the hero's name should be a stark contrast with his overall wonderfulness. The base player, Sergei Lapin, suggested, "How about Vasya?" Khavtan was appalled: "Anything but that!" But it was too late. Vasya won, and a hit was born (Kurii).

Twenty years later, during their unimaginatively named "Bol'shoi kontsert" (Big concert, 2011), Kasta announced "a little surprise" ("From the south of Russia... We're not gonna tell you what it is...") before launching into their own, hip-hop version of the Bravo song. Rapping the lyrics rather than singing them, they made only one alteration: "Vasya" was now "Some Vasya or something" (*Kakoi-to Vasia*). In Russian, that is just one extra word added to the chorus and the song's title, but it was a word that changed the song even more than Kasta's rap stylings.

Vasya, short for Vasily, is the quintessential hick name in contemporary Russia. Old-fashioned but still not rare, Vasya is somewhere between "average Joe" and Cletus from *The Simpsons*.[1] This is particularly the case when preceded by *kakoi-to* (some sort of), and the lead vocalist of Kasta pronounces the phrase with precisely the sort of disdain that usually accompanies it (the "v" in Vasya is drawn out with an expression of contempt).[2] Where Bravo uses the name Vasya to play against type, Kasta doubles down on the contrast: Vasya isn't even a proper name anymore but a type of its own. As a result, the song virtually deconstructs itself: how can a high-society heartthrob showing off so much cultural capital over the span of just two verses and a chorus be "just some Vasya"? For a hip-hop band of provincial upstarts, the paradox is irresistible.

"Just some Vasya" indicates the speaker's superiority based on geography, class, and cultural capital. Aside from the name, there is nothing specifically Russian about finding a way to denigrate this category of people. But, as the previous chapter has shown, the entire category of the "common people" is fiendishly complex after nearly a century of allegedly egalitarian socialism barely concealing the elitism of educated urbanites. Soviet ideology was fuzzy on the boundaries between the social and the biological, with the emergence under Stalin of the category "hereditary proletarian" suggesting a pseudo-Lamarckian sublimation of class into blood.[3] This chapter examines the variety of post-Soviet figurations of the "backward" common folk, many of which straddle the line between class-based disdain and quasi-eugenic contempt.

But the paradox in the original Bravo song, amplified by Kasta's playful cover, is our introduction to another of the main themes of this chapter: the propensity for a collective image of the "average" or even the laughable to be reclaimed as an exemplar of virtue or as a status symbol. In this case, the very ordinariness of the name Vasya suggests possibilities for its elevation to a point of pride.

Something happened to poor Vasya in the years between Bravo and Kasta: he ceased to be Soviet and now was simply Russian. Not that Vasya was ever *not*

Russian, but the Soviet civic identity provided an easy way to generalize without emphasizing ethnicity. In late Soviet times, someone heaping abuse on the sovok could be condemned as "anti-Soviet"; what, then, would be the appropriate way to dismiss someone peddling stereotypes about Russians? Accusing them of Russophobia.

The idea of Russophobia has a long and complex history, which I treated in *Plots against Russia*.[4] The short version is that the term was coined in the nineteenth century, revived by the antisemitic dissident mathematician Igor Shafarevich in the 1980s, and brought into the mainstream of Russian political discourse under Putin. In the twenty-first century, the Russian government and its defenders chalk up virtually any criticism of state policy or actions as Russophobic, while the stories of Russian interference in elections in the United States and Europe have finally begun to stoke actual, sustained Russophobic sentiment in the West.

Though undoubtedly a real phenomenon among specific people at discrete moments in history, Russophobia is also an invaluable tool in the analytical arsenal of the Russian conspiracy theorist. External enemies are motivated by irrational hatred for Russia, while internal critics are guilty of the very phenomenon elaborated in the introduction to the present study: self-hatred. The Russian post-Soviet successors to sovok fall under the umbrella of self-hatred, but only if the "self" at issue covers the entire Russian nation, ethnicity, or state. There is a convincing case to be made for the near-total identity of sovok and the Soviet people, in that the term's polyvalence (describing a person, a system, and a country) meant that the burden was on individual Soviets to prove that they were not sovki. The wide scope of sovok is also appropriate thanks to a prehistory of universalizing Soviet and anti-Soviet typologies (the New Soviet Man, Homo Sovieticus, Homosos).

The terms treated in this chapter (Vasya, Dmitrii Bykov's "Vaski," bydlo, and vatniki) have a different connection to self-hatred. They isolate presumably undesirable qualities and project them onto a stigmatized class, a subset of the larger group. Where sovok smacked of totality, these other terms function as synecdoche. The result is homologous to the exiled Soviet dissident writer Andrei Sinyavsky's explanation of antisemitism: "From my point of view, Russian anti-Semitism represents a kind of alienation of evil. It is a popular, mythic, almost fairy-tale notion that the people cannot be bad. Our people are good. They are our people. But some outsiders have wormed their way into the government, and they are to blame for everything" (13). In the cases discussed in the present chapter, the alienation is internal. The people *can* be bad, or at least specific groups among them can bear a burden that is far more banal than evil: it is the shameful yoke of the yokel. The speaker who identifies others as one of these various heirs of sovok is implicitly claiming an identity that stands in counterdistinction to an embarrassing, retrograde behavior or worldview. The speaker is engaging in a version of what the sociologist Lev Gudkov called "negative identity" (*negativnaia identichnost'*), a "self-constitution by contradiction, from another significant subject or concept, but expressed in the form of denying some qualities or values of its carrier—as another's, disgusting, frightening, menacing, personifying everything that is unacceptable for members of the group or community" (271, as quoted in Beumers and Lipovetsky, 64). For Gudkov, negative identity is wrapped up in violence (discursive and otherwise), but this would be too strong a formulation for the phenomena discussed in the present chapter.

Though he is the culmination of nearly a century's discourse on the next stage in socialist evolution, the sovok is only the beginning of an uncomfortable reckoning with the "common people" in a country that touted equality while cherishing social hierarchy.[5] The late- and post-Soviet imaginaries offer up an intriguing variety of ways in which to stigmatize a particular subgroup based on a range of possible strengths and deficiencies, while still never making the stigmatized group alien enough to reject as entirely other. The horror will always lie in an uncomfortable self-recognition.

But where the sovok was framed as a holdover from a dead or dying system, his successors crystallize anxieties about the new world being shaped in real time. Labeling someone (or something) sovok was an inherently ideological gesture, in that it encoded a jaundiced view of the Soviet system. But it was political only in the sense that ideology is political; the term appeared at a time just before "politics" became a set of open, public questions (perestroika). By the time the successors to sovok arrive, politics (electoral politics, government policies, and especially questions of economics) are contested openly in the mass media. The heirs of sovok are now bound up in these political processes.

In the current chapter, we look at the successors to the sovok, the imaginary types who embody a disdain of the common folk, crystallizing anxieties about the possibility of ever overcoming "backwardness." This is the common people as sociocultural ballast, a form of self-hatred projected by the elites on the poor and undereducated. After a brief examination of Dmitrii Bykov's "Vaski," a complex parody of the common folk disdained by elites, we examine the common slur *bydlo*, which covers the great unwashed characterized by their limited intellect and political primitivism. Finally, we turn to the Vatnik Internet meme, a political caricature of Russian nationalists and xenophobes. With the exception of bydlo, all of these categories will be subject to reclamation as sources of pride, superiority, or aesthetic charm, continuing the love-hate dynamic already established by sovok.

Bums, Shamans, and Holy Fools: Dmitrii Bykov's *Living Souls*

In 2006, the Russian writer Dmitrii Bykov published a novel that offered a perverse revisionist reading of Russia's past, present, and future. Entitled *ZhD* in Russian, the initials lend themselves to numerous interpretations, from "railroad" to "live souls." A version of the latter phrase, suggesting a counterpoint to Gogol's *Dead Souls*, became the somewhat less evocative title of the English translation, *Living Souls*.[6]

In *Living Souls*, we learn that Russia has long been the battleground between the Varangians (the modern Russian population) and the Khazars (the Jews).[7] Caught in the middle is the "native" population, who either live in isolated villages or, ignorant of their own roots, become assimilated in the big cities. Occasionally, some of these urban-based natives undergo a kind of midlife crisis, drop out of society, and join the growing ranks of the homeless. In the English translation, the women among them are called Mashkas and the men, Joes. In the Russian, however, the men are Vas'kas (I will omit the apostrophe in the name from here on out).[8] Vaska is a variation on Vasya, with an ending that implies either the speaker's condescension toward an inferior or warm feeling toward a friend who is something of a scamp.

Most of the action takes place in a time that appears to be an alternative version of the very near future, but with repeated references to the early post-Soviet years. The book presents two, seemingly contradictory, views of the Vaskas. When they are referred to as the natives, then they are simply the latest iteration of a peaceful, nonconforming group of bystanders who prefer to stay out of the way of history. Most of the time, however, they are a more of a social problem, a reinterpretation of the crisis of homelessness that began with the collapse of the Soviet Union. Vaskas are repeatedly rounded up and moved into shelters, but now there is hope for a limited reintegration into society: the new "Salvation Plan" allows families to adopt Vaskas and bring them into their homes, like pets. When one of the characters expresses his dissatisfaction with the program, another remonstrates with him: "'You're saying it was better when they cluttered up the streets and subways?' Shura said lazily. 'It was you who kept writing "Something must be done!" And now something's been done and still you aren't happy!'" He adds: "What's the alternative, Slava? Remember what it was like when Luzhkov was Mayor? What do you suggest, turn them into sausage meat?" (203).

We learn about the Vaskas because of one particular case of adoption: "Since she was eleven, Anka had dreamt of having a Vaska" (201).[9] She knows she wants a full-grown adult rather than a child. The entire episode is disturbingly like a story about a child adopting a dog (indeed, it even resembles the beginning of the Disney film *Lilo and Stitch*):

> One tried to juggle with two balls, another struggled to do a handstand, putting his legs against the wall and tumbling down again and again. Two more Mashkas of about sixty clapped hands and sang a Russian folk song with a sad rakish tune, although she couldn't make out the words. She noticed a couple of young ones sitting thoughtfully over a game of chess, moving the pieces at random: the Syndrome clearly made it impossible for them to learn the rules.
>
> She had discounted the idea of a child Vaska from the start. She liked one of about thirty-five, with a long face and big teeth and glasses, but at that moment he did a somersault and gazed up at her with such dog-like devotion that she wanted nothing more to do with him. Her eye fell at last on an elderly Joe with thin straw-colored hair, who had been sitting quietly in the corner gluing a little box and not trying to impress anyone. (209)

Anka chooses the old man and is sent home with instructions about his care and feeding: "No tobacco or vodka of course, and feed him strictly as prescribed.... Plenty of black bread and iron and outdoor exercise and daily walks" (210). This particular Vaska is a bundle of contradictions. On one hand, we find out that he is one of the "natives," and a highly respected one, at that. Indeed, his people esteem him as a kind of sage. On the other hand, his midlife breakdown and transformation into a Vaska is both socioeconomic (like the dislocation that struck so many middle-aged people after the fall of communism) and overtly medicalized. He and all his fellow Vaskas suffer from something called "Vasilenko Syndrome," a condition whose name is meant to be the source of the group's nickname ("Vaska" for "Vasilenko").

Bykov is, in fact, playing multiple games with the variations on "Vaska." The man adopted by Anka is named Vasily Ivanovich, which means that Vaska is a version of his real name. More important, his name, while ordinary, is also immediately recognizable. The most noteworthy Vasily Ivanovich in Russian culture is Vasily Ivanovich Chapaev, the Red Army commander who became famous during the Russian Civil War. The writer Dmitry Furmanov, who served as commissar under Chapaev, published one of the most popular novels of the early Soviet period based on his experience. Titled *Chapaev*, it came out in 1923 and served as the inspiration for an even more popular film in 1934 (by the Vasiliev brothers—more Vaskas!).

In the novel, Furmanov is simultaneously impressed and frustrated by Chapaev, who demonstrates a tactical genius but an otherwise simplistic worldview.

In the movie, he is prone to portentous aphorisms. But he found his greatest success in Soviet jokelore, with endless anecdotes about Chapaev and fellow protagonists Anka and Petka; in most of them, he appears to be a dolt.[10] All of this became grist for the mill of the premier post-Soviet satirist Victor Pelevin, whose 1996 novel *Chapaev and the Void* (published in the United States as *Buddha's Little Finger*) splits the difference by portraying the commander as an inscrutable Zen sage.

It would be difficult for a Russian reader not to think of Chapaev when encountering Bykov's Vasily Ivanovich, if for no other reason that the fact that the jokes never use his last name; though they are referred to as "jokes about Chapaev," they are always about Vasily Ivanovich, Petka, and Anka. And of course, the girl who "adopts" Vasily Ivanovich in *Living Souls* is named Anka.[11]

On one hand, Vasily Ivanovich is so helpless that Anka has to take him for walks every morning. Anka's family friend, Gurov, thanks her for taking care of Vasily Ivanovich ("He's completely useless when it comes to practical matters, as you know"), prompting Anka to ask, "Is it a bad case of the Syndrome?" Gurov's answer, like everything related to Vasily Ivanovich, is frustratingly vague: "Yes, or rather the highest form of it, I'd say. But forget the Syndrome, what he has isn't an illness, it's part of his nature, and I'm happy you're friends with him. Now listen carefully. This man could be the salvation of you and your family" (224). He adds: "my job's simply to make sure we lose as few of ours as possible, and Vasily Ivanovich is one of our best. Don't be surprised, Vaskas are never what they seem" (224).

On the other hand, when Anka eventually travels with Vasily Ivanovich, she sees that he is received by his fellows as a kind of shaman savant, a more docile variation on the holy fool. Yet he is also clearly a *bomzh* (Russian slang for the homeless), as Bykov spells out earlier in the text. What exactly is Bykov doing?

In a much more complicated fashion, Bykov is playing the same game as Bravo and Kasta: indulging the audience's familiarity with a negative stereotype while also (at least in Bravo's case) revealing the yokel's hidden gifts. In much of his work, Bykov delights in frustrating moral and aesthetic expectations. (His novel *Justification*, for example, reveals the Gulag to be a testing ground for finding the country's best people.) *Living Souls* is an odd variation on the alternate history genre, in that it is really an alternate near-future based on two important deviations from our historical reality: first, the discovery of a new fuel source that renders hydrocarbons irrelevant; and second, the transformation of conspiratorial or secret histories from speculation to fact (the Khazars and the Varangians).[12]

The Vaskas are a key feature in what turns out to be a phantasmagorical exploration of both Russian chauvinism and Russophobia. When removed from the philosemitic fantasies of Arthur Koestler and his acolytes, the very idea of the

Jews as the Khazars fits a familiar paranoid paradigm of a sinister nation within a nation. But conservative Russian nationalists are simultaneously undermined by the identification of Russian state power (the government, the military) as Varangian rather than native to Russia. If the natives are the "real Russians," then their depiction is simultaneously Russophilic and Russophobic. Consistent with the snobbishness and classism behind phrases like "some sort of Vasya," at best they live a step removed from utter squalor. As the homeless, they are a blight on the post-Soviet urban landscape; as genetic defectives reduced to incompetence in midlife, they are the phenotypic expression of Russian backwardness. But as fonts of wisdom, however Zen or absurd that wisdom might be, they are truly in touch with the land, and they preserve gentle moral values forgotten by both Varangians and Khazars. In this sense, they are a twisted version of a Slavophile fantasy.

The Vasyas of popular song and the Vaskas of Bykov's novel remind us how easily these stigmatized identities switch valences and become glorified, and how easily they move from one category to the other.

Cattle Call

There are, however, a few terms that resist reclamation, in particular the epithet that has the broadest, least specific scope in the Russian arsenal of projected stigmatization: *bydlo*. Bydlo is a Polish and Ukrainian collective noun that originally referred to cattle, but in Russian denotes the brainless, unwashed masses who follow the crowd, believe what they are told, and, of course, have terrible taste. Compared to bydlo, the concept of sovok is practically optimistic: Soviet holdovers will inevitably pass, but stupidity is forever.[13]

As an insult, bydlo functions multidirectionally: one might hear a (possibly liberal) snob dismiss, say, Putin's supporters as bydlo, but one might just as easily hear someone who claims to represent the common people attacking the elites, saying, "They think we're all bydlo." Indeed, even though the word *sovok* has its roots in words related to politics, it is *bydlo* that has the stronger political component (along with its obvious concerns for social class). Sovok, we recall, implicated everyone who came of age in the USSR, to one degree or another. As an attempt at alienating the negative from one's concept of the collective self, sovok could never be an unqualified success. Bydlo, in contrast, is an ideal tool for alienation. Moreover, it is universal: every culture can have bydlo, but only some can have sovki.

As the scholar and journalist Sergei Medvedev put it in a 2012 article, "Fenomenologiia bydla": "In the 1990s, we disdainfully tried to distance ourselves from the sovok, while in the 2000s, instead of the sovok we began to speak of bydlo."[14] The decline of sovok and the persistence of bydlo puts sovok in context. Like many countries, Russia has a long history of alienation between the elites and the masses (terms that should really be put in scare quotes, since their definition is both provisional and malleable), traceable in no small part to the long serfdom of the majority of the ethnic Russian population before 1861. In Pushkin's time, this was expressed in disdain for the unwashed *chern'* (from the word black, it connoted an intellectual rather than physical darkness). In the last six decades of the nineteenth century, the common people (*narod*) were fetishized across the Russian political spectrum, from the Slavophiles (who saw the peasants as the bearers of true Russian values) to the Populists (whose movement to "go to the people" was a dismal failure) to the varieties of Marxists (who saw the future in the proletariat).

In 1908, the Symbolist poet Aleksandr Blok wrote his famous essay, "The People and the Intelligentsia," lamenting the naive one-sidedness of the intelligentsia's infatuation with the common folk:

> But from the other side—ever the same faintly ironical smile, the knowing silence, the gratitude for "instruction" and apologies for "ignorance," with an undertone of "for the present, till our time comes." A dreadful laziness and dreadful torpor, it always seemed to us; or else the slow awakening of a giant, as it seems to us more and more. A giant waking with a singular smile on his lips. No intelligent smiles like that; one would think we knew all the ways of laughing there are, but in face of the muzhik's smile—which has nothing in common with the irony that Heine and the Jews have taught us, or with Gogol's laughter through tears, or with [Vladimir] Solov'ev's loud laughter—all our laughing instantly dies; we are troubled and afraid. (359)

For Blok, the people and intelligentsia might as well be warring nations: "Between the two camps—the people and the intelligentsia—there is a line at which they can meet and agree. No such uniting line existed between the Russians and the Tatars in their frankly hostile camps" (360). Blok sees in this conflict an oncoming disaster, borrowing from the metaphor of Gogol's troika at the end of *Dead Souls*, and suggesting that the Russian troika might be on the verge of trampling the intelligentsia beneath its hooves. A hostile interpretation of the Russian Revolution would hold that Blok was prophetic.

But Blok's giant *muzhik* or runaway troika are (like the sovok) the historically contingent and ultimately short-term metaphorical manifestation of a centuries-old problem that is not going away. In Blok's time, this split between the elites and the common folk is appropriately framed in terms of impending catastrophe, while the late- and post-Soviet sovok is an image of inexorable decline. When each moment passes, we are left with something that is, at least structurally, the same gap as before (if we do not include the intelligentsia in the sovok category, as do Pelevin and Bykov). It is an algebraic formula, with one variable representing some notion of the elite, and the other standing in for some notion of the common.

As the post-Soviet period wears on, we start to see a possible deideologization of this gap, starting in the late 1990s, when the bydlo can be merely crass, and coming to an abrupt halt in Putin's third term. The contempt for bydlo (or, to borrow a Soviet-style formulation, "Bydlo and the Struggle against It") goes farther than the disdain for the sovok. Sovok-hatred is preoccupied primarily with taste, while bydlo-bashing rests at the dangerous intersection of taste, intelligence, and, eventually, politics.

When it comes to culture, the sovok's lament was that culture wasn't being produced with him in mind anymore. His alienation from post-Soviet trends in art, entertainment, and literature was a constituent element of his personal story. As Western and Westernized mass culture come to dominate the post-Soviet media ecosystem, the anxieties center around (1) the incredibly poor quality, lack of sophistication, and sheer stupidity now on offer; and (2) the audience that is presumed to enjoy this stuff and even want more of it.

Bydlo functions simultaneously as national and global; global, in that the contempt for bydlo easily inscribes itself within a worldwide tradition of elite disdain for the unwashed masses; and national, in that the critique of bydlo so often plays out in terms of shame for a specifically Russian "backwardness." Even this, however, could be framed as a kind of progress: self-hatred does not have to rely on the Soviet experience anymore.

Watching the Defectives

Unlike its Internet successors, bydlo is a creature of television. That is, bydlo is posited as the ideal audience for the stupefying messages conveyed by state television. Even worse, the bydlo threatened to become not just the audience but the subject matter of mass entertainment. This would certainly be the case in Russia, as in the rest of the world, when Internet streaming technology made video blogging accessible to the masses (YouTube's motto was, famously, "Broadcast yourself"). But before YouTube and its imitators, in the age of the dial-up modem and the 2400-baud connection, national television was already moving in the direction of turning its least sophisticated viewers into entertainment in their own right. The most notable example was the TV6 program called *Znak kachestva* (Seal of Quality).

Initially a ten-minute series of clips aired twice a day on TV6, after three years on the air *Znak kachestva* changed to an hour-long format in June 1999, only to be cancelled in 2001 due to low ratings. In its classic, pre-1999 format, *Znak kachestva* was a step toward the democratization of television, even if some of the audience probably watched it in horror. The show had an uncomplicated premise, giving virtually anyone the chance to express themselves before the entire country at no cost, whether that expression took the form of (frequently terrible) singing and dancing or the recitation of poems that were unlikely to grace the pages of selective literary journals. Paid announcements and advertisements were also included, but in a manner consistent with the rest of the show (commercials were not prerecorded).

Because most episodes had no grand design beyond the program's basic conception, virtually any random episode can be taken as representative of *Znak kachestva*'s typical content. The only differentiating factor was that the daytime broadcast tended to favor children and teenagers a bit more than the evening version, which relied heavily on amateur exotic dancers trying to win a never-ending "erotic show" contest promising work in Russia and abroad. An episode that aired on May 26, 1999, presents two different colorfully garbed women reading tarot cards, lighting candles, staring at icons, and gazing into crystal balls. Madame Sofia offers her help removing curses and finding success in love and business, in a deadly earnest tone that her central-casting witch's outfit renders all the more comical. She is followed by a young man playing the guitar and singing off-key, then by a set of erotic dancers. Immediately after the erotic dancers we see a group of five teenage (and preteen) girls, performing basic aerobics moves while lip-synching to the song "Ia uchus' tantsevat'" ("I'm Learning to Dance"). *Znak kachestva* was a late-twentieth-century twist on the nineteenth-century physiological sketch, offering up peculiar character types for the viewer's entertainment, if not edification.

Indeed, the elements that compose *Znak kachestva*'s minimalist frame reinforce this sense of a parade of character types. At least twice during every sequence, the performances are interrupted by an animated clip of a spaceship with the *Znak kachestva* logo as it lands in front of Red Square. When the door opens, out come a violinist in a tuxedo; a big-haired, big-breasted woman in the skimpiest of bikinis; and a young man listening to his boom box: *Znak kachestva* is a freak show from outer space. Yet immediately after the last cartoon character leaves the ship, telephone numbers flash across the screen, reminding the viewers that they, too, can be transported through the ether and end up on the nation's television screens. Thanks to *Znak kachestva*, the idiot box is no longer a one-way means of communication: anyone in the audience can become part of the show.

But who, exactly, is the audience, and why are they watching the show, let alone performing on it? The amateurs who dance, sing, and declaim are, more often than not, painfully sincere: the would-be exotic dancers hope to land paying gigs, while the singers' and poets' dreams of stardom are almost palpable. From its very beginning, *Znak kachestva* held out the promise of fame and fortune as a distinct possibility. *Znak kachestva* created its very own girl band through an amateur competition: the bland but relatively successful Strelki. But the innovation of *Znak kachestva* is not so much that it takes no-talents seriously as that it has it both ways: the amateurs perform their hearts out, smiling or looking soulfully at the cameras, but the producers add their own editorial comments in the form of quips and *chastushki* printed at the bottom of the screen. The commentary, while sarcastic, does not break with the show's overall level of sophistication and taste: these ready-made aphorisms may make it all the more difficult to take the performers seriously, but they show no more evidence of talent than do the singers and dancers themselves. The aforementioned guitarist probably doesn't realize that his picture is accompanied by the phrase "Radost' derzhi v karmane, a gore na ekrane" (Keep your joy in your pocket, and your misery on the screen), nor do the aerobics girls know that while they are jumping and waving, the audience is reading the words "My uchilis' tantsevat', chtoby doma ne skuchat'" (We learned to dance, so as not to stay at home bored).

Znak kachestva may well be the first Russian example of self-conscious popular entertainment with such polyvalent irony. It appeals to both the earnest amateurs and the skeptical hecklers, living up to its self-proclaimed status as a *narodnaia peredacha*: it has something for everyone. The show exploits the irony inherent in the very name, *Znak kachestva*: initially referring to Brezhnev-era attempts to improve consumer goods by affixing a "seal of quality" to various products, the *znak kachestva* quickly became the stuff of Soviet anecdotes, implying the exact opposite of the intended meaning. It is an official emblem of high quality that the savvy consumer immediately realizes is a sign of no quality. This symbol was supposed to alert the consumer to the arrival of an extraordinary product but actually meant more of the same shoddy merchandise. The irony of the Brezhnev-era *znak kachestva* is affixed to the post-Soviet amateur performers, who themselves play the role of the defective goods elevated to high-quality status.

Playing a complicated game with its audience, *Znak kachestva* invited them both to identify with and mock the people on screen, who were essentially audience members who might have been better-off never leaving their couches. Critics hated it, of course, because the "people's show" showed the people to be hopeless fools. Nearly twenty years after the show went off the air, however, what is striking is how harmless and good-natured it actually was. A product of the free-wheeling 1990s, *Znak kachestva* did not invite its viewers to draw political conclusions; culture and politics were still largely separate spheres.

It can only be a coincidence that the show changed to a moderated, MC-facilitated format just a few weeks before Putin first became prime minster, but the fact that the show went from giddy chaos to controlled tedium on the eve of the next great political transformation of the post-Soviet era is certainly evocative. The show's 2001 cancellation, no doubt attributable to both the failure of the new format and the limited shelf life of novelty programming, was also well-timed. When next we see the bydlo take to the airwaves, the stakes will be much higher.

A Coat of Not Many Colors: Vatnik

In 2011, the cartoonist Anton Chadsky invented a meme that would, a few short years later, become a mainstay of political discourse and satire: Vatnik.

The Russian word *vatnik* originally and primarily refers to a cotton-padded jacket that was part of the Soviet army's winter uniform from the 1940s through the 1960s, also serving as standard-issue winter clothing for prisoners in the Gulag. In a 2014 interview with *Snob*, Chadsky explains how he turned the vatnik into an Internet meme: "It was in 2011, a couple of months before the mass protests against the falsified Duma elections. I decided to draw a character who would embody all the negative qualities of the typical Russian citizen (*rossiianin*). By analogy to SpongeBob Square Pants, Rashka Square Vatnik (Rashka-Kvadratnyi Vatnik) was born." Chadsky also cited American satirical cartoons as an influence, claiming that they can help people "set their brains right": *American Dad* and *Family Guy* "are cartoons that poke fun at the flaws of American society. I want my readers to look at themselves from the outside, get more rational, and not fall for propaganda." For better or worse, Vatnik takes visual inspiration from SpongeBob (he is roughly the same shape) and satirical inspiration from the work of Seth McFarlane.

Where SpongeBob is a bright and healthy yellow (well, healthy for a sponge), Vatnik is gray. Where SpongeBob smiles vacantly, Vatnik looks like a mean drunk. One of his eyes is always blackened, the other purple and closed shut. His teeth are few and far between, and his face is usually covered with a five-o-clock shadow.

As a mouthpiece for the kind of reflexive chauvinism known in Russian as *urapatriotizm* (hurrah patriotism), the Vatnik meme quickly spread throughout the Internet. Obviously, this is fundamentally different from the way in which the idea of the sovok spread in the 1980s and 1990s, before the Internet was a mass phenomenon. The sovok's origins were verbal, as part of oral folklore;

subsequently, artists could create caricatures of the sovok, but they were always multiple and secondary: there is no single representation of the sovok.

The sovok started as, and remained, a character type; Vatnik was a character intended to *suggest* a type. When aggressive patriotic sentiment came to the forefront during the war in Ukraine, Vatnik was ready. And this is where Vatnik's trajectory differs from that of the sovok. Where the sovok was a concept known primarily by people who could, at least theoretically, fall within its target group, Vatnik took a different path.

Vatnik was now both a specific character (as seen in the Internet meme) and a general category, a distinction I am trying to highlight here by capitalizing the word as a proper name for the character and using the definite article (with no capitalization) when referring to the type. Within Russia and the Russian-speaking community, *vatnik* was less an ethnic slur than a political label. Putin's critics reserved the label *vatnik* (and its more generalized corollary, *vata* [cotton]) for a part of their own society that they found loathsome. Internally, vatniki were essentially politicized, pro-Putin bydlo.

In Ukraine, vatnik as a designation for the Russian enemy inevitably became an ethnonym. Slurs are casually tossed about on all sides of the conflict: Russians refer to Ukrainians as *ukropy* (dills), while Ukrainians, who have long complained of *moskali*, now also call Russians *kolorady*. With the possible exception of kolorady (based on the apparent resemblance of the St. George's ribbon, a Russian military symbol that has recently been adopted for patriotic purposes, to the Colorado beetle), these terms have no independent negative meanings. Ukrainians are called "dills" because the Russian word *ukrop* shares its first three letters with Ukraine, and *moskali* simply comes from Moskva (Moscow). They are offensive only because they are meant to be offensive.

As a Ukrainian ethnopolitical slur, vatnik has little to recommend itself; it is just one item in a sadly growing vocabulary for denigrating a nation's external enemy. Within Russia, the vatnik follows the path of the sovok and the bydlo toward alienating a subsection of one's own, larger group. No doubt the vatnik is a compendium of national and ethnic stereotypical traits easily identifiable with Russians: the rowdy, aggressively patriotic vodka-swilling drunk is not exactly an original idea. The critique, however, is less ethnic or national than it is ideological: the vatnik is an object of scorn not because of his ancestry but because of his behavior and his worldview. Or rather, the only ancestry that is important for understanding the vatnik is figurative: he is a descendant of sovok.

Vatnik's own creator, Anton Chadsky, makes the link clear: "Vatnik's success comes from the fact that it has filled an available niche, just as the term *sovok* did in its time. Some people made fun of Russian nationalists, others of communists, still others of pagans, but there was no single, collective image. Vatnik combined all of that into himself, becoming a universal symbol" ("Sozdatel' 'Vatnika'"). In another interview, he extends the comparison:

> In my opinion, Vatnik is the anthropological continuation of the activity and way of thinking of the sovok. There's no Soviet Union, so there are no sovki. The people who are nostalgic for the USSR today I would also call vatniki. Vatnik is the grandson and son of the sovok, he thinks in the same categories, but under contemporary Russian conditions and realities. But again, that's if you think of the word *sovok* negatively. But Genis himself doesn't put negative connotations into the word; his definition has nostalgic notes to it. I would consider the image of the sovok as a more parodic and more caricatured negative, just as I see in the image of the vatnik a person living according to the stereotypes delivered to him by the state on television screens. ("Vnuk 'sovka'")

It makes sense that Chadsky sees the sovok in such a strongly negative light, since it is negativity that both characterizes and drives his idea of the vatnik. Under Chadsky's pen, Vatnik is difficult to love: ugly, bruised, and aggressive, his features are usually contorted to express the feeling that his creator identifies as central to the vatnik's existence—hatred.

Compared to the vatnik, the sovok looks positively gentle. The sovok, after all, is the quintessence of Late Socialism, preoccupied with consumption, culture, and work avoidance. But the vatnik, even if he is the "grandson" of the sovok, has a more troubling and more complicated historical context. Chadsky designed him to represent his own era, an era that he understands in terms of a more distant Soviet past: the Stalin years. Though the coat that gave Vatnik his name was a mainstay of military life during World War II, Chadsky specifically connects it to the Gulag. The vatnik lives in two times at once, as Chadsky himself told an interviewer: "The vatnik is the Russian citizen [*rossiianin*] who, to this day, still mentally lives in Stalin's camps and is fine with that" (Zhogov). Thus, according to Chadsky, the key to the vatnik is hatred, whose targets include but are not limited to: America, the West, sexual minorities, liberalism, and Ukraine (2015).

The sovok oscillated between representing a maligned segment of the post-Soviet population (people who clung to their old Soviet ways and worldview) and encompassing virtually everyone who was raised in the Soviet system, ruefully acknowledging kinship with a character type that, while not flattering, may have had its charms. The vatnik's role in the Russian imaginary is much more clear-cut. Chadsky acknowledges that some people might try to appropriate Vatnik as a positive representation of their own self-image but is convinced that this would be a misunderstanding of what Vatnik is all about. The sovok was abject, but the vatnik is the *politicized* abject. The vatnik is the (presumably liberal)

Russian's ideological opponent in political debates and processes that are real, relevant, and current. To put it simply: an American vatnik would be a cartoon character made out of a MAGA hat.

Chadsky may be right when he identifies the vatnik with hatred. For that matter, if we believe in the importance of authorial intent, he has to be right, at least in the initial stages, before the Vatnik Internet meme spreads both with and without him. But even if we accept that the hatred is initially the product of Vatnik and the people he parodies, hatred inevitably becomes a two-way street. Loving Vatnik-as-parody is difficult to disentangle from hating the vatnik as an object of parody. Which raises the question: is Vatnik an instrument of Russophobia? The image of Vatnik is so hostile (however hilarious) that accusations of Russophobia begin to look rather credible.

Vatnik is not just a condensation of Putin-era patriotism and aggressive chauvinism; he is a symbol, or perhaps symptom, of contemporary Russia's political polarization (again, see MAGA hat). Appreciating Vatnik places the viewer in a very particular subject position, that of someone who is fed up with everything Vatnik represents. Chadsky rejects the possibility of a positive reappropriation of Vatnik and does not offer as a possible alternative the *overidentification* with Vatnik—Vatnik as *styob*. Styob is a particular form of humor pioneered (or at least initially identified) in the late Soviet era, in which the straight-faced adoption of Soviet cant or ritual serves to undermine the very thing adopted. In the United States, the most obvious example would be the right-wing person Stephen Colbert created for *The Daily Show*.

But it is precisely the question of the vatnik's reappropriation that shows the limits of Chadsky's vision. Fair enough: the visual image of Vatnik is so repellent that it would appear to defy positive self-identification. In her 2016 article on "conspicuous patriotic consumption," Vera Skvirskaja traces the path of the vatnik from liberal satire to nationalist point of pride, with particular emphasis on the resurgence of the original vatnik (the coat) in contemporary Russian fashion. Many of her examples are about people either wearing the vatnik or proudly claiming to *be* vatniki. But once we move to appropriation, Vatnik, the image from the Internet meme, starts to fade from view.

A quick search of the Internet reveals multiple instances of Russian speakers proudly claiming their vatnik identity, even if they are dwarfed by content targeting the vatnik for ridicule. In 2015, Andrei Iurevich Lukin, a self-published poet and science fiction writer, composed a poem called "I Am a Vatnik," subsequently set to music by Vasily Rodin and a YouTube slide show by the Tula Creative Association of Orthodox Writers. Its greatest success online (with 13,930 views as of March 19, 2020, though the account has since been deactivated) is a video of the poem as read by the actor Yuri Nazarov, a mainstay of Soviet and Russian film and cinema, best known in the West as the heroine's father in *Little Vera*. Nazarov, a signatory to a 2014 open letter by cultural figures in support of Russia's invasion of Ukraine, brings both theatrical talent and nationalist street cred.

The poem assembles the characteristics usually associated with the vatnik, but combines them with the tropes of Soviet patriotism, in precisely the same manner used by defenders of sovok. In fact, the poem invokes sovok in its very first line (as always, the unrhymed, inelegant translation is my own):

> I'm a vatnik, a hereditary sovok,
> Born in the USSR in the days of yore.
> I'm black bread. I'm a pleather boot.
> I'm the military oath's sonorous word
> And the triumphant red banners.

It turns out that the defenders of the vatnik are obliged to follow the same strategy as those who ridicule him: assembling a list of stereotypes and touchstones to define him through metonymy. When the vatnik is the object of satire, those touchstones are thoroughly negative: drunkenness, blind devotion, nostalgia, poor hygiene. In Lukin's poem, some of those traits are present, but they are outweighed by the familiar tropes of Soviet patriotism:

> I'm the son of a different time and age.
> Within me burns *How the Steel Was Tempered*,
> And the soldier's medal in May . . .

Lukin moves swiftly from the revered Soviet heritage to the ideological battles of the present, implying a connection between past glories and the conflict in Ukraine:

> I'm guilty before Europe
> Because I'm happy beyond measure at Crimea's return.
> I remember the Crimean Spring,
> And am not ashamed of my country.

Defending the vatnik inevitably relies on one of his most unappealing characteristics: his anger. Lukin turns that anger into proud defiance:

> I'm a vatnik. So those who destroy our monuments
> Don't recognize me!
> I'm a holiday!
> I'm a solemn fireworks display!
> I'm the laurels given to the fallen.
> I'm the wind blowing through the St. George's ribbon.

I'm not ashamed to cry on Victory Day.
I have not forgotten!
I remember!
I'm proud!

Svirskaja's thesis about the reappropriation of the vatnik is convincing in the abstract, especially when shifting the focus from the meme to the actual item of clothing that inspired it. If, however, we stick with the meme (and the hostile caricature behind calling someone a vatnik), then the patriotic reading is on shakier ground. This may be because, online, Vatnik-the-meme is in his natural habitat; patriotic and Putinist vatnik revisionists are fighting a rear-guard battle. Compare Lukin's roughly fourteen thousand views on YouTube to the popularity of a satirical song with the same title, this time by a YouTube performer and chan denizen posting under the name bitard671. His song, which spares no venom in its portrayal of the vatnik, had 93,927 views as of March 19, 2020.

Styob may surround the vatnik as an item of clothing, but the path for converting the vatnik stereotype into something positive relies on turning vices into virtues, on turning a portrait of regressive nostalgia into a point of pride. If anything, Anton Chadsky himself, along with his various antics in the past several years, resembles an exercise in a styob of a different kind: at times, Chadsky appears to be engaging in styob whose object is not the Russian chauvinist but the "Russophobic" Russian liberal.

This begins with Chadsky's name, which is both a pseudonym and a portmanteau. "Chadsky" combines "Chaadaev" (the nineteenth-century intellectual whose critique of the barrenness of then-contemporary Russia led the authorities to declare him insane) and "Chatsky" (a name whose orthographic difference from "Chadsky" yields to homophony when either one is spoken aloud). Chatsky is the protagonist of Alexander Griboyedov's 1831 play, *Woe from Wit*, about a man who, on his return home from abroad, is appalled by Russian reality. (Tradition has it that Chatsky himself was based on Chaadaev.)

Styob may well be the best framework for Chadsky's most scandalous public art action on a visit to Ukraine that turned into extended exile. On January 12, 2015, a video posted online caused a minor stir on Russian social media: filmed at an event in Kyiv titled "Junta und vata" (a multilingual reference to the Russian media's characterization of the post-Maidan government as a "bloody junta" and the Vatnik-inspired term *vata* (cotton) to characterize Russian nationalist sentiment), it was called "Poedanie russkoiazychnogo mal'chika" (Eating the Russian-Speaking Baby, or Eating the Russophone Baby) ("V Kieve razrezali"). Most likely this video was inspired by an earlier scandalous political art action in 1998, when the artist Yuri Shabelnikov baked a life-sized (or perhaps, death-sized) cake baked in the shape of Lenin's corpse, to be consumed by those in attendance at the performance (Rivituso). Chadsky's event was even more macabre. In this case, the base of the cake is decorated in the colors of the Russian flag, on top of which lies the shape of an infant, complete with diaper and pacifier (also, naturally, made of cake rather than human flesh). As the theme to the 1980s evening soap opera *Dallas* inexplicably blares in the background, the revelers laugh and ask to eat various baby parts ("I want the belly!") and shout about the "bloody Kyiv junta."

Events like these are easy to dismiss as bad taste (though in his interview with Dmitrii Zhogov, Chadsky noted that "the baby was excellent. Very tasty"). But to take them at face value is both to misunderstand the styob and succumb to elementary trolling (which, come to think of it, is often tantamount to a weaponized form of styob). In this case, the choice of a baby was a pointed reference to an infamous case of propaganda in the summer of 2014, when Russian state television aired a false report about a Russian boy publicly crucified by Ukrainian fighters in the city of Slovyansk.

The baby also subverts the very premise of this sort of propaganda. What, after all, is a "Russophone" baby? At the surface level, we know exactly what this means: the child of Russian-speaking parents. But on reflection, we realize the absurdity of the term. A baby cannot be Russophone because a baby cannot speak. This renders the banana cake baby the perfect simulacrum of an ideological concept that has no counterpart in real life: the banana cake construct is just as much a fake baby as a biological baby is a fake Russophone. As an idea, eating a Russophone baby is an atrocity, but as a reality, it cannot be a crime, because there is no Russophone baby to eat.

In the hands of a different artist, then, the Russophone Baby action could serve as a critique of language-based nationalism throughout the entire Eastern Slavic region, or even reinforce a common Russian dismissal of the existence of Ukraine itself (on the basis that Ukraine and the Ukrainian language are simply variations on Russia and Russianness). Yet this is manifestly not Chadsky's intent, as seen in his response to his critics, whom he called in his interview with Zhogov, "fainting, drooling maniacs and rapists, hysterical maidens, sighing over the banana cake baby while gladly swelling the real corpses Russia makes with your approval in Eastern Ukraines."

Unless Chadsky is engaging in some sort of next-level styob that even my cynical eyes can't recognize, it is hard to miss just how saturated his condemnation of the "hate-filled" Putinists is with unadulterated hate. To be clear: this is neither a "plague on both your houses" nor a "good people on both sides" argument; it is quite possible to sympathize with Chadsky's politics while being put off by his rhetoric. Which brings me back to the main feature distinguishing the vatnik phenomenon from the sovok: where the sovok is engaged in a subtle back-and-forth game between identification and alienation, the vatnik (like the MAGA hat) leaves no room for even rueful, ironic identification. The sovok is a symbol of backwardness and poor taste, but also of nostalgia for a time when the cash nexus was relatively powerless. Vatnik is an icon of ideological civil war.

If we look back at the four axes around which these stigmatized identities revolve (culture, wealth, effectiveness, and criminality), Vatnik, the Vaskas, and the bydlo all cluster around the same section of our imaginary map: all of them prove deficient in culture and wealth. All of them serve as a proxy for socioeconomic class, a category that, even three decades after the collapse of the Soviet Union, is still murky. None of these identities are in any way aspirational; there is little about being dismissed as bydlo that could serve as a cause for envy. But before bydlo and their brethren came to the fore, and after sovok had already begun to recede, another group became the target of mockery: the semicriminal businessmen known as the New Russians. In a time when millions of Russians saw their savings dwindle into nothing, the New Russians managed to make wealth unappealing. This, in fact, is the lesson of Kasta's appropriation of Bravo's song from the beginning of the chapter: a Vasya with piles of money is ultimately still a Vasya.

4
WHATEVER HAPPENED TO THE NEW RUSSIANS?

Exactly one decade after Sascha Baron-Cohen made the post-Soviet yokel a hilarious international embarrassment in the *Borat* movie, another British entertainer, Robbie Williams, released a music video that targeted a much narrower group. His 2016 song, "Party Like a Russian," was a musical time warp: his invocation of the tacky rich Russian suggested that Williams was actually partying like it's 1999.

Williams's song is easy to hate. The combination of uninspired pop and canned Prokofiev ("The Montagues and the Capulets") is the worst thing to happen to Romeo and Juliet since the end of *Romeo and Juliet*. Plodding away at a soporific slow tempo, Williams deploys lazy Russian clichés with a lack of verve that is less Snoop Dogg and more Droopy Dog. Maybe it's on account of the molly and the Stoli that Williams brags about in one of the verses.

In her much livelier response to the video, Marijeta Bozovic notes that the song "might offend all 147 million people in Russia." That may be the case, but offense would more appropriately be taken by the top 1 percent. Or perhaps the top 0.1 percent—147,000 might be a better census result to describe the superwealthy people targeted by the video. And the rest of the country never liked them much, anyway.

Not that the video endeared itself to the Russian public, or at least to Russian pundits. The nightly newscast *Vesti* devoted six minutes to discussing Williams's video on September 30, 2016, pointing out the numerous inconsistencies in its representation of Russia. The criticism was rather restrained; no one on *Vesti* was labeling Williams a rabid Russophobe. Less than a month later (on October 27), a *Vesti* correspondent interviewed Williams in London. The singer was at great pains to express his love of Russian culture, his lack of hostile intent, and even (after refuting the allegation that the song was somehow about Russia's president) asserting that Vladimir Putin would be on the top of his list of famous guests for a dinner party.

The *Vesti* commentators surmised that Williams gathered his impressions about Russian partying from his concerts in Moscow and his presence at the corporate celebratory events Russians call *korporativy*, speculating that he might no longer be welcome at such venues in the wake of the scandalous video.[1] But he might have formed his opinion without even leaving home. Thanks to the unforeseen consequences of brain drain and capital flight, the rich Russian presence in London is visible enough to have earned the British capital the nickname Londongrad.

Like Baron Cohen, Williams gives Western audiences a simplified take on a complex post-Soviet type. In both cases, the British artists' appropriation evokes the complications that arise when the post-Soviet character braves the frontier and ends up in foreign lands. True, Baron Cohen was the initial border crosser thanks to his legendary vacation in Astrakhan, but all of Borat's subsequent adventures took place in England and America. Williams, too, may have gotten an eyeful on his trips to Russia, but the only reason his partying Russian is legible to pop audiences is that rich Russians have garnered a reputation for conspicuous consumption in countries that had long been accustomed to their own homegrown plutocrats.

Not that Williams's video required a great deal of inside knowledge in order to produce it. If it had, then the result might not have been as easily understood by non-Russian audiences. What we are left with is a predictable range of easy targets. Williams name-checks Rasputin (admittedly, as part of a clever rhyme with Louboutin).[2] He makes numerous allusions to corruption and conveys Russian wealth (and possible money laundering and capital flight) through the unsurprising metaphor of the matryoshka:

> There's a doll, inside a doll, inside a doll, inside a dolly
> (Hello, Dolly)
> I put a bank inside a car, inside a plane, inside a boat
> It takes half the western world just to keep my ship afloat

Also, Russians don't smile without a good reason ("And I never ever smile unless I've something to promote/I just won't emote"). And I have little hope of ever figuring out what it means to "Ave like an oligarch."

The song's bridge is sung by a heavily accented, Red-Army-style male chorus, mentioning that there is "revolution" in the air (because, Russia). Every now and then, Williams lip-synchs to a voice shouting *Spasibo*! (Thank you!). You're welcome?

Beyond the lyrics, there is, of course, the visual aesthetic: cold, beautiful women decked out as S&M ballerinas, with signs of crass opulence as far as the eye can see. Williams and the women cycle in and out of Russian-inspired military costumes for no apparent reason, and the camera occasionally focuses in on the prison-style tattoos on the singer's fingers. And, speaking of fingers, the second to last scene shows Williams sitting on the stairs, surrounded by beautiful ballerinas, flipping the bird to his adoring viewers.

"Party Like a Russian" is a mess. The jumble of stock Russian visual signifiers stripped of context and the verbal references to Russian-related topoi fail to mesh into even the most elementary postmodern citational collage. Perhaps the best thing to say about it is that it makes Billy Joel's "We Didn't Light the Fire" look like a worthy pop equivalent to a Don DeLillo novel.

As failures go, however, Williams's song and video are instructive. As social satire, it manages to be neither timeless not timely, a reminder of its target's simultaneous longevity and extinction. The rich Russian is still very much with us; despite Williams's inane references to revolution, when it comes to capitalist exploitation and income inequality, Russia gives the United States a run for its money. But the economic and biographical fact of rich Russians' persistence is no guarantee that their role as a discursive phenomenon remains unchanged since the 1990s.

When the Russian Federation shook off the dust of the shattered Soviet Union, it awoke to the birth of a new, quasi-folkloric character type: the crass, acquisitive, nouveau riche known as the New Russian. The New Russian was the butt of a seemingly endless series of jokes, the subject of novels and films, and the convenient object of class resentment and scorn.

But at some point in the early years of the twenty-first century, the New Russian died. Unmourned, he is survived by his real-life counterpart, the rich Russian; his former employees and epigones, sometimes called the "new middle class" or the "creative class"; and the millions of ordinary people who don't have him to kick around anymore but appear largely unmoved by his passing.

But what, exactly, was he? Where did he come from? And where did he go?

Secret Origins of the New Russians

In 1999, when my study of Russian mass culture was at the stage where I was still casting my net widely, I decided to investigate the new Russian romance novel. The results were not encouraging—so disheartening, in fact, that I decided there was no need to include the topic in my research.

What I found in my admittedly unscientific survey of Moscow bookstores was hundreds of translated bodice-rippers (mostly from the Harlequin line) and virtually no Russian-sounding names on the romance shelves. In the end, I found only two to take home. Their titles did not simply speak volumes; they obliquely spoke to the absent volumes of locally produced romance fiction. One was called *Bogatyi muzh* (Rich Husband), and the other bore the title *Zamuzhem za novym russkim* (Married to a New Russian).

Were I to do a similar search now, I would find a treasure trove of love stories written by and for Russian women.[3] The paucity of such tales in 1999 struck me as a useful data point, however. The small number of books showed how new this particular market niche was, and the painfully generic titles only reinforced this conclusion. In English-speaking countries, calling a romance novel "Rich Husband" is like calling a crime novel "Murderer." You might be able to get away with it, but only when you still have the market cornered.[4]

The titles also suggested a potential problem for the genre's Russification. Less than ten years after the end of communism, where is a wealthy suitor to be found? And if he is found, what are the chances that he is not a criminal? Just as Prince Charming is hard to locate in the absence of hereditary titles, rich men who came by their money honestly were not exactly thick on the ground. In fact, they were nigh on inconceivable.

Unfortunately, my copy of *Married to a New Russian* has not survived the two decades and, at last count, nine different offices since I rescued it from a crowded bookshelf on Tverskaya Street. Its lack of an Internet footprint would be the envy of a fugitive oligarch but does not help me reconstruct its contents. So I am left judging this book not even by its cover but solely by its title.

Luckily, *Married to a New Russian* is a title that says it all. The phrasing—reminiscent of the 1988 American comedy, *Married to the Mob* ("Zamuzhem za mafiei" in Russian)—combines wealth with an appropriate whiff of criminality. Russian literature's long-standing problem with positive heroes had come to a crisis point in the early post-Soviet years: who could the "good guys" possibly be? Or, in terms more appropriate for the romance novel, was a good man ever harder to find?

Romance novels might seem like a perversely oblique entry point into the phenomenon of the New Russian, but the genre actually highlights two fundamental features that define the phenomenon. First, to state the obvious, the New Russian is male. This could simply be a matter of grammatical gender and the tendency to consider a human type masculine unless otherwise specified, but even a cursory survey of the term's uses show that it has little room for women. The *novyi russkii* is a man, and there was initially no corresponding *novaia russkaia* to denote a rich Russian (business)woman. When Serguei Oushakine did research on popular notions of the "new Russian woman," the term he used was *novaia russkaia zhenshchina*, which, far from a term of art, proved open to a wide variety of interpretations and imagined lifestyles ("Quantity of Style"; "Fatal Splitting"). The recent television series based on Elena Kolina's *Dnevnik novoi russkoi* (Diary of a new Russian woman) series may have made the *novaia russkaia* more available as a term, but now that the New Russian phenomenon has become part of a bygone historical moment, it seems unlikely to catch on.

The second feature appears obvious but holds the promise of intriguing cultural ramifications. The New Russian is, of course, rich. As a fictional character, he is more obviously at home in the genres of crime, political/economic intrigue, and humor. His inclusion in romance fiction puts the character type under a particular stress that emphasizes the moral complexity underlying the New Russian and his role in post-Soviet culture. For the New Russian to be a worthy partner to a romance heroine, he has to have the admirable qualities that, in his "home genres," he so demonstrably lacks.

The New Russian is not just simply a bad or crass rich person; his riches are tainted by the original sins of post-Soviet capitalism. Late capitalism in the West fosters the illusion of the deservedly rich or, at the very least, the socially responsible rich (largely through philanthropy). The New Russian could not have inherited his money; nor could anyone say with a straight face that he came by it honestly.

Were we to stop there, the New Russian would appear to be an understandable target for simple class-based resentment, and his story might end with the beginnings of economic justice after a latter-day storming of the Bastille—or, more appropriately, the chichi Moscow neighborhood known as Rublyovka. But the deployment of the New Russian rarely seemed to point his readers and viewers in the direction of social engagement. In fact, the New Russian served a dual role in popular consciousness: he represented not just the injustices of the new system but also a deep discomfort with the problem of wealth itself.

Despised as he may have been, the New Russian crystallized a range of ambient anxieties about humans' relationship to money. Money in the Russia of the 1990s and early 2000s was like a radioactive isotope in a 1950s monster movie or a 1960s Marvel comic: it had a distorting, mutating effect on those exposed to it directly. Money was the radioactive spider that bit the New Russian Pyotr Parker. Sadly, with great power came great irresponsibility.

Words Fail Us

To understand the New Russian phenomenon, we must first deal with an unfortunate but productive fact: the phrase is a terminological nightmare. According to a 2002 article commemorating the term's tenth anniversary, the phrase "New Russian" first appeared in the September 7, 1992, issue of *Kommersant-Daily*. One theory has it that the term is a play on the French phrase "nouveau riche" (which came into Russian as a single word (*nuvorish*); from there, it is just a phonetic hop, skip, and a jump to *nouveau russe*. How *nouveau russe* allegedly found its way into Russian is left to the imagination.

A more likely explanation blames English rather than French and has the advantage of a paper trail. "New Russian" is less a sociological description than the uninspired name of a sequel, based on a persistent misunderstanding of the nature of the Soviet Union. The culprit here is the award-winning *New York Times* reporter Hedrick Smith.

Smith was the *Times*' Moscow bureau chief from 1971 to 1974, and he achieved the pinnacle of foreign correspondent-hood by using his experience in the Soviet Union as the basis for a reader-friendly, journalistic account of life behind ideological enemy lines. Smith's book was called *The Russians*, and that is where our trouble begins. *The Russians* was a title that was immediately legible to the book-buying public and infuriating to those of us who already knew something about the subject. Though it might seem like a moot point now (and I'd be happy to argue that it actually is not), the casual conflation of the Soviet Union and "Russia" encouraged a troubling ignorance about the USSR. It should come as no surprise to readers of this book to hear that Russia was one of fifteen constituent republics of the Soviet Union and that, while Russian was the lingua franca for the USSR, even the Russian Soviet Federative Socialist Republic (RSFSR) contained sizable minorities who would not be considered "Russian" by anyone in the Soviet Union. But the title of Smith's book really left us a problematic legacy when he decided to follow it up with a sequel. Even by the mid-1980s, Smith's *The Russians* was an inadequate guide to life in the USSR. So Smith went back, interviewed more people and published another bestseller in 1990, *The New Russians*.

My search of the Universal Database of Russian Newspapers would confirm the Hedrick Smith hypothesis. Doing a search for *novyi russkii* or *novye russkie* is a slog, given how common both words are on their own (and given the system's stubborn resistance to look only for the words as a single phrase). But the earliest mentions I could find (as a noun phrase, and not as a descriptor for another noun, such as "new Russian book" or "new Russian film") were brief reviews of Smith's book in 1991, where the title was inevitably translated as *Novye russkie*. Within two years, the phrase started to appear in reference to a new class of rich business people.

The term's origins had to be foreign, for precisely the same reasons that it is problematic. No one in the last years of the Soviet Union or even the first years of the Russian Federation would have used the word *russkii* as part of the name for this phenomenon. As explained above, it would have been inappropriate and quite simply puzzling for a Soviet citizen to use "Russian" as a generic term for people in the USSR; doing so would have been making a nationalist or ethnic point that is absent from the earliest New Russian discourse.

After the collapse of the Soviet Union, using *russkii* would have been even more fraught. The sudden independence of the multiethnic, multilingual, and multiconfessional Russian Federation required terminology that was generally inclusive, as well as a way of indicating when such inclusivity was not the point. The language still contained adjectives for "Russian" that distinguished between Russia-the-state/empire and Russia-the-ethnicity/language, based on the current term for Russia (*Rossiia*) and the medieval term for the state that gave rise to Russia, Ukraine, and Belarus (Rus'). *Russkii* referred to the language, the culture, and the ethnicity. *Rossiiskii* referred to everything related to the Russian state/Soviet federative republic. In late Soviet times, *rossiiskii*, though available, was not in great linguistic demand.[5]

Nouns were slightly more awkward. Though *russkii* is technically an adjective, it, like so many adjectives in Russian, functions quite happily as a noun. In Soviet times, the plural *russkie* were Russian-speaking, ethnic Russian Slavs, whose ancestors were Russian Orthodox. If your parents were ethnic Ukrainians, but you were born in the Russian Republic and spoke only Russian, you were still technically a Ukrainian (and "Ukrainian" would appear on the notorious "line 5" of your internal identity papers). Particularly confusing to Americans, Jews whose ancestors lived in Russia for generations would still never be "Russians" on their IDs; instead, they would be Jews.

Calling everyone who lived in the Russian Federation *russkie* was simply not an option. Fortunately, there was an old-fashioned word just waiting to be resurrected through the dark magic of the census bureaucracy: *rossiianin*. Like *rossiiskii*, it comes from the modern word for Russia, and therefore does not have any particular ethnic connotation. When talking about a Russian in the sense of "citizen of the Russian Federation," *rossiianin* and the feminine *rossiianka* are the correct terms. Unfortunately, when Smith published *The New Russians* and when it was noticed in the Soviet press, there would have been no reason to translate the title as *Novye rossiiane*. So Russia was stuck with a phrase that suggested an oddly ethnic specificity.

Who Were the New Russians?

This is one of many questions not answered in the current chapter. The aim is not to provide empirical studies of the lives of self-identified "new Russians," nor to develop an economically based definition of the category. As a concept, the New Russian floats free from any actual lived experience, financial portfolios, or criminal holdings. Indeed, I will not be the first to argue that the New Russian never actually existed.[6]

If I stress the imaginary nature of the New Russian more than I do that of the sovok or vatnik, it is because the latter terms are so clearly a matter of stereotype and projection rather than sociology. No one would expect a census to give us a sovok head count, but one might reasonably expect to be able to determine who the New Russians were and how many of them were out driving their Mercedes or BMWs at any given time.[7] After all, the New Russians were all about wealth, and wealth is quantifiable.

But if the New Russians were characterized by wealth, the accumulation of assets did not necessarily make someone a New Russian. Like the sovok, the New Russian is a set of assumptions and projections, but with an important difference: the sovok could be observed (or at least imagined) up close, while the New Russian kept his distance. One of the many compelling images of nineteenth-century literature can, predictably, be traced back to Pushkin: in his story, "The Stationmaster," a sad, pathetic "little man" finds himself chasing after an important person's carriage on foot, unable to catch up. In post-Soviet terms, that little man may or may not be the sovok, but the person in the carriage is a New Russian.

There are many reasons why the New Russian in the carriage (or, less anachronistically, the imported luxury automobile) will always remain out of reach. The most obvious is the disparity of power and wealth, but the ramifications of that disparity are greater than one might imagine. It is not just that the poor and the rich live in two different worlds, but rather that the life experience and newly invented habitat of the new rich is so far from everyday experience that this world is being imagined in an empirical vacuum. Most ordinary people will never interact with the superrich, in any culture; but when the rich have been with us for decades or even generations, their lives have been assimilated into an imaginary construct that becomes familiar, and that presumably has some connection to the world of the actually existing rich. The rich are celebrities (Donald Trump, for instance, even if he is probably more celebrity than rich) or from famous families (the Rockefellers). By comparison, the New Russians are generic, impersonal, and created almost entirely out of whole cloth.[8] The New Russian is a figure of urban folklore.

We find ourselves once again confronting the problem of origins. The established rich in countries that have long tolerated a class of the inordinately wealthy tend to have a "just-so" story to explain why they have (and even deserve) the privileges and power they have accrued. The wealthy man (and it is usually a man) is a "genius," most recently in the world of high technology, often ascribed talents and accomplishments that he clearly lacks (Bill Gates didn't even write MS-DOS, but in the Nineties, he was commonly assumed to have invented the Internet, a tech phenomenon his company was very late to grapple with). The wealth may be inherited, but it is the result of a genius founder (Carnegie, Morgan) or goes far back enough in history to confer nobility or be the result of nobility (the Windsors).

The premise is that the system for the accumulation of wealth is somehow rational, perhaps even just. While there are plenty of reasons to be skeptical that this is the case, there are nonetheless narratives that sell the system's validity. Even the reverse scenario, in which a person or family's rise to wealth is interpreted as part of an evil conspiracy (the Rothschilds), is still based on the premise that the accumulation of capital is understandable.

The post-Soviet case is another matter entirely. Here we have the accumulation of massive wealth in a manner that is almost entirely opaque to outsiders, with little effort wasted on legitimation through public relations (PR). Two seemingly opposite but essentially homologous scenarios are usually invoked: people became wealthy from the massive theft of state property, or they got rich by making money out of nothing at all. In each case, wealth is detached from the part of the economy that seventy-plus years of Soviet rule always put at the center of everything: production.

In the 1990s, evidence of Russian industrial or consumer production was hard to come by. Instead, starting with the institution of the mysterious system of "vouchers" that kicked off the privatization process, stories about rich people were peppered with names of mysterious "financial instruments" and other foreign phrases ("promissory notes," "futures," "derivatives"). I would be lying if I claimed to understand these terms (and probably would be richer if I actually were proficient in their use), but I have had an entire lifetime of knowing that I know nothing about them. An underinformed Westerner slowly steeps in the waters of finance for years, while most Russians found themselves thrown in the deep end without the benefit of lessons, time, or flotation devices.

Russian capitalism was the perfect storm of injustice, theft, and deceit, not to mention the complete abandonment of years of rhetoric about the collective good. Economic exploitation, sudden and dramatic inequality, and grotesque consumerism were shocking and diffuse. All of this makes for an abstract enemy; a real, concrete enemy has the virtue of an identifiable face. Such a face has endless possibilities: you can punch it, you can spit at it, and you can laugh at it. In this regard, the New Russian was a gift to the people. Because the New Russian gave all these negative phenomena a face.

Is a Crocodile Longer Than It Is Green?

In 2002, Pavel Lungin released the film *Oligarkh* (Tycoon), adapted from Yuli Dubov's 1999 novel, *Bol'shaia paika* (The big slice), which in turn was inspired by the life and career of one of Russia's most notorious oligarchs, Boris Berezovsky.

The oligarch and the New Russian are not entirely overlapping categories; actual Russian oligarchs look restrained in comparison to the New Russian of folklore, while the New Russian need not be rich enough to be an oligarch. Yet the English and French translations of the film's title render the terms equivalent. The full English title is *Tycoon: A New Russian*, while France cuts to the chase and calls the movie *Un nouveau russe*. Lungin's film is a touchstone for the post-Soviet representation of the new rich; even with the caveat about assuming that the New Russian and the oligarch are the same thing, *Tycoon* is an unavoidable part of any analysis of the New Russian phenomenon.

Early in the film, when the future oligarch Platon Makovsky and his friends are still university students, the impending transition from ossified state socialism to savage, unrestricted capitalism is established and parodied in a lighthearted scene that could have turned tragic for one of its participants. One of Platon's friends, Viktor, has made the political mistake of arguing in a certain Professor Koretsky's class that the Soviet economy is shrinking and on the verge of collapse. Koretsky's response is not to engage with the substance of the argument, but rather to pontificate in a familiar Soviet vein:

> KORETSKY: If I understand you correctly, when you say "ineffective economy," you mean the economy of socialism?
>
> VIKTOR: I was solving a theoretical problem. This is mathematics, not ideology.
>
> KORETSKY: Don't try to weasel your way out of it. So the socialist economy is not viable? And what about Marxism-Leninism? Do you propose repealing it as well? . . . For the future of our country, for the life we have today, generations of Soviet people went hungry, gave their lives for the ideas that you are trampling under your feet.

To the untrained ear of a viewer born after the Soviet collapse, his words might seem simply laughable, but older generations, who managed not to sacrifice their lives for Soviet ideals, will easily recognize Koretsky's tirade as a direct threat to Viktor's future.

By this point in the film, we already know one important thing about Platon's circle of friends: they live life to its fullest when testing the boundaries of convention. These are men who play with fire. In the previous scene, after a night of drinking in a four-person train car packed with revelers, one of the main characters, Mark, wakes up naked next to a similarly disrobed train conductress. She informs him that they had a fabulous night together, and that if he doesn't follow up on his promise to marry her, she'll file a personal complaint against him that will ruin his life. Mark's friends reassure him that being married to a conductress is not so bad; it has its perks, and he'll get used to it. Then they all burst out laughing, and Mark realizes that the whole thing is a practical joke.

Now, when Viktor is facing actual danger in his confrontation with Koretsky, it is Mark who calls Platon and tells him to come to Viktor's rescue. What follows is a moment that turns Viktor's brush with career tragedy into comedy gold.

> PLATON: Forgive me for interrupting you, but it seems that Comrade Koretsky is overdramatizing the situation. We are just sharing ideas, including controversial ones.
> KORETSKY: Strange logic you have there!
> PLATON: Logic cannot be strange. It either is, or it isn't. On the level of logic, you can prove anything. How about I show you that, say, a crocodile . . . [draws on the chalkboard]? Yes, that looks about right. Does it look right?
> AUDIENCE: Yes!
> PLATON: A crocodile is more long than it is green. Because it's long on top and below, while it's green only on top.
> KORETSKY: This is a circus!
> PLATON: Just for Comrade Koretsky I'll prove that the crocodile is more green than it is wide. The crocodile is green lengthwise and across, but wide only across. Thank you!

Why include such a scene early in the film, especially when it is nowhere to be found in the novel on which it is based? And, for that matter, why discuss it at such length now?

The crocodile scene fulfills a variety of important functions for this film. First, there is the obvious one, involving entertainment: it's funny. If we look further, however, we see a discursive clash waged before our very eyes. We are in the role of the audience at the lecture, watching a debate that has serious implications. If we assume that the classical economics on which Viktor must be basing his conclusions is somehow neutral or objective (an assumption that the entire enterprise of the transition to capitalism takes for granted), then Viktor is the voice of cold reason, a representative of what some in Washington derisively call the "reality-based community." Koretsky does not even attempt to refute Viktor's arguments, presumably because he can't (i.e., Viktor is objectively right). So

Koretsky switches registers, proving himself a past master of Soviet cant. Or to put it more bluntly, Soviet bullshit.

The philosopher, Harry Frankfurt, famously turned "bullshit" into a term of art, distinguishing it from mere lying:

> It is impossible for someone to lie unless he thinks he knows the truth. Producing bullshit requires no such conviction. A person who lies is thereby responding to the truth, and he is to that extent respectful of it. When an honest man speaks, he says only what he believes to be true; and for the liar, it is correspondingly indispensable that he considers his statements to be false. For the bullshitter, however, all these bets are off: he is neither on the side of the true nor on the side of the false. His eye is not on the facts at all, as the eyes of the honest man and of the liar are, except insofar as they may be pertinent to his interest in getting away with what he says. He does not care whether the things he says describe reality correctly. He just picks them out, or makes them up, to suit his purpose. (55–56)

At this point in *Tycoon*, we could allow for the possibility that Koretsky is sincere, but over the next two hours of screen time, the professor evolves into Platon's primary antagonist, and his motivations are anything but noble.

Marxism-Leninism, the philosophy Koretsky so pompously evokes, would lead us to expect arguments in the form of a dialectic (thesis-antithesis-synthesis). Any argument that takes that form would be reaffirming the premises of Marxism-Leninism even if explicitly refuting them. But it is Koretsky himself who makes the dialectic all but impossible by responding to reason with bullshit. Enter Platon, who replaces the synthesis with an absurdist argument that exposes the absurdity of the entire debate. Platon's "crocodile" proof could be seen as a synthesis only if we do what Platon himself is doing: ignore the content entirely and focus on the underlying problem of logic itself. The result would be a dialectic of "reason-bullshit-metabullshit."

Yet the stakes of the bullshit argument could not be higher, and this is why the crocodile scene pairs so well with the previous train conductress episode. In each case, a real or imagined transgression could lead to personal ruin. When Mark implores Platon to come to Viktor's rescue he uses the same word (*personalka* or "personal complaint") that the conductress used in her threat against Mark himself. The conductress's blackmail threat was based on a falsified incident (Mark hadn't actually slept with her, and she didn't want to marry him), while Viktor endangers himself by insisting on "facts" and "reality" in the face of falsity and bullshit.

Taken together, these two scenes are concise allegories of both the film's central conflict and the rise of the New Russian. The three-part, nondialectical argument about economics and crocodiles points to the actual tripartite relationship that drives much of the film: a love triangle. Right after winning the argument, Platon races back to the woman whose bed he left two hours before: Masha Koretskaya, Koretsky's wife. Not only does this ensure Koretsky's lifelong hatred of Platon, but it also easily symbolizes Platon's approach to his surroundings. The world as it exists is nothing but an imperfect arrangement of raw materials, from which he can take the best and leave the rest. Given the familiar, indeed, clichéd trope of the female character standing in for Russia (or the USSR) itself, Platon is seizing the country from a man who no longer knows how to husband it.

If Russia is going to belong to the Platon Makovskys of the world, it is because these New Russians, rather than simply accepting the world as given, hack the world as if it were a vulnerable computer system. They zero in on weakness after weakness, exploiting them precisely because they are available, and because no one else has gotten to them first.

Using the model developed by Mark Lipovetsky, we might say that Platon Makovsky is a trickster. But he is not just any trickster, in that the film continually links him to Soviet literature's master of this particular art: Ostap Bender, the protagonist of Ilya Ilf and Evgeny Petrov's 1928 novel, *The Twelve Chairs*. The connection suggests itself early in the film, when we see that one of Platon's first schemes involved the inexplicable overproduction of short, Russian-style brooms (*veniki*)—150 million of them, in fact. This is all part of a complicated scheme to acquire wealth without cash changing hands and is an ironic counterpoint to one of the many quotes from Ilf and Petrov's novel to become part of everyday speech: "the company does not make brooms" (*firma venikov ne viazhet*). The expression has come to be something of a boast, or at least a confirmation of quality: "I did a good job remodeling your apartment? Of course I did—the company doesn't make brooms." In Platon's case, the company actually *does* make brooms, but it is their production, rather than denial of production, that suggests a kind of illicit success.

The Twelve Chairs also reminds us of the two scenarios of New Russian enrichment discussed above: theft from the state and conjuring money out of thin air. Among Bender's many other catch phrases is his response to a demand he deems unreasonable: "What else do you want, the key to a room full of cash [*kliuch ot kvartiry, gde den'gi lezhat*]?" Indeed, this was the first phrase the authors associated with him as they wrote the book; the entire character was built around it (Ilf, xvi). Bender attributed this dubious sentiment to his interlocutors, but it was actually his primary motivation. Platon, with his knack for determining just which state property can be had for a song, builds his empire in part because he finds the keys to rooms full of cash.

Like Ostap Bender, Platon claims to be dealing with concrete items (Ilf and Petrov's chairs, for example), but his success looks more like magic. He conjures up deals, schemes, and money through the dizzying force of his argumentation, convincing his audience while still leaving them confused. From the outside, Platon's generation of money from nothing may as well be magic. In Russian, one of the main verbs for casting a spell or enchantment is *zagovorit'*, a word whose root (*govor*—speak) suggests the verbalization of magical thinking. Russians cast spells by speaking them into existence, a capacity at which Platon excels. Take, for example, the scene when he explains his broom scheme to his partners: his description of the relationship among three cooperatives, none of which can actually deal with money, and his plan to circulate brooms and vacuum cleaners through this system of exchange until they somehow turn into automobiles, has the same effect on his audience as his crocodile proof: everyone in the room is reduced to amazed laughter. But they are also convinced.

When the New Russian simply appropriates state property, he is getting something that, as the Russians would say, "is just lying there for the taking" (*plokho lezhit*), like the mythical room full of cash. But when he works his economic trickster magic, following a logic most of us can only marvel at, the choice of the crocodile for his absurdist proof starts to make sense. Yes, the crocodile is a dangerous creature hiding behind a smile, but Platon is assessing its color. The future New Russian oligarch fights "Red" platitudes by measuring something green. "Green," of course, is precisely what matters to the New Russian. It is not just the color of the crocodile, it is the color of the money that he conjures out of thin air. The switch from red to green is the measure of the New Russian's success. Compared to him, ordinary Russians may as well be colorblind.

Loved Labours Lost

If New Russian were just a synonym for oligarch, we would not need the phrase at all. The term may include oligarchs, but it is far more capacious. There is a spectrum of New Russianness, with oligarchs at the far end. Who might be found on the way to other side?

If we start with the New Russian as an economic pseudophenomenon—or perhaps a pseudoeconomic phenomenon—we of course return to wealth. But not to the mere fact of *having* wealth, something that will end up falling under the Putin-era category of "glamour." Being a New Russian is about *gaining* wealth, and that is where our trouble begins.

Like all countries, the Soviet Union needed its citizens' labor to survive. Where it stood out was in the creation and inculcation of labor as a cult. Initially a

Marxist correction to a capitalist system that typically valued intellectual or "white collar" work over actual physical labor (whether on farms or in factories) while validating the ownership of capital above all else, the notion of Soviet citizens as laborers took center stage in Stalin's time. The most famous example is that of Alexei Stakhanov, who in 1935 repeatedly broke records for the amount of coal mined in a single shift or even half-shift. Feted as a national hero, he inspired an entire movement of "Stakhanovites," dedicated shock workers who committed themselves to constant feats of industrial and agricultural labor.

The Brezhnev era provided a countermyth: the image of the Soviet worker as a lazy, often drunken, shirker, indifferent to the poor quality of the goods he made. The unofficial literature of the time certainly bears this out, from Venedikt Erofeev's tale of epic goldbricking in *Moscow-Petushki* (1969) to the many sections of Zinoviev's *Homo Sovieticus* disparaging the skill and enthusiasm of the Soviet worker. In the popular parlance, the labor problem was summed up with a joke: "We pretend to work; they pretend to pay us."

This discrepancy between the official cult of labor and the unofficial assumption (or recognition) of the shoddiness of Soviet industry, the surliness of the Soviet service sector, and the inadequacy of Soviet goods should remind us that there is no reason to expect that actual economics and labor should be identical to their representation or popular understanding. Privatization in the 1990s was an incomprehensible mess, whose results were not exactly inspiring for ordinary people: unemployment and plummeting living standards for a large portion of the population accompanied by spectacular wealth for an infinitesimally small layer, with thriving criminal enterprises somewhere in between.

It was not just jobs that were disappearing; the fig leaf of socially useful labor had been stripped away. "We pretend to work; they pretend to pay us" was a joke, but it was also a tacit social compact. In Soviet times, unemployment was not just virtually unknown but technically a crime. The legal charge against the unemployed was *tuneiadstvo*. Often translated as "parasitism" or "social parasitism," the term does not have the same biological connotations, but the discourse surrounding it made abundant use of variations on the Russian word *parazit*. Not working was tantamount to exploitation of those who worked.

When we look at the categories of people who get labeled "New Russians," while they all may be frenetically active, what they do would not have been called "labor" just a few years before. Buying and selling, brokering deals, making connections with organized crime, and, most important, focusing on profit were all considered unproductive, even parasitic. The notion that the New Russian rich weren't actually "producing" anything helps explain the widespread acceptance and enthusiastic participation in pyramid schemes such as MMM. MMM was accused of simply printing worthless paper and making useless promises;

how was anyone supposed to tell the difference between that and "legitimate" business?

Generally speaking, three types of people are usually covered by the classification "New Russian": oligarchs, successful or would-be businessmen several rungs below oligarch status, and organized crime leaders. What unites them, and potentially makes "New Russians" a meaningful category, are the following features.[9]

(1) Money. In Soviet society, cash was not king. Certainly, money was always welcome, and a huge portion of the country could legitimately consider itself underpaid. But where capitalism manages scarcity through the medium of money (making money scarce), scarcity in Late Socialism was primarily a matter of goods and access. After the reforms of 1990 and the subsequent end of the USSR, money became paramount. The New Russians' perceived comfort—if not obsession—with money, their proficiency in the magic of currency manipulation (foreign exchange, "dark money," "noncash" money that technically existed only in bank accounts and could not easily be turned into paper bills), and the financial instruments that surrounded money put them in a category of their own.

(2) Labor. Virtually nothing that the New Russian did to generate this money qualified as labor in the Soviet sense. This does not mean that the New Russians were not active (indeed, hyperactive) in managing their affairs. But they were not working with their hands, not producing goods, not providing recognizable services, and not engaged in typical intellectual labor. The New Russian was the parasite triumphant.

(3) Taste. Like the sovok, the New Russian was ridiculed for his bad taste. But the form and content of this bad taste were altogether different.

(4) Conspicuous consumption. Here the New Russian was the anti-sovok: accumulating luxury goods and name brands with an impressive single-mindedness.

(5) Corruption. The New Russian was generally assumed to have broken laws and traded influence to get where he was.

(6) Spiritual and social vacuity. The New Russian presumably had no social conscience and no sympathy for those less fortunate than him.

(7) Absurdity. The New Russian was easy to laugh at.

The Putin-era successors to the New Russian neutralize most, though not all, of these complaints. Bad taste and gross conspicuous consumption have given way to glamour. Asocial selfishness takes on the guise of philanthropy and political engagement. Corruption gets folded into a system in which the state, rather than private business, has primacy. The next chapter witnesses the transition from New Russians to merely rich Russians.

5
RICH MAN'S BURDEN

The collapse of the Soviet Union left Russians with a surprisingly impoverished vocabulary for describing social class. In this regard, as in so many others, Russia and America play the role of nonidentical twins. The United States, with its national myth of individual initiative and complete social mobility, not to mention its historical preoccupation with race and skin color at the expense of class, has drained nearly all meaning from the phrase "middle class" by using it to include the majority of the population. Poll after poll shows people in the top 10 percent of the country's wealth bracket identifying themselves as middle-class, while proposals to increase the tax burden on the superrich for the benefit of the less fortunate inevitably invite charges of "class warfare."

The Soviet Union, in contrast, was supposed to be the land where class warfare had been openly waged, and one class triumphed: the proletariat. The "dictatorship of the proletariat" was meant to give rise to a classless society. In the absence of capitalists, class would presumably become irrelevant. Clearly, this was not the case. While the salaries of factory workers and bus drivers could be greater than those of white-collar professionals with advanced degrees, social stratification remained, even if money was a less important component. The perks of being a party member, and in particular being part of the nomenklatura, were well-known: privilege expressed itself primarily in *access* (to better housing, to automobiles, to vacation resorts). Privilege was supposed to be earned but often turned out to be inherited: the children of privileged homes lived lives that were far from the Soviet ordinary. Access, like property, can be handed down the generations.

When the Soviet Union collapsed, it was not a matter of total equality being replaced by unheard-of stratification. Indeed, one complaint commonly heard was that those with access before 1991 became the ones with money and property after 1991: party and Komsomol networks were resources to be exploited, and people in powerful positions were able to direct the spoils of privatization into their own coffers. The end of communism was like a game of musical chairs: if you found a comfortable seat for yourself at an opportune moment, you could become a winner.

The Soviet system did not end inequality, but it sharply limited both the range of inequality and its visible manifestations. As Alaina Lemon notes in *Technologies for Intuition*, Western accounts of the grayness and deprivation of late Soviet life were conditioned by the relative economic privilege of the visitors themselves, who were more likely to be comparing Soviet living conditions to comfortable, middle-class Western lifestyles than to the lot of the working poor, an observation that Lemon's own working-class background made obvious to her (xvi–xvii). The New Russians made the drastic inequalities of Russian capitalism not just visible but unavoidable. Like the caricatured capitalists of 1920s Soviet propaganda (whose top hats and tails made them look like they had stepped out of a game of Monopoly), the New Russians embodied unfair, unearned wealth that flaunted itself at every opportunity.

But if the capitalist fat cat of the 1920s was a class enemy to be extinguished, what was the role of the New Russian? If the 1990s was simply the beginning of capitalist accumulation, could the New Russians legitimately be considered the beginning of a new social class? From a Marxist view, casting them in class terms might be both obvious and depressing, as a harbinger of even greater exploitation to come. But a capitalist class framework also held out the possibility for a limited kind of optimism. If the New Russians were analogous to nineteenth-century North American robber barons, then eventually they might settle down, throw off some of their most offensive attributes, and (re)join civilization as philanthropists and job creators. The New Russians might be an inevitable but short-lived step on the path toward a capitalist radiant future.

The question of social class becomes one of temporality: did the New Russians have a future? And, if so, what would it be? Two decades after the peak of the New Russian phenomenon, the question would seem to have an obvious answer: no, the New Russians did not have a future, because they are no longer on the scene. But that is not what the "future" question is about.

Rather, the New Russian suggests three possible temporalities: first, the capitalist teleology discussed above. This is the scenario in which the New Russian is a temporary but necessary evolution from the sovok to a civilized upper class. In this framework, the New Russian does not necessarily create anything or even mean anything; he is the tacky, awkward age of a capitalism that is undergoing growing pains.

But if we combine the capitalist teleology with both the starry-eyed optimism implied by Hedrick Smith's *New Russians* and the century-long tradition of imagining a new people who either inhabit or create a new world, the New Russian is a parodic counterpart to the New (Soviet) Man. That he so closely resembles Mayakovsky's *Philistinius vulgaris* from *The Bedbug* suggests the active creation of a future that looks suspiciously like a relatively recently rejected past. This temporality is both retrospective (looking to the anticapitalist, antibourgeois sentiments of the 1920s) and conditional-subjunctive: the New Russian is creating a capitalist world, but it is not that of North America or Western Europe. It is the imaginary capitalist hell of Soviet propaganda, in which the rich run wild and the poor have no rights or resources whatsoever.

The third temporality is much broader than simply the world of the New Russians. This is the pervasive fantasy of a future that recapitulates not simply the recent, Soviet past or a lost capitalist Neverland but a precapitalist, medieval system of estates or castes, in which the power of the aristocracy over the peasants (read: the poor and dispossessed) is virtually limitless.

This is a vision of social stratification that uses capitalism as a waystation to serfdom. Where F. A. Hayek famously argued that the road to serfdom was paved with government overreach, central planning, and the rejection of individualism (83–88), fantasies of a New Russian, oligarchic feudal system ignore the boundaries between capitalism and communism, focusing instead on the persistence of an elite privilege that, while it may change its outer form and expressed ideology, inevitably leads to a new medievalism.

New medievalism can mean many things to many people; in political science, it usually refers to the decline of the nation-state and the rise of supranational entities that impinge on sovereignty. For the Russian philosopher Nikolai Berdiaev, who wrote *Novoe srednevekov'e* (The new Middle Ages) in 1924, it was about the turn away from rationalism and humanism, a spiritual revolution that emphasized the collective over the individual. But the feudal fantasy that is relevant to the New Russians ends up emphasizing the socioeconomic structure of feudalism over its spirituality, even if spirituality is often invoked as its justification in both satirical and sincere new medieval Russian futures.

The best-known vision of a feudal twenty-first-century Russia is that of Vladimir Sorokin, in his books *The Day of the Oprichnik* (2006) and *Sakharnyi Kreml'* (Sugar Kremlin, 2008). Cut off from the world by a Great Wall, the tsarist Russia of 2028 is carefully policed by security forces bearing the name of Ivan the Terrible's vicious enforcers. There are no New Russians in the novel per se; instead, they have been replaced by a restored nobility—one that, unlike the rich men of the 1990s, is painfully aware that it exists at the sufferance of the state. Tatyana Tolstaya's dystopian 2000 novel, *The Slynx*, also features a return to medievalism, this time against the backdrop of a world recovering from a nuclear holocaust. Here, too, New Russians are not a going concern. For a firm connection between feudalist fantasy and New Russian absolute power, we must turn to the work of Vladimir Tuchkov.

The New Russian and the American Psycho

Vladimir Tuchkov's cycle of stories *Smert' prikhodit po internetu* (Death by Internet) is a New Russian master text and one of the main literary examples highlighted by Lipovetsky in "New Russians as a Cultural Myth." Published in 2001, Tuchkov's book bears the revealing subtitle *A Description of Nine Unpunished Crimes Secretly Committed in the Homes of New Russians*. As the subtitle suggests, the recurring theme is that of New Russian excess and the sense that New Russians are people to whom no rules actually apply. The pleasure is that of reading good satire, but also the thrill of watching people get away with the unthinkable.

The collection's first story, bearing the Gogolian title "Strashnaia mest'" (A terrible vengeance), sets the stage with a tale of a New Russian's unlimited power and total lack of mercy. The fabulously wealthy businessman Nikolai spends all his time managing his business empire, leaving his wife, Olga, to dedicate herself just as doggedly to hosting a nonstop array of high-society orgies. But when her parade of meaningless sexual encounters gives way to real feelings for one of her guests (a TV personality), Nikolai will not stand for it. Nikolai imprisons her lover in their house, informing him that although he will remain alive, Nikolai is taking away his life and identity. The lover is replaced on television with a double, and after a few weeks, Nikolai has the man's four front teeth removed and replaced with a steel bridge. The man is given ratty clothes to wear and released back into the general population. No one believes his claims that he is a well-known public figure, and he is eventually institutionalized for delusions of grandeur.

In "A Terrible Vengeance," the businessman's wealth and influence defy all rules and laws. In the United States, people used to say that Apple's founder, Steve Jobs, had a "reality distortion effect," which meant that his sheer persuasive enthusiasm seemed capable of convincing his interlocutors that he could achieve the impossible. Nikolai goes one step further: he is literally the master of all he surveys, meting out "justice" to those around him with the impunity and confidence of a feudal lord. Even his imprisonment of his rival is couched in terms of magnanimity and hospitality. Olga's love is maintained in Nikolai's mansion under more than comfortable conditions; when Nikolai's project is complete and his rival has now entirely lost his identity and become a "new person," Nikolai tells him: "Well, now, at last you can abandon my hospitable home, where you have been inappropriately happy for someone of your former social status" (18). Nikolai's destruction of his rival efficiently hits him where gender and class intersect, simultaneously stripping him of the attributes of wealth and success and the physical features that presumably make him attractive. The punishment administered by Nikolai is a feat of socioeconomic alchemy; standing at the pinnacle of a complex social hierarchy, he has performed the class equivalent of what used to be called gender reassignment surgery.

"A Terrible Vengeance" surrounds Nikolai with the aura of the powerful feudal lord, but the connection to a medieval ethos is still a matter of simile and transposition. Nikolai is analogous to the lord of a manor, but he functions within a contemporary context, however exaggerated his capacity to exert his will might seem. The second story has no need of comparison or analogy, in that its protagonist's entire project is to literalize the metaphor inherent in his New Russian status.

"Stepnoi barin" (Lord of the steppe) is about a rich banker named Dmitry who buys land outside of Moscow in order to set up his own feudal estate. He has no overt political agenda, although in the hands of a different sort of satirist at a different point in time, his localized New Middle Ages might look like a comment on Stalin's attempt to "build socialism in one country." Once the estate is operating, he seems to be interested solely in satisfying his own desires and indulging his own whims. But the origins of his impulses are more complex.

As the first line of the story tells us, "Dmitry was the product of great Russian literature" (20). But where the implied reader of the Russian classics is presumably moved to compassion for the downtrodden, disdain for material riches, and other such "spiritual" concerns, Dmitry learns the opposite lesson. Having virtually memorized the complete works of Dostoevsky and Tolstoy, he finds the greatest pleasure in the scenes in which evil and cruelty triumph: "Thus he was an unusually shameless, calculating, mean, and cruel person in relation to those who stood lower than him on the social ladder" (20). Where generations of readers were taught to empathize with the proverbial little man chasing in vain after the carriage speeding in front of him, one imagines Dmitry responding to the same scene as if it were the social class equivalent of hard-core pornography.

Naturally, Dmitry builds a luxurious house for himself, but then he immediately turns to the construction of twenty-five "dilapidated" huts, complete with holes in the walls and crooked windows. Once these are finished, he begins hiring serfs. The serfs sign a contract (laser-printed, in duplicate) listing all the agricultural implements that will be at their disposal, requiring them to live full-time in the country, and promising them two thousand dollars per year. In exchange,

Dmitry gets the fruits of their labor, along with the right to impose physical punishment, authorize or forbid marriages, and unilaterally resolve any disputes. The serf has the right to break the contract, but only on Yuri's Day (the autumn St. George's Day, November 26, when serfs were allowed to change masters before 1597).

Dmitry starts administering harsh punishments on the second day of his reign. Soon he is raping peasant women, sometimes in the presence of his wife (whose moral degeneracy now matches his own). Recalling that some feudal masters had theater troupes composed of serfs, he stages a production of Alexander Griboyedov's *Woe from Wit* with an all-female, all-nude cast, which is instructed to spend most of the play beating each other. When Yuri's Day arrives, he arranges a feast, provides copious amounts of vodka, and all his serfs extend their contract for another year.

Within three years, the serfs have adapted completely:

> They started to see their master not as an eccentric rich man, but as their own father, tough, but fair, constantly worrying about their well-being. Deep in their hearts each one of them knew that without their master, they wouldn't plow, and they wouldn't go to church, and would start killing each other.... So the serfs, whose psyches were so seriously reconfigured, were wrong to have counted on the possibility of returning to contemporary society. They couldn't live there; its laws would strike them as wild and inhuman. (26)

Even Dmitry is stunned by this turn of events and starts to consider "reforms" (such as cutting their quitrent by twenty percentage points), but by now he's gotten old, and his eldest son Grigory has taken charge. The story ends with the observation that the serfs have started having children who look exactly like Grigory.

Lipovetsky is correct when he argues that Tuchkov's New Russian heroes are better understood along a "spectrum of social roles" (2003, 63) rather than through psychological realism, and that they exemplify a "trickster archetype" (2003, 64) that serves as a "negative variant of a cultural hero" (2003, 64). But I must disagree with his analysis of the role of power, that his "bankers do not care about power over somebody or something; they desire power as such, as a fetish, and they realize that this kind of power tolerates no compromise" (2003, 63).

But how can power function as an absolute in a social context? Tuchkov gives us New Russians whose obsession with power absolutely requires that other people suffer in its exercise. *Death by Internet* rarely shows the protagonists deriving actual sensual pleasure from their abuse of their underlings; Tuchkov's New

Russian is no American Psycho. Yet the New Russians in these stories dehumanize their victims just as efficiently as Bret Easton Ellis's sadistic serial killer, not by taking pleasure in their pain but by being indifferent to it. These New Russians hold the human life of the underclass in such low regard that they cannot even be bothered to enjoy their victims' suffering.

Both the American Psycho and the New Russian are incapable of empathy, and in each case their callousness is easily interpreted as a comment on the worlds that made them. But where Ellis's Patrick Bateman is the perfect extrapolation of a heartless capitalist world, Dmitry in "Lord of the Steppe," as the product of Great Russian Literature, is even more demonic: he has spent his life surrounded by cultural inputs that demand an empathic response, only to identify with the purveyors of cruelty. Culture is no insurance against savage exploitation; on the contrary, virtually any cultural production can be appropriated to teach an unintended and undesirable lesson.

Tuchkov's New Russians, then, are the men who, through some murky combination of nature and nurture, are best equipped to take advantage of post-Soviet chaos and recreate their surrounding microworlds according to their needs. In the language of Lev Gumilev, whose pseudoscientific theory of ethnogenesis grew in popularity at roughly the same time as the New Russians appeared on the scene, Tuchkov's New Russians are passionaries, albeit unforgivably selfish ones: they are people whose sheer vital energy and drive move those around them toward creating a new a new collective identity.

The New Russians of *Death by Internet* would make excellent cult leaders. For that matter, so would Platon Makovsky from *Tycoon*. But rather than prophesy the end of the world, the coming of aliens, or transcendence into a higher realm, Tuchkov's New Russian cultists gravitate toward the feudal or medieval. The greatest threat of his imaginary New Russian is that he will recreate a feudal social structure by sheer force of will.

Jokes and the New Russian Body

Tuchkov's psychopathic, faux-medieval oligarchs take the popular discourse of the New Russians to its logical extreme. After all, how do we spot a New Russian? All the urban folklore reinforces the conclusion that the New Russian is identified in relation to his possessions. The New Russian may be described as a physical type, but the most important attributes are metonymic: the cell phone, the clothing, the Mercedes 600, and, behind all this, the money. A feudal scenario in which people themselves become the New Russians' property therefore makes a great deal of sense; the New Russian cannot relate to others as actual subjects (i.e., as people) but only as objects for him to manipulate. In Martin Buber's terms, he is incapable of an "I-You" intersubjective connection, only "I-It."

Certainly, the popular jokes about the New Russians and their satirical representation in film and fiction reek of class resentment, but they lack an important element of representations of the "lifestyles of the rich and famous" both in the West and, just a few years into the twenty-first century, in Putinist Russia: a palpable sense of envy. How hard can it be to make people want a fancy car and the latest gadgets? But when paired with the New Russians, fancy commodity fetish objects and the money that purchases them manage to look unappealing.

Jokes about New Russians were fertile ground for scholarly analysis in the 1990s and early 2000s, most notably by Emil Draitser and Seth Graham. Both Russians and Russia watchers seized on a phenomenon that was strangely reassuring: after several years in which the previously reliable folklore genre of political and topical jokes (*anekdoty*) had dried up, suddenly Russia was undergoing a renaissance of jokelore. Soviet political jokes often focused on the self-seriousness and hypocrisy of the regime and its leaders, a subject that lost its relevance after 1991. If Russian humor had found a new topical target of ridicule, surely this had to mean something.

A sizable portion of the New Russian jokes I've heard and read do, in fact, focus on commodity fetishism, mocking the New Russian obsession with things without simultaneously engaging in the older, Soviet moralizing about *veshchizm*. One of the classics is about two New Russians talking about a tie. One of them says, "Check it out, I bought this tie for $1,500!" while the other replies, "You idiot! You could have gotten it for $2,000!" At the usual risk of killing humor by explaining it, I want to point out the obvious detour from conventional values that is at work here. As a means of exchange, money is presumably valued for what it can buy, but for the New Russian, what he can buy is valued in accordance to how much money he can spend on it. Curiously, the obsession with material things threatens to dematerialize them entirely: they exist only as excuses for money to change hands.

In another joke involving the inevitable Mercedes, a New Russian gets into a car accident. He survives but moans repeatedly, "Oh, my poor Mercedes! My Mercedes." An onlooker notices that the New Russian has lost one of his arms. "Forget about the car! What about your arm?" The New Russian looks in the direction of his now-missing arm: "My Rolex! My Rolex!" Again, his values are distorted, this time in favor of objects at the expense of his own body.

In still another joke, the New Russian body is whole but is rendered little more than a vehicle for his beloved gadgets:

> Three New Russians are engaged in conversation, when one notices something odd about another New Russian's finger.

The second New Russian explains that he has a pager implanted in his finger.

Then the first New Russian's ear starts to buzz. He explains that this is his portable telephone getting a call.

Soon the third one's stomach starts to rumble, and he appears about to vomit. "What's happening?" they ask him. "I'm getting a fax."

In such jokes, the New Russian is a nightmare vision of the posthuman. He is not simply a cyborg (as in the previous joke), not merely obsessed with the material objects and gadgets he could potentially be using to extend his sense of self beyond the human body. Rather, he is an emptied-out self that has transferred virtually all of its value and all of its meaning into items beyond his own flesh, without compensating for this deprivation through even the vaguest appeal to the spiritual, intellectual, or sublime. He is the posthuman who has not transcended but descended.

Thus the New Russian embodies (to the extent that he can even be said to have a body anymore) a reflexive, undertheorized rejection of humanism, from the liberal humanism that animated Western Europe after the Renaissance to the sentimental humanism of Russian literature and culture (Radishchev's appeal to empathize with the downtrodden, the nineteenth-century Russian validation of the "little man"). To him, other people are like objects, and not particularly valuable objects at that.

In one anecdote, two New Russians are talking about remodeling their homes. One asks, "Who does the work on your house?" The other replies, "Tajiks. How about yours?" "The Swiss." "Why not Tajiks?" "Do you have any idea how expensive it is to ship Tajiks to Switzerland?"

In another, a New Russian refuses to provide funding to scientists in need of support, but he is generous in his handouts to beggars. Someone asks him why, and he responds, "You never know, someday I could be a beggar too. But I'll never be a scientist." This is not just selfishness or self-centeredness; it is the inability to think of other people in terms outside of himself and his needs.

The sheer vacuity of the New Russian, both as a self and as a body, is particularly clear in the last joke I want to tell for the moment:

A husband returning from a business trip sees a Mercedes 600 parked in his driveway. Inside, he sees a crimson jacket on a hanger, a cellular phone on the table, and his wife in bed with a man. The husband pushes the man:

"Hey, what are you doing here?"

"What do you mean? Don't you see? We're making New Russians." (Quoted in Draitser 2001, 449.)

Here the New Russian is reduced to his essence, a set of external attributes used to conjure him up through sympathetic magic (plus a healthy dose of adultery). The body to go along with all the possessions is merely an afterthought.

The joke works because before the husband encountered the couple, he saw a Mercedes 600 in the driveway, a crimson (probably raspberry) jacket on a hanger, and a cell phone on the table. The New Russian's identity was tied so closely to these (and a few other) particular objects that the listener is supposed to get the joke immediately.

Why these three things? The Mercedes could theoretically be any fancy, expensive car, except that linking all New Russians with one particular model of automobile suggests that little personal assessment is going on. This is not a matter of a man with money picking out the car that suits him best; it is a rich man who buys the car that everyone else of his status already possesses.

The cell phone obviously would not work even a few years later, now that nearly everyone in the country (or at least the big cities) has one of their own. But the presence of a lone cell phone in a crowd of people without phones is particularly disruptive, and not simply because of envy. The caricature has it that the New Russian is always yelling into his phone, heedless of the reactions of those around him. Cell phones may or may not still be annoying, but they are no longer marked as belonging to a particular category of person.

The raspberry jacket, however, takes some explanation. This jacket first appeared as part of Versace's 1992 collection, which was excellent timing from the point of view of a New Russian trying to show off. Soviet officials and factory heads were not exactly fashion icons; the drab grayness of Soviet men's style was as pervasive as their clothing options were limited (Molchanova; "Pochemu novye russkie"). What better way to stand out than with a bright red jacket (probably not from Versace, but who would notice)?

The raspberry jacket quickly became shorthand for New Russian. Sergei Mavrodi, the founder of the MMM pyramid scheme, traded in his customary track suit for a raspberry jacket for his televised 1993 New Year's address to his "partners" (read: "dupes"). In Aleksei Balabanov's 1997 hit film, *Brother*, one of the criminal leaders is a bald man in a raspberry jacket who is constantly laughing at the folk sayings and clichés out of which he constructs nearly every one of his utterances. His absence of imagination in fashion is outweighed only by his lack of wit when it comes to speaking. Balabanov returns to the 1990s criminal business world in his 2005 film, *Zhmurki* (Dead Man's Bluff), casting a backward glance at a bygone era. Naturally, he gives the film's most iconic character, Mikhailych, a raspberry jacket.

This jacket is fashion for the man who wants to be considered fashionable but has no inclination to spend the time actually assessing the clothing he is to wear, just as the Mercedes 600 is a default rich man's car. So perhaps we should give the New Russian a break: perhaps it is not that he has bad taste, but that he simply has no taste at all?

Alas, no. For the New Russian to fulfill his discursive function, his taste has to be terrible. Fortunately, he is up to the task.

Bad Taste, Revisited

One of the many functions of New Russian jokes is to take a potentially threatening, disturbing figure and reduce him to a laughingstock. There is nothing inherently funny about amassing millions of dollars through quasi-criminal enterprises, siphoning off state resources, or hiring hitmen to solve your problems. But a fool who shows off his terrible taste and total ignorance of high culture every time he throws his money around is entirely another matter.

As I indicated in chapter 2, the New Russian as a folk figure is the mirror image of the sovok. Where the sovok is flummoxed by the new capitalist consumer paradise, the New Russian revels in it. Where some versions of the sovok combine consumer cluelessness with a reflexive, often laughable fixation on high culture as framed by decades of Soviet education, the New Russian is incapable not just of appreciating but even of recognizing art. What unites the New Russian and the sovok is that both of them exemplify terrible taste.

The New Russian's bad taste has two components. The first is the assumption that aesthetic value depends on flashiness and expense. In this, the New Russian resembles the American stereotypes of lottery winners and shares an aesthetic with Donald Trump (often derided as "a poor person's fantasy of what a rich person is like").

Hence the joke about a New Russian who brings a gold ingot to a jeweler and asks him to make him a ring. The jeweler says, "Which one?" and starts to show him a catalog. The New Russian just looks at him. "What are you, an idiot? Just drill a hole!" Or the joke where the New Russian brags to his brother about his amazing new, custom-made BMW. The body is platinum, the bumper is gold, the tires are silver. It has a diamond-encrusted steering wheel, and pearls all over the exterior. "How often do you drive it?"—"I never do. It uses too much gas."[1]

The New Russian's tackiness would not be complete, however, if it merely consisted of his positive, or active, bad taste. Even worse than what he likes is the vast aesthetic and cultural world that he is incapable of appreciating. His ignorance of Culture-with-a-capital-C is so vast that he does not even recognize the huge gaps in his knowledge.

So we have the New Russian going back to the jewelry store, this time to buy a crucifix, since everyone is wearing them nowadays. He wants a gold one, of course, as heavy as possible. The clerk finally finds a huge gold crucifix, almost to the New Russian's liking. "Just one thing—Can you get me one without the gymnast?" (*Anekdoty nashikh chitatelei*, no. 33 [1997]: 6, as quoted in Graham 2003, 41).

In Paris, the New Russian points to the Eiffel Tower and asks the tour guide, "So have you guys found oil yet or not?"

One New Russian asks another: "So who are these guys, Bach and Beethoven, anyway?" The answer: "They're the guys who write the ring tones for our phones." Or, at a classical concert, one New Russian gestures toward the stage, asking, "Is that Beethoven?" Answer: "It's hard to tell from the back." Another joke has a New Russian relaxing with some music. His wife asks, "What are you listening to?" He answers: "Tchaikovsky. Piano Concerto no. 1, with orchestra." "Then why is the disk labeled 'Led Zeppelin III?'" "Damn it! I'm always getting them mixed up."

From the standpoint of the (post-)Soviet intelligentsia, the New Russian's values are literally reversed: he loves flashy garbage and cannot be bothered with the heritage of high culture. It is bad enough that men with money now rule the world, but even worse that they are so irredeemably vulgar.

Emil Draitser (2001), Seth Graham (2009, 134; 2003, 48), and Helena Goscilo (1998) have all noted the resemblance between the protagonist of New Russian anecdotes and a much more established butt of Russian jokes: the Chukchi. The inhabitants of a Siberian peninsula separated from Alaska by the Bering Strait, the Chukchi feature in an endless parade of jokes, the popularity of which is in direct proportion to the overall ignorance about them on the part of the average Russian. Non-Chukchi Russian citizens outside of Siberia could easily go their entire lives without meeting a Chukchi; thus while the Chukchi jokes are unequivocally racist, they are not based on any animus toward Chukchi in particular.[2] Instead, the Chukchi is used as a shorthand for backwardness, lack of culture, and lack of civilization.

Draitser argues quite convincingly for the role of Chukchi as the generalized fool but also for the Chukchi as a stand-in for the Russian himself: "In Chukchi jokes, one cannot help but sense a certain compassion for the simpleton. Such relatively sparing treatment of the Chukchi man can be explained by a high degree of identification of the Russian joke tellers with the butt of their jokes" (1998, 94). For the New Russian, though, there is precious little compassion and even less reason to try to cultivate it. The Chukchi's ignorance is posited to be either situational (i.e., he's culturally deprived) or, worse, biological (the jokes' racism). The New Russian has all the resources in the world available to him, and all he wants is more gold.

In framing the sovok as the Soviet intelligentsia, Victor Pelevin compared him to the estate owners in *The Cherry Orchard*. The New Russian calls to mind another of Chekhov's plays: *The Three Sisters*. The women of the Prozorov family are revolted by their brother's fiancée, and eventual wife, Natasha, who dresses badly and throws temper tantrums. The embodiment of the *poshlost'* (vulgarity) that triumphs over their refined sensibilities, by the end of the play, Natasha is the mistress of the house. While she does not sell or chop down a cherry orchard, she can't wait to completely transform the grounds, planning to plant "[cute little] flowers, flowers, flowers!" (*Tsvetochki, tsvetochki, tsvetochki!*).

Like Natasha in *The Three Sisters*, the New Russians are a reminder to their audience that the world no longer belongs to them. The jokes about the New Russians, by turning the new would-be aristocracy into figures of fun, soften the blow.

The New Russian in the Rearview Mirror

When Aleksei Balabanov made his cinematic return to the world of Russian criminal business with *Dead Man's Bluff*, he treated the eight years that had passed since the release of *Brother* as if they were eighty. The film begins in a crowded lecture hall, with an instructor standing in front of a blackboard announcing the day's topic: *nakoplenie nachal'nogo kapitala*, which can be translated either as "accumulating start-up capital" (if you're an MBA) or, with a bit of a stretch, "the primitive accumulation of capital" (if you're a Marxist). She explains that getting start-up capital "in our time" is very difficult, but in the 1990s, it was a different story. State property was being divided up, and all our current "so-called oligarchs" got their money back then.

A student comments: "I think back then it was easy to make money from nothing, both for start-up capital and for the rest of your life." She brings up the problem of pyramid schemes, which the instructor is quick to pick up on. The instructor notes that there were also "criminal structures" which had become intertwined with the state authorities, who also got their start-up capital at that time.

Balabanov then jump-cuts to the scene of one man torturing another in a morgue, ending in a bloodbath. In the same amount of time it takes for the instructor to explain 1990s capitalism, three men die, with two more killed thirty seconds later. In the first scene, although the classroom has students of both sexes, the conversation about the criminal economy is conducted entirely by women, with the men either silent or trying to get out of the lecture. In the second, all the speaking parts are male, as are all the murderers and victims, but the action unfolds against a backdrop of naked female corpses. What could be more Nineties than that?

This aesthetic contrast is as important as the change in subject matter (economics lecture vs. indiscriminate murder), leaving open the possibility that what Vadim Volkov called the "violent entrepreneurs" of cutthroat capitalism can be hygienically sealed off from the calmer, more civilized world in which the lecturer and her students now live. Though the classroom scene is a prologue, its function is reminiscent of the epilogue of Margaret Atwood's dystopian novel *The Handmaid's Tale*. After two hundred harrowing pages immersing the reader in a repressive, patriarchal regime of scheduled rape and mandatory childbirth, Atwood jumps hundreds of years into the future to a scholarly conference for historians who study this miserable time in their world's past. The tone is now matter-of-fact, if not lighthearted, a jarring counterpoint to the intense desperation of the novel's first-person narrator. This epilogue (much like the historical appendix on Newspeak in George Orwell's *1984*, whose most important feature is that it is *not* written in Newspeak), though not necessarily a pleasant reading experience, smuggles optimism into a bleak story. At some point, we know, conditions (will) change.[3]

The criminal New Russians of *Dead Man's Bluff* are not quite so hermetically isolated from the world of their frame story, however. The connection between the two reinforces both the film's satire and the instructor's own words about the origins of the current "so-called oligarchs." The film does not return to the classroom, but it does end with the revelation that our main gangster heroes have now cleaned themselves up and found a comfortable place as part of the apparatus of state, rather than private, corruption.

This, in fact, is the most common folk explanation for the fate of the New Russians. By "folk" I mean nonscholarly, lay explanations. Again, my concern here is not the actual socioeconomic transformation of post-Soviet Russia but its representation through media. I will, however, gesture toward the political developments that fostered a new environment for entrepreneurs in the 2000s.

A recurring refrain of the 1990s was that criminal organizations and the newly minted oligarchs (to the extent that this distinction even meant something to people at the time) needed be brought in line. Someone with a "firm hand" needed to put an end to *bespredel*, the boundary-less, terrifying chaos that allowed rich men and thugs to commit crimes with impunity. A weak central government run by an erratic, drunken president (Boris Yeltsin) gave way to a new administration under Vladimir Vladimirovich Putin. Over the first few years of the 2000s, Putin strongly centralized state authority (appointing governors rather than letting them be elected), allowed the development of a low-level personality cult focused on himself, and brought the oligarchs to heel. The message to the superrich was clear: if you want to keep your wealth and your freedom, you must recognize that you are subordinate, rather than superior, to the state. Meanwhile, oil prices and general prosperity began to rise as crime began to fall.

The New Russian was a fixture of an era when the state barely seemed relevant, and when money meant more than state power. The point I am making has less to do with how much *actually* changed in the 2000s than with the mood fostered by the media and entertainment industry. The culture had little room for the New Russian as anything more than a figure of fun, which meant that new models of wealth and power would inevitably arise.

On a discursive level, the decline of the New Russian and the resurgence of state power recapitulate a surprising Soviet pattern: the personal trajectory of the socialist realist hero. As Katerina Clark famously demonstrated in *The Soviet Novel*, the hero of socialist realism operated according to the dialectic of spontaneity and consciousness (15–24). Initially, the hero's strength is connected to his relative lack of attachment to the sometimes bureaucratic structures of the Party and the factory; he brought the very initiative (spontaneity) that the inertia of these structures discouraged. However, in the course of the story, the hero would manage to do two things: successfully accomplish the task that the forces of consciousness/inertia thought impractical while recognizing the necessity of subordinating (or at least incorporating) himself to the wisdom of the very organization that had discouraged him.

As the New Russian, the wealthy Russian recognized few strictures on his behavior, let alone a moral framework within which he must operate. Reborn as simply the rich Russian, he now functioned within the framework of the state, allegedly for the good of the state (or at least, not against it). For the state, this scenario presents one problem: If the New Russians/oligarchs are not responsible when things go bad, who is?

Loving the Leviathan

Consider two post-Soviet Russian dramas about the struggle for ordinary people to hold on to their land in the face of overwhelming opposition. In 1995, the veteran actor Yevgeny Matveev directed and starred in a film that turned out to be the first in a trilogy: *Liubit' po-russki* (Love, Russian style). The sequel, released the following year, was called *Love, Russian Style 2*. I leave it to my more perspicacious readers to guess what the final entry in the series was called when it came out three years after that.

Love, Russian Style tells the story of a group of former collective farmers whose plans to work their land are threatened by the insidious machinations of a local gang leader, who steals the land out from under them when a valuable source of mineral water is discovered on it. Our heroes are a motley group of salt-of-the-earth types: a former collective-farm director (Matveev); a rugged young man who seems to style himself after the 1970s Russian bard Vladimir Vysotsky, singing the film's theme song, Vysotsky style, from his prison cell; and a female refugee—but a "good" one, an ethnic Russian fleeing violence in a former Soviet republic. Their opponent is a rich, repulsive New Russian, while their means of resistance only reinforces the heroes' old-fashioned purity (they actually find a cache of World War II weapons, fighting the New Russian's hired thugs with a fabled *tachanka*). The iconography of their struggle could not be clearer.

Love, Russian Style was not a memorable movie (I seem to be one of the few who hasn't managed to forget it), and its sequels, as is so often the case even with better films, brought diminishing aesthetic and financial returns. Yet it shares an overall plot with one of the most highly acclaimed Russian films of the twenty-first century, Andrei Zviagintsev's 2014 *Leviafan* (Leviathan).

Though based on an actual event that took place in the United States ten years earlier, *Leviathan* establishes a conflict that is structurally equivalent to the one that motivates *Love, Russian Style*. In this case, a car mechanic named Kolya refuses to sell the land his house is built on, but the antagonist is not a private citizen. He is the town's corrupt mayor, who supposedly wants to set up a telecom tower on Kolya's land, but in the end builds a church at the behest of the local bishop (who is one of his friends).

Where *Love, Russian Style* embraces the optimism of a feel-good melodrama, *Leviathan* wallows in arthouse misery. The heroes' success in the 1995 film and Kolya's defeat almost twenty years later are each appropriate to their respective genres, but the difference in the status of the films' villains also plays a significant role. Hating the New Russian in the 1990s was not just acceptable; it was practically a national pastime. And no matter how much power the New Russian might have, and no matter how many strings he was able to pull, he was still not the state. In fact, *Love, Russian Style* mediates among three separate constituencies (a kind of hate triangle), with the state still available as a possible force for good. The problem with the state is not that it is evil but that it is weak, and leadership positions can still be filled by good people (over the course of the trilogy, the former collective-farm director is elected governor). In *Leviathan*, private wealth and state power have merged (and formed a threesome of their own with the Russian Orthodox Church). Kolya has no other avenues of recourse, no means of (re)mediation. The ethically bankrupt New Russian can have people killed, but it is the state that can crush the soul. The state is Leviathan; the New Russian is somewhere between a piranha and a guppy.

We Need a (Rich) Hero

The neoliberal hope for the New Russian was not that he would lose his wealth or even his power, but that he would acquire a veneer of civilization and use even the tiniest portion of his wealth in support of culture, rather than as the unwitting instrument of its destruction. For the New Russian to cease to be the New Russian, he needed two things: a conscience and taste.

Taste proved relatively easy to acquire, a topic I'll come back to. But where was the New Russian supposed to find a conscience? Jiminy Crickets were an endangered species, just as likely to be stomped on as adopted. If the New Russian needed a conscience, he was going to have to grow his own. Or, more to the point when it comes to the popular consciousness, we were going to have to *watch* him grow his own.

The standard trajectory for the New Russian plot followed the logic of tragedy: gifted and somewhat likable heroes, as they climb the ladder of success, become increasingly corrupt and difficult to admire. Such is the case with the aforementioned *Oligarch*, as well as Denis Estingeev's 1994 film, *Limita*, and, to a lesser extent, Pyotr Buslov's 2003 *Bumer* (Bimmer). Yet one of the most popular television miniseries during Putin's first term was a gangster story that, by the end, was close to a Bildungsroman about building a better New Russian: Aleksei Sidorov's 2002 *Brigada* (sometimes known in English as *Law of the Lawless*).

Over the course of fifteen episodes that unfold from 1989 to 2000, *Brigada* brings its viewers into the lives of four best friends (the "brigade" of the title): Fil, Kosmos, Pchola, and their leader, Sasha Belyi. Together, they build a small criminal empire, fighting off competitors and engaging in increasingly high-stakes activity (including, indirectly, the First Chechen War). The series stands out for its charming and compelling protagonists, especially Sasha Belyi, played by the young heartthrob Sergei Bezrukov. The heroes' appeal would set off a minor moral panic about the series' allegedly pernicious effect on its teenage viewers, much as the prostitute drama *Intergirl* did thirteen years earlier. In 2018, Pavel Maikov, the actor who played Pchola, denounced the series as a "crime against Russia," making boys want to grow up to be gangsters ("Pchela iz 'Brigady'").

Of course, there are no data on the effect of this particular miniseries on young male Russians' career choices. Instead, I would like to offer another interpretation of *Brigada*, one that does not nullify concerns about the romanticizing of banditry but rather supplements them with the possibility that the last few episodes offer the beginnings of a romanticizing of the Russian rich.

In 1998, Sasha Belyi's sworn enemy, Vladimir Kaverin, is running for the State Duma. After Pchola is put into a coma in a botched assassination attempt, Sasha decides to join the race. At first he is motivated by revenge, but something happens during the campaign. His initially cynical tactics for rehabilitating his image start to become real. He distributes aid to the poor, sponsors the construction of Russian Orthodox churches, and campaigns for social justice and equality.

During the televised debate, Kaverin accuses him of hypocrisy, given his criminal past. Sasha's response is not to cover up but to admit it. Yes, he's violated laws, but who in Russia hasn't? Lawlessness in Russia started at the top, with the people in power, and his task will be to put an end to the chaos. Unlike politicians, Sasha Belyi "answers for his words."

Just one word away from one of the most common Russian criminal sayings ("answering for one's *bazar*"—slang for spoken statements), Sasha's declaration is about bringing the best part of the world of crime (a sense of "justice," of "rules") to an unjust but technically legal world. If we're going to be covered by thieves, wouldn't we be better off if those thieves had a code?

The makers of *Brigada* were caught in a moral bind: they wanted Sasha to be appealing, and even to grow as a person. But ending a fifteen-episode television series with the outright triumph of a gangster-turned-politician would have been too strong a break with the conventions of the genre, either a celebration of criminality or an openly cynical statement about politicians and criminals. So in the last few episodes, Sasha does grow a greater sense of responsibility and moral nuance, even if he can't be allowed to win.

The story of Sasha Belyi is based on a dialectic of selfishness and empathy, self-centered utilitarianism and social responsibility. As a gangster and budding New Russian, Sasha is out for himself; the only thing that saves him from becoming a mobster Ayn Rand is his attachment to his mother and his loyalty to his three best friends. As time passes, Sasha marries, has a son, and the circle of his selfishness expands to include his new family. When he runs for office, he sees the opportunity to combine his own self-interest with the greater good of his fellow citizens.

Empathy and communal responsibility do not come naturally to the New Russian, but Sasha's development provides a model for *learning* empathy through the gradual widening of his circles of community. Despite the many deaths that can be laid at the feet of Sasha Belyi, he inspires the hope that the New Russian might not be *entirely* a sociopath or psychopath. With the proper socialization, perhaps the New Russian can learn to fake human connections and communal responsibility until they finally become real.

The New Russian would prove to be a bad fit for the new millennium. Already taking a serious hit from the 1998 financial collapse, he embodied so much of what Putinism was supposed to overcome: the limitless power accrued at the intersection of wealth and crime.

The devaluation of the ruble in 1998 was an obvious disaster for the economy, but one that presented real opportunities for a certain type of entrepreneur. As

Tycoon demonstrated, the New Russian business model was about import and resale, not production. The post-1998 environment, by making imports expensive, encouraged actual industry.

A little less than two years later, Putin began presiding over a country with a rapidly growing economy. Rising oil prices were its engine, but industry grew by 76 percent. The introduction of a flat tax in 2001, while obviously regressive, helped refill government coffers. During his first term, Putin and the oligarchs came to something of an understanding (at the cost of some oligarchs' wealth, freedom, and lives): the oligarchs kept their money and their business, and Putin could count on them to support the government. The rich Russian was therefore no longer such an ideal target in the media and culture industry. What could replace him?

In 2002, *Brigada* had teased with the possibility of a rich hero: an ex-criminal, a reformed New Russian with a social conscience and the resolve to use at least some of his ill-gotten gains for the greater good. Just two years later, one of the oligarchs, Mikhail Prokhorov, set up a foundation to support culture, education, and science throughout Russia's regions. The rich Russian as citizen and patriot was becoming thinkable.

It should be no surprise, then, that one of the fictional models of this civic-minded rich Russian should emerge out of a project conceived by an actual rich Russian, Konstantin Rykov. Rykov was one of the early content entrepreneurs on the Russian Internet in the 1990s, and his career has included serving on the State Duma, being an adviser to former Russian President Dmitri Medvedev, and becoming one of the most powerful television and Internet content producers in the Russian Federation. A staunch supporter of Putin, he was also a target of opposition leader Alexei Navalny's anticorruption campaign. During the 2011–2012 opposition protests, Rykov made several tweets threatening violence against the protesters.

One of the keys to Rykov's success, both as a producer and a political figure, is his capacity for crafting both entertainment and political messaging that appeals to the country's younger citizens. Like Putin's gray cardinal Vladislav Surkov, he is able to combine nationalist/conservative politics with a countercultural aesthetic. He can make Putinism "cool."

In 2009, he launched a massive literary "project" called *Ethnogenesis*. Based on the highly influential crackpot theories of Lev Gumilev (the son of the poets Anna Akhmatova and Nikolai Gumilev), *Ethnogenesis* is a series of young adult novels spanning time, space, and genres, all connected by two threads: the Gumilev family and a set of mysterious, animal-shaped objects (*predmety*) that endow their owners with a particular power (teleportation, mind control, clairvoyance, and so on). All of the sixty novels and six novellas that compose this never-completed project either have one-word nouns for titles (*Blockade, Dragon*) or are named after famous people (*Che Guevara*).[4] One particular subset of the *Ethnogenesis* novel that bears consideration for our discussion of the New Russian and the rich Russian: the trilogy called *Milliarder* (Billionaire). The fact that this title is so generic is in keeping with the project's naming conventions, but the announcement of a billionaire as not just protagonist but hero is another thing entirely.

The Man Who Has Everything

The *Billionaire* trilogy was begun by Elena Kondrateva before Kirill Benediktov replaced her for the second and third installments.[5] It centers on a rich protagonist who is a titan of industry, a paragon of virtue, and a man with an impeccable pedigree: Andrei Lvovich Gumilev. Gumilev is the grandson of the famous poet mentioned above, himself the protagonist of two other *Ethnogenesis* series, and the even more famous poet Anna Akhmatova, who barely merits a paragraph in one of the novels about her husband, as well as the son of Lev, the man whose theories give the series its name.[6] And perhaps the most unbelievable aspect of these novels—which also involve transparent alien artifact hunters, a lost tribe of yeti, and a cryogenically frozen Adolf Hitler maintained by a colony of cloned Valkyries on a secret Antarctic base—is the fact that Gumilev never once brings up his famous forebears.

This is surprising not only because the hero's name was famous long before he himself ever was, but because Gumilev, who repeatedly rejects the term "oligarch" as offensive, prefers to see himself and his kind as "aristocrats." This trilogy and the series about Gumilev's daughter, Marusia, actually confirm his argument, albeit on different terms: the Gumilev family is special because its members carry a strain of alien DNA, either attracting the mysterious objects (in Marusia's case) or endowing them with special abilities of which they themselves might not be aware (in Andrei Lvovich's case).

Andrei Lvovich is both the culmination of his storied ancestry and, as befits a series titled *Ethnogenesis*, the founder of a new and prosperous future for both Russia and humanity. Marusia is only the first of several of his descendants to appear in the books, and the technology he pioneers in the *Billionaire* trilogy will make the interplanetary, Russian-centered civilization in the twenty-fifth century (in the *Sleepwalker* trilogy) possible. He is also one of the first of a new breed of rich Russians who develop, rather than exploit, their country.

In fact, Andrei Lvovich shares the popular contempt for the "classical oligarchs":

> As for the fact that the resources sold by [such] oligarchs to the West, along with the entire raw material infrastructure that allowed them to pump petrodollars from Tyumen and Yugorsk, belonged to them only by the whim of the liberal "fathers of privatization," these people tried not to think about that. Just like their responsibilities to "this country," as they liked to call Russia.[7] Gumilev, who tried to develop an economy of innovation for the good of all Russia, found these resource oligarchs unpleasant.[8]

By contrast, we are told in the very beginning of the novel that, after the 1998 financial collapse, Gumilev "quickly understood that the implementing the technologies his center developed in Russia would be much more complicated and expensive than in the West, but that did not stop him."

Indeed, one can't help but wonder if Gumilev is meant to be an idealized version of . . . Konstantin Rykov: "While he was still in college, Gumilev patented an array of IT inventions and became the first businessman to make millions on the Russian Internet." If that is the case, the mastermind behind the *Ethnogenesis* series should find the *Billionaire* trilogy to be an unending source of flattery. The handsome Gumilev attracts nearly every woman he meets (though he is primarily monogamous) and keeps in such good shape that he manages to have "not a single gram of excess fat" on his body.

As befits a self-made billionaire, Andrei Gumilev combines concern for his motherland with an ethos of self-reliance. How else can one explain devoting an entire chapter of the first book to a business subplot that goes absolutely nowhere? After making an attempt on Gumilev's life, a young man named Krasnov is arrested and about to be sent away for life. But Gumilev intervenes: he must find out why the man hates him so much. It turns out that Krasnov's father had a genetic engineering research start-up that Gumilev bought for much less than it should have been worth, ruining the father's life and leaving the son embittered ("You're just a common pirate! You stole from my father, you stole his business! What do you need genetic engineering for?"). Gumilev patiently listens to the youth's rantings, then calls in the father, pressing the elder Krasnov to admit the truth: he had embezzled from his company and racked up enormous gambling debts and begged Gumilev to buy him out.

At this point, both father and son are humiliated. But Gumilev is merciful and arranges to have Krasnov imprisoned under relatively decent conditions, with the prospect of a job on his realize. He also offers a job to Gordeev, the young man who helped apprehend Krasnov after the botched assassination attempt. He sees that Gordeev is a decent but directionless person who could use a sense of purpose and doesn't want to reward him with mere cash:

> Handing out money is against my principles. But giving you a good, well-paying job, that I can do. By the way, you're no match for the would-be killer; he's a unique specialist who will get his diploma, work for a while—he'll be priceless. While you were kicked out of school. And when your grandmother left you her apartment, you sold it to buy a motorcycle instead of, say, investing it. Or even just putting it in the bank. The moral? You live from day to day. Do you know how many people like that there are in Moscow?

Gumilev's behavior with Krasnov *père* and Krasnov *fils* proves him to be a man who has not only earned his money honestly and in the best interests of his country but has also not allowed himself to see money as the immediate solution to all problems. The caricatured New Russian is trapped within a very simple equation of money and goods, and he cannot think his way out of it. But Gumilev knows better than to simply throw money at a problem; instead, he uses the social and cultural capital that money has made available to him in order to help others solve their own problems.[9] It's not just a matter of believing in self-reliance. Although money is one of our most pervasive vehicles for symbolic exchange, the New Russian's understanding of it is confined to the realm of the Imaginary. Money means access to material wealth, while material wealth demonstrates the possession of money. For Gumilev, money functions on a level closer to the Symbolic: money provides not mere possessions but possibilities.

Gumilev is the rich Russian who can be admired because he *deserves* to be rich. In fact, the source of his wealth and power transcends the problem of origins that haunts the New Russian, who cannot reasonably claim to have come by his wealth by legitimate means. He prefers to think of himself as an aristocrat (with alien DNA), and his storied lineage would certainly support such a claim. But it is the ability his DNA grants him that turns wealth into his birthright.

Early in the first novel, the narrator tells us that Andrei Lvovich's strategy of investing in technology and employing the best and the brightest paid off better than anyone else would have imagined. He also has a knack for picking stocks that will pay off: "When he was asked how he calculated which shares he should buy, Gumilev only smiled and gently touched his finger to his forehead. Some interpreted that gesture as a not-so-humble reminder of his outstanding mental capacity, but Andrei had in mind his intuition. Intuition had always been his strongest suit."

This intuition has made him master of all he surveys. As we see later in the first novel, when he is looking down at Moscow from his office building: "The entire city was at his feet—and not just figuratively. Andrei Gumilev was the sort whom one called the master of his life, someone who has it made, a self-made man."[10]

Which is it, then? Is he a self-made man who picked himself up by his bootstraps, an Ayn Rand hero in a post-Soviet young adult (YA) adventure novel, or an aristocrat who was born into the role? *Ethnogenesis* combines all three scenarios. In the concluding volume of the *Billionaire* trilogy, the former Federal Security Service (FSB) general and artifact hunter Ilya Sviridov explains to Andrei Lvovich that he does not need an artifact because "you yourself are an artifact.... There are people in this world who can do things without an artifact":

> Andrei Lvovich, how did you earn your billions? Did you simply go for a walk and find a wallet with a billion in it? Or maybe you got an inheritance from a rich aunt in Australia? ... You earned your money, and earned it honestly. And since that's almost impossible in our country, one has to assume that something helped you.... You have an unbelievably developed intuition. On a level that an ordinary person could never reach.

Andrei Lvovich's superpower, then, is a way out of the (anti)utopian closed circle of post-Soviet capitalism. Just as the imperfect ideologues of the new (Soviet) world were not the ideal people to populate it, there was no place for creating a system of "fair" capitalism that was not based on corruption. The billionaire's intuition skips over all the messiness normally associated with 1990s wealth creation by invoking a power that comes from beyond economics.

Such a move is entirely appropriate for the *Ethnogenesis* series as a whole. Lev Gumilev's theory assumed a rising level of "passionarity" that sparked the creation of a new ethnos. Where did this energy come from? Gumilev's response was pseudoscientific hand waving: it came from "the cosmos" (space). Rykov's *Ethnogenesis* series fills in the gaps by making this alien energy literal and material, manifesting it in both the artifacts (which give their bearers superpowers) and the inborn abilities of those, like Andrei Lvovich, who bear alien DNA.

The *Billionaire* trilogy, then, is not just a reassuring just-so story about good rich Russians; it is a myth of origin about rich Russians not so much as an aristocracy (as Andrei Lvovich would prefer), but as either the passionaries who will reinvigorate the Russian ethnos or the beginning of a new ethnos of their own.

The right kind of rich Russians will be rich because they deserve it, and they will deserve it because they are special. Unlike Tuchkov's neo-feudal New Russians, these rich Russians will use their wealth for the betterment of the breed. The rest of us just need to be wise enough to appreciate their wisdom.

Born This Way

Billionaire, and to a lesser extent *Brigada*, point the way out of the New Russian paradigm and into something more respectable.[11] Sasha Belyi needed to launder more than simply his money; he needed to clean up his backstory. Andrei Gumilev, essentially a superhero, embodies the culture's wish-fulfillment fantasy regarding its superrich: neither he nor his past need laundering because he has always been deserving of wealth, and his road to riches, rather than strewn with corpses, is paved by his efforts on behalf of the country he calls home. Gone are the New Russian's corruption, boorishness, and selfishness; in Andrei Lvovich's own words, what we have instead is an aristocracy.

The lack of an aristocracy has always haunted the New Russian; indeed, it is one of the reasons he exists. Recall the paucity of rich Russian bachelors as love objects in the early romance novels; without inherited wealth, the rich Russian hero could not escape the taint of his money's origins.

In her excellent sociological study, *Rich Russians: From Oligarchs to Bourgeoisie*, Elisabeth Schimpfössl interviews dozens of people who fit the category announced by her title. The book is a treasure trove of revelations about Russia's new masters of the universe; Schimpfössl deserves credit for her thoroughness, envy for her access, and admiration for her ability to listen to what she is being told without erupting into class-based rage.

Schimpfössl is quite clear-eyed about the contradictions inherent in the rich Russians' self-image. On one hand, many of them want to give credit entirely to their own effort and grit: "When rich Russians talk about the roots of their post-Soviet fortunes, they often cultivate an image of rags-to-riches billionaires who can lay claim to humble beginnings and to having made it without enjoying any advantages, neither the cultural and social advantages they got from their parents, nor the vital social networks they enjoyed during their university years. Instead, they often cherry-pick elements of their work biographies" (30).

On the other hand, it is these cherry-picked biographies that offer more interesting, if no less problematic, explanations for their success. One of the most intriguing parts of Schimpfössl's book are when her rich Russian subjects offer lengthier explanations for their success and justification for their exceptional economic status. Some of her subjects like to stress that their parents and grandparents were members of the Soviet intelligentsia, giving themselves an aura of inherited culture and intellectual heft. This provides support for their efforts to be a more sophisticated wealthy class than the New Russians.

The intelligentsia connection can be considered primarily sociological, a reference to the social and cultural capital that enabled the rich Russians' rise. But a number of Schimpfössl's sources suggest that they owe their success to "good genes." As one tells her, "Listen, I got genes from my parents. Of course, these genes allowed me to develop myself and all the qualities that led to success" (69). Another says, "This is thanks to God and thanks to genes" (71). Schimpfössl notes, "Genes and God were the most frequently cited reasons for success, and the people I spoke to sometimes identified themselves as 'chosen ones'" (71).

This faith in the power of genes did not occur in isolation, according to Schimpfössl:

> Although justifying success by reference to genes is in many ways ad hoc and improvised, it is not random. This kind of essentialist reasoning is strong in Russia, not because everybody is obsessed with genes, but because it offers a convenient justification for inequality. What is supposedly grounded in nature is difficult to argue against. In addition, secular ways of "naturalizing" the social and the historical have a strong tradition in Russia. This is despite the fact that Marx considered consciousness to be determined by being. (72)

For the rich Russians, it's not just genes; it's genealogy. In order to be legitimate, in order to be a true modern aristocracy, they need a respectable origin story. The New Russian's story was anything but that: it was about money, access, criminal ties, and, yes, cleverness. It is not enough for the New Russian simply to transform himself into something more refined, because his origins do not change. Instead, the New Russian has to be transformed into a vanished missing link in the evolutionary chain of the post-Soviet bourgeoisie.

6

RUSSIAN ORC

The Evil Empire Strikes Back

Since sending its "polite little green men" into neighboring Ukraine in 2014, the Russian Federation has had an image problem. A large segment of the Western media has reduced the birthplace of Dostoevsky and Tolstoy to a caricature of invasion-happy, gay-bashing ultranationalists led by a shirtless man on a horse. So of course, the obvious solution was to deck the skies of Moscow with one of the most internationally recognized symbols of evil this side of the swastika. In late 2014, in honor of the final installment of the eighty-seven-part Hobbit film series, the Russian art group Svechenie decided to crown the Moscow International Business Center with the All-Seeing Eye of Sauron.

To be sure, this was not a government project; indeed, the group of hard-core Tolkien fans who constructed the Eye claimed to have been taken aback by an outpouring of criticism whose intensity rivaled Mount Doom itself. As soon as word got out about the group's plans for the Eye of Sauron, the Russian Orthodox Church head of public affairs at the time, Vsevolod Chaplin, denounced the Eye as a "demonic symbol": "Such a symbol of the triumph of evil is rising up over the city, becoming practically the highest object in the city. Is that good or bad? I'm afraid it's more likely bad. Just don't be surprised later if something goes wrong with the city" (Walker 2014).

For Chaplin, this was par for the course; the man could find demonic symbols in his breakfast cereal. And, to be fair, the Russian Orthodox Church leadership is not the only religious group to go overboard with its warnings about the forces of darkness lurking in popular culture. Recall the fundamentalist US Protestants fuming over the "satanic" magic in the Harry Potter series (Halford). But the

Russian Orthodox Church hierarchy had been prevented from issuing such proclamations about mass culture for seven Soviet decades; in the last ten years, it seems as though they're determined to make up for lost time.

In any case, the Eye of Sauron was quickly closed, and unlike in the original books, it did not even require a thousand pages of turgid prose and relentlessly merry ballads for this worthy quest to reach its completion. But what was the Eye of Sauron kerfuffle really about? If we take the Svechenie art group's spokesman at his word, the last thing they had in mind was politics. If that is the case, then Svechenie was displaying a shocking geopolitical naiveté. Nothing says "Evil Empire" like the Eye of Sauron.

A bit later in this chapter, we will examine precisely how and why *The Lord of the Rings* has gained so much resonance in Russian culture, to the point where one of the series' most loathsome antagonists (the Orcs) becomes a self-mocking symbol of post-Soviet Russia.[1] But in order for that discussion to take on its proper resonance, we need to address the larger question of Western mass culture and non-Western audiences during and after the Cold War.

For all its complexities, the Cold War constituted nearly five uninterrupted decades of simmering conflict within a persistently dualistic framework: the United States vs. the USSR, capitalism vs. communism, freedom vs. totalitarianism, exploitation vs. economic justice, racist colonialism vs the brotherhood of nations. It is a patently reductive model, whose failures and omissions (China, anticolonialism, religious revival, environmental degradation, and the full spectrum of women's and minority struggles for equal rights) outweigh its value as an analytical tool. But discursively, one of the few things that both the United States and the USSR agreed on was the centrality of the competition between the two blocs' political and economic systems.

However, the two sides waged their war for hearts and minds on different fronts. Soviet mass culture featured relatively few stories of the standoff between the Soviet Union and the North Atlantic Treaty Organization (NATO) or the United States (in film and fiction, World War II was where the action was). Instead, Cold War antagonism played itself out in the news and in explicit propaganda, particularly the posters that were an unavoidable part of the Soviet visual landscape. In the United States and Western Europe, the story was different, in that the conflict was very much a story. Not only were there endless spy dramas involving the Soviets and their lackeys, and fantasies of a future World War III between the superpowers, but the very structure of the conflict replicated itself throughout Western popular culture.

Whether by accident or design, the Cold War coincided with a boom (or several boomlets) in Western mass entertainment that recapitulated the binaries of the conflict between the Eastern and Western Blocs. Binarism is an integral part of adventure fiction and war drama, with the struggle between "good guys" and "bad guys" transformed into a central feature of the superhero comics that had become popular in the run-up to World War II. High fantasy, as revived by Tolkien in the 1950s, tends to rely on a Manichaean metaphysics that often dispenses with all subtlety: good battles evil, or the forces of light fight the forces of darkness.

Dualistic Western mass entertainment is arguably a more important contributor to the Cold War imaginary when it is not directly telling stories about the Cold War itself. The James Bond franchise has plenty of subtexts, but its Cold War plots are all simply text. Moreover, fictional narratives that are actually *about* the Cold War travel badly across the East/West divide: from *Ninotchka* to *The Hunt for Red October*, the obvious failures at depicting Soviet reality preclude real identification by Soviet or post-Soviet audiences. When Western Cold War dramas move east, they become little more than kitsch.

When Cold War dualism is transferred to the more purely imaginary realms of fantasy and science fiction, to worlds other than our own, authors can decide whether or not to hint at the Cold War, and audiences can choose whether or not to see or impose the ideological conflicts of the "real" world onto the entertainment they are reading or viewing. My argument is not that all dualistic fantasy and science fiction (F&SF) mass culture of the Cold War era is an allegory of the Cold War; to the contrary, I would reject such a reductive interpretation with all the resolve Aragorn's army of elves, hobbits, and men demonstrated at the Battle of the Pelennor Fields. Instead, I argue that dualistic storytelling popularized *during* the Cold War lends itself to being understood as an allusion to the Cold War, regardless of the authors' intentions. More important, these stories' Manichaean frames also worked in the opposite direction, allowing audiences to understand the Cold War in terms of fantasy tropes about good heroes and evil villains.

Sith Lords of the World, Unite!

Among the many proxy battlefields that took the place of armed superpower conflict during the Cold War, we should also count the war for the popular imagination. When it came to "good guys" and "bad guys," the Soviet Union after World War II specialized in only one type of story: the fight between the Soviets and the Nazis. This story structure proved both powerful and productive, and it remains one of the primary filters imposed on Russia's post-Soviet struggles. We see this in the post-Maidan conflicts in and with Ukraine, as I discuss at some length in chapter 6 of *Plots against Russia*: the enemies of Russia inevitably become the "fascists." It was, however, of limited utility for framing the Cold War when the Soviet Union still existed, and of virtually none after the USSR's collapse. And, like American stories of the fight against Soviet espionage or expansionism, it did not travel well to the other side.

American and Western European dualist dramas, in contrast, were context-independent; rather, in depicting fantasy worlds, they carried all the context they needed with them like a snail carries its shell. *Lord of the Rings, Star Wars,* and *Harry Potter* have captured audiences' imaginations the world over, and all of them are Anglo-Saxon story worlds based on the struggle between the forces of good and the forces of evil (with only the post-Cold War Harry Potter series treating the subject matter with any attempt at nuance). As such, they address themes that could reasonably be considered universal. After all, what culture manages to do without stories about heroes and villains? Ideally, fantasy gives us virtual worlds which we can inhabit regardless of our background and baggage. Everyone can be Luke Skywalker or Frodo Baggins, because no one actually *is* Luke Skywalker or Frodo Baggins.

The problem is that the very last people who can determine what is universal and what is specific about such stories is the Anglo-Saxon audience. In the case of Russian audiences, we have, as is so often the case with late- and post-Soviet interactions with global popular cultures, a delicate question of timing. Tolkien, as we shall see, makes some headway in the USSR in the 1970s, much more in the 1980s, and is already a mass-culture juggernaut by the time Peter Jackson's first installment of *The Lord of the Rings* appears in 2001. *Star Wars* was not available in the USSR in the 1970s, although it was frequently discussed (and reviled) in the Soviet press; the first two films were popular bootlegs when videocassettes became available and were screened at two Soviet theaters in 1988, with spotty distribution of the films throughout the 1990s (by which point they had already saturated the VHS market). The post-Cold War Harry Potter comes to Russia with virtually no time lag whatsoever. Western fantasy's capture of the Russian popular imagination coincides with the decline of the Soviet Union and the chaotic 1990s.

It is fitting that the entanglement of Western mass fantasy and Cold War politics should be highlighted by America's Hollywood president, the former cowboy actor Ronald Reagan. On March 8, 1983, Reagan gave his notorious "evil empire" speech, named after the phrase he used to describe the Soviet Union, in which he called on his countrymen to commit to the fight against communism as a "struggle between good and evil." Fifteen days later, Reagan announced the Strategic Defense Initiative, immediately ridiculed as "Star Wars." Two months after that, George Lucas concluded his trilogy with *Return of the Jedi*.

Conservatives lauded Reagan for bringing moral clarity to the superpower conflict and reminding his countrymen that there was nothing ordinary about the ideological clash with the USSR. Liberals ridiculed him for endorsing a simplistic worldview that was likely to turn a Cold War hot. In fact, Reagan's rhetoric was a departure for US mass media and culture. Despite the enduring caricatures of Soviet villains in spy stories, the more liberal-leaning Hollywood (which nevertheless managed to produce the right-wing Reagan) preferred stories that humanized the Soviets rather than demonizing them. For example, Norman Jewison's 1966 film, *The Russians Are Coming! The Russians Are Coming!*, portrayed both the Soviet and American characters as flawed, lovable doofuses who, by eventually working together, manage to avoid bringing their two countries to all-out war.

Even popular science fiction and fantasy with explicit Cold War parallels often nudged its audience toward a more complex understanding of the enemy. The Klingons of the original *Star Trek* series were an obvious Russian stand-in, but at least one episode (1968's "The Day of the Dove") pushed the two sides toward a peaceful resolution of their conflicts. When the series was revived as *Star Trek: The Next Generation*, the Klingons were the Federation's allies (granted, they were also now culturally closer to stereotypes of the Japanese).

Reagan's use of the term "evil empire" was part of a call for his country to recommit to binary, black-and-white thinking but couched in language that pointed beyond politics and even metaphysics: the phrase "evil empire" invites its listeners to understand their world in terms of fantasy. We now reach a strange convergence of genre and high theory: Lacan's and Zizek's identification of ideology as a form of shared fantasy and Reagan's notorious slippage between fiction and fact. The Soviet Union as an enemy was not just real but complicated, in a way that no amount of world building would complicate Mordor or the Galactic Empire. This is not to say that all fantasy is as simplistic as Reagan's "evil empire" speech; Reagan needed the straightforward morals of *Lord of the Rings*, not the messy ethical compromises that, decades later, would be the hallmark of *Game of Thrones*.

Evil Empire: Love It or Leave It

When a film has millions of viewers, those millions of viewers are not all watching the same film. We all bring our own baggage to any text that confronts us, and we all pay attention differently to different things.

Scholars of media long ago abandoned the mid-twentieth-century assumption that audiences passively received the messages transmitted to them, instead focusing on the ways in which diverse audiences encounter a media object in order to create or wrest meanings for themselves. This is most starkly the case when the implied audience and the actual audience diverge: LGBT audiences and people of color, for instance, might use the lack of characters for obvious identification constructively, reading allegorically in a way to reclaim a space for themselves in stories ostensibly not about them (as in the case of American gay men's postwar appropriation of *The Wizard of Oz*).

The grand dualistic fantasy entertainments I've mentioned so far (*Star Wars, Lord of the Rings, Harry Potter*) are inherently reassuring to Anglo-Saxon audiences, as the heroes act according to familiar cultural scripts, and, in the first two cases, are coded to be essentially stand-ins for Americans or Brits, while in the third, they simply *are* British. This does not mean that international audiences cannot identify with the heroes; quite obviously, they can. But when we step away from the individual characters to the general framework in which they operate, geopolitical allegories can become obstacles.

To some Russian audiences, the villains can start looking uncomfortably ... Russian. Or, in a pinch, Soviet (a distinction Western entertainment was never particularly good at maintaining in any case). In his 1986 study *Konveir grez i psikhologicheskaia voina* (The conveyer belt of dreams and psychological warfare), Kirill Razlogov warns his readers (most of whom had probably not had the chance to see the films yet) that the *Star Wars* trilogy must be seen in the context of Western propaganda:

> It cannot be ruled out that, under the conditions of anticommunist hysteria, in the West the "black star" [Death Star?] ... may appear to the mass audience as the center of "world communism"—"the evil empire," according the US president's famous phrase. Such an interpretation is supported by the television productions and films where in similar space adventures the villains are quite simply KGB agents, and the protectors of 'innocence" are 100-percent Americans from the CIA. (Quoted in Dubogrei.)

In *Gollivud: Kontrasty 70-kh* (Hollywood: Contrasts of the 70s), Elena Kartseva notes that the emperor's favorite, Grand Moff Tarkin, has a Russian-sounding surname and looks like the "sly Bolsheviks ... in anti-Soviet films." The enemy's frozen territory shown in *The Empire Strikes Back* would apparently remind American audiences of Siberia, while the imperial uniforms in *Return of the Jedi* look like they come from the Warsaw Pact.

How likely is it that the resemblance noted by Soviet critics was intentional? This is a question to which we will return but one that, for the moment, is not particularly relevant. Instead, if we assume that at least some Russian-speaking viewers would see parallels with the USSR (or start to see them after someone else points them out), how are such viewers supposed to situate themselves in relation to the films? Luke Skywalker and his friends invite identification on an individual level, but through visual cues spotted by some Russian viewers, the forces of evil suggest kinship on a group level.

Consuming entertainment that seems to identify the forces of evil with one's own culture presents serious challenges. One can assume a stance of distanced, amused irony, such as in Victor Pelevin's *Generation P* (also published in English as *Homo Zapiens*), in which the narrator muses about whether it was worth trading in the "evil empire" for an "evil banana republic that imported its bananas from Finland." Also possible is outrage, based on the supposition that a Russophobic West is intentionally encoding anti-Russian messages into its popular entertainment as part of an overall plot to weaken the Russian Federation in the eyes of the world.

But what has proven especially productive for some is a strategy of acceptance and identification, whether based on pride in the motherland's continued status as dangerous threat (and therefore a force to be reckoned with), as *styob* (ironic overidentification), or as a combination of the two (*styob* that over time becomes serious, like the gradual process in which online trolls can move from ironic appropriation of fascist tropes to espousing fascist views in all sincerity).

All of this brings us back to the Eye of Sauron, which, however inadvertently, captures the dynamic perfectly. The Eye is both viewer and viewed, an audience that watches and an audience that watches itself being watched and transforming what it sees through the very act of observation. The Eye is a case study in reification, turning the other into a fixed object of unmitigated evil that reifies at the same time, an image of what could be an intersubjective relation but collapses into mutual objectification and deliberate misprision.

The Eye of Sauron is a basilisk.

The Fellowship of the Wrong

Given the obvious associations between Reagan's "evil empire" and *Star Wars*, not to mention the far greater cultural weight of the Star Wars phenomenon in North America before Peter Jackson's movies came out, Western observers might be surprised to find Tolkien looming so large in internal Russian discourse about the culture's relationship with the West.

After all, other upstart Dark Lords have made a name for themselves since Tolkien first wrote *The Lord of the Rings*. Presumably, Darth Vader's genocidal home base would have been as powerful a symbol as anything associated with

Mordor, but Death Stars, like old Soviet color televisions, have an unfortunate tendency to explode. And as for Voldemort, even He Who Must Not Be Named trembles before the might of J. K. Rowling's legal team.

Nor can the plan to project the Eye of Sauron onto a Moscow skyscraper be patronizingly chalked up to a local culture's misunderstanding of an imported work of art. If anything, *The Lord of the Rings* is one of those foreign classics that has so permeated the culture as to have become all but Russian. As someone who long ago found himself reading John Galsworthy's *The Forsyth Saga* and Astrid Lindgren's *Karlsson-on-the-Roof* to remedy embarrassing gaps in his knowledge of Russian culture, I truly believe this is not an overstatement.

Indeed, I find it difficult not to view the entire Eye of Sauron affair as a postmodernist prank. A tale of the forces of Light fighting the armies of Darkness, *The Lord of the Rings* easily lends itself to allegorical readings. Tolkien created the better part of his secondary fantasy world during World War II, allowing simple connections to be drawn between Mordor and fascism. But, as Michael Moorcock shows in *Wizardry and Wild Romance*, the implications of the triumph over evil, dark-skinned hordes by pasty-faced hobbits and porcelain-skinned elves are disturbing.

So projecting the All-Seeing Eye of Sauron over the capital of a country that is developing a reputation for xenophobia and excessive media surveillance could seem like a rather pointed political statement. But if we throw Gogol into the mix of our wandering body parts, perhaps the Eye of Sauron is a bit too "on the nose"?

Writing in the hardline newspaper *Sovetskaia Rossiia* on December 30, 2014, Svetlana Zamlelova included the Eye of Sauron controversy in her end-of-the-year column, whose headline, "The Americans Have Announced Sanctions Against Us," would become the title of her essay collection the following year. After a brief reference to Reagan-era attempts to bring the "evil empire" to heel and listing all the anti-Russian events of 2014, she turns to the Tolkien fans' idea for commemorating the release of Peter Jackson's *The Hobbit*:

> The Eye of Sauron—Tolkien's main symbol of evil—was supposed to light up over the capital. Why Moscow and why the Eye of Sauron? We can only guess. And if we recall that "Putin is capable of any atrocity," and Russia is a "Mafia Country," that is, the epicenter of evil, then there's no reason to be surprised. After all, Mordor—Sauron's country—is the same thing as the "evil empire," only updated. The "Evil Empire" is old-fashioned, pathetic, and boring. But Mordor is dynamic, "trendy," and young people, including Russians, understand it. There's even a kind of "message" to Russian youth: if you don't want to live in Mordor, change the system, get rid of Putin/Sauron and his butchers.

Zamlelova is not one to see light-hearted humor, let alone *styob*, when there is an opportunity to uncover a Russophobic conspiracy. On the contrary, she wants to make sure her readers understand that the real Eye of Mordor belongs in America. Knowingly or not, she is situating herself in a decades-long Russian tradition of Tolkienist allegory, even if, by 2014, nationalist rereadings of Tolkien had far surpassed her own in terms of sheer ingenuity. For years, the most active venue for deconstructing *The Lord of the Rings*' political implications has been Russia itself.

Although an official, complete Russian translation of *The Lord of the Rings* would appear only in 1992, numerous Russian-language manuscripts of the trilogy had been circulating in samizdat since the 1960s (Hooker, 17–25). While the danger of being caught with an unauthorized edition of *The Two Towers* could not reasonably be compared with the possession of, say, *The Gulag Archipelago*, Tolkien's unofficial circulation certainly added to his work's subcultural mystique. And if *The Lord of the Rings* had become the model for epic fantasy in the West, its centrality would only be greater in a literary environment that was largely inhospitable to elves.

The Abuses of Enchantment

Politics, like fantasy and science fiction, is the art of creating and selling an imaginary world. It can be the world yet to come: Stalin called on his people to create a "radiant future," Bill Clinton built a "bridge to the twenty-first century" (as if we would not have gotten there without one), and Reagan's "morning in America" promised the optimism of a brand-new day. It can just as easily be a restoration of past glory: Trump bellows his plan to "make America great again"; Milošević proclaimed a return to Serbian purity; and Putin, after "saving" Russia from an imagined imminent dismantling, is restoring his country to "great power" status after years of humiliation.

Particularly telling is the increasingly frequent application of the American term "paleoconservatism" to Putin's program; paleoconservatism, like the Paleo Diet, connotes a return to a Stone Age informed less by archeology than it is by *Clan of the Cave Bear*. Linking one's politics to a purely fantastic world is but a small step. This might suggest Frederic Jameson's famous connection of politics with science fiction and utopia, but the example I have in mind is a more comfortable fit with "heterotopia": we are dealing with political fantasies rooted in a different, not necessarily better world. I bring you word of a small but vocal community of Russian patriots who voluntarily, if ironically, proclaim that Russia is not, as the old Soviet joke goes, "the motherland of elephants," but rather, the motherland of Orcs.

Through a philologically suspect reading of J. R. R. Tolkien's *Lord of the Rings*, this community has appropriated the trilogy's largest contingent of villains in defiant response not just to the Manichaeism of Tolkien, but to the equally primitive binaries of the Cold War and its aftermath. Although it is the result of a clever and subversive appropriation of the tools of postmodernism, the identification of Russians with Orcs is not deconstructive. Even when the same Tolkien references are used by the liberal opposition, the inherent dualism remains undisturbed. Productive irony cannot save either group from the fact that they are simply reversing Cold War binaries rather than undermining their foundation.[2]

This tacit acceptance of dualism is consistent with the source material. J. R. R. Tolkien has been accused of many things, but subtlety is not among them. Nor is there even the faintest whiff of moral relativism in his most famous works. After all, one of the hallmarks of old-fashioned high fantasy is a straightforward, dualistic cosmology, a worldview that encompasses works as apparently disparate as *Lord of the Rings* and *Star Wars* (a film series that is essentially epic fantasy with droids instead of dragons).

Such heroic stories bring an extra appeal to the familiar F&SF phenomenon known as world building: we are not only invited to share in the imagining of Tolkien's (or Lucas's) imaginary world but also to find clear and compelling ethical positions for our own imagined selves to adopt. This is the unjustly maligned escapism that features the simplicity and moral clarity that the real world should best avoid. (After all, Aragorn is basically trying to "make Middle Earth great again," something even Tolkien's fantasy world rejects when Frodo joins the elves in the exodus of magic from the land.)

We have in *Lord of the Rings* a famously complex fantastic geography, history, and ethnography, in which all the forces of good just happen to have languages and cultures with clear Anglo-Saxon roots, while the "dark" and "savage" enemy offers little resistance to familiar racist, orientalist tropes. The very fact that Middle Earth contains "evil" races is, at the very least, problematic. F&SF practitioners as varied as Michael Moorcock, David Brin, and China Miéville take Tolkien to task for his nostalgic feudalism and displaced racism, while the scholarship and commentary on Tolkien's racial politics continues to grow.[3]

It is the racism that is key here. Where Russian critiques and reappropriations of Tolkien will be preoccupied with a geopolitical framework, English-language discussions are rarely concerned with international relations. This makes sense, in that each community is reading Tolkien in line with its own most pressing concerns.

In 2001, Andy Duncan, after noticing that the early-twentieth-century segregationist senator, Theodore G. Bilbo, shared a last name with one of Tolkien's most famous characters, wrote a short story imagining the senator, now recast as Bilbo's descendant, leading a racist campaign to keep nonhobbits from immigrating into the Shire. The story gained little attention until it was republished in Duncan's 2018 short story collection *An Agent of Utopia*. After the author was interviewed in episode 336 of the *Geek's Guide to the Galaxy* podcast (Adams and Kirtley), the question of Tolkien's racism led to a brief culture war skirmish, ridiculed in *The New Statesman* (Jefferson) and *National Review* (Timpf), as well as on rt.com ("Tolkien Was 'Racist' to Orcs?").

Reactionary defense of Tolkien could be dismissed as a familiar fandom phenomenon: (mostly male) "curatorial" or "affirmational" fans, who reject any attempt to reinterpret or play with beloved source material, and "transformative" fans, for whom the original stories are a springboard for creating something more interactive, resonant, and inclusive. But even this divide in fandom has obvious political content, and it is exacerbated when dealing with faux-medievalist high fantasy such as Tolkien's. As controversies online and at the International Congress of Medieval Studies have shown, the alt-right is preoccupied with the Middle Ages as an imagined utopia of Whiteness, a preoccupation that spills over from scholarship and pseudoscholarship into fan communities.[4]

In 2013, N. K. Jemisin, an African American woman who is among the most critically acclaimed writers of F&SF in the United States, wrote a post on her blog, "From the Mailbag: The Unbearable Baggage of Orcing":

> Awhile back I got an email from a reader which asked, "When are you going to write some real fantasy, y'know, with Orcs? [...]
>
> I have a problem with orcs. I'm orc-averse, you might say; even orcophobic. I know, I know, orcs are everywhere in fantasy; from Tolkien to Warhammer; by saying I hate orcs I invite the wrath of ... well, the fannish horde. (Groan. Sorry.) But here's something I want you to think about: what *are* orcs?
>
> Seriously. In most of the fantasy works I've consumed, orcs are violent, mindless or less intelligent than human beings, brutal and thuggish and Always Chaotic Evil. But these are adjectives, not nouns. All mythological creatures have a real-world root. Dryads are trees + humans + magic. Mermaids are fish + humans + magic, or maybe porpoises + magic. Unicorns are deer or horses + magic, maybe with a bit of narwhal glued on. Dragons are reptiles + magic, or maybe dinosaur bones + magic—paleontology. So again: what are orcs supposed to be? [...]

> They are human bodies + bad magic—*the essence of humanity*, for whatever value that essence might hold: a soul, a mind, aestheticism, whatever. And therefore, in most fantasy settings in which I've seen orcs appear, they are fit only for one thing: to be mowed down, usually on sight and sans negotiation, by Our Heroes. Orcs are human beings who can be slaughtered without conscience or apology.
>
> Think about that. Creatures that look like people, but aren't really. Kinda-sorta-people, who aren't worthy of even the most basic moral considerations, like the right to exist. Only way to deal with them is to control them utterly a la slavery, or wipe them all out.
>
> Huh. Sounds familiar.
>
> So maybe now you can understand why I'm not very interested in writing about orcs.

Jemisin commends the serious and sincere attempts to redeem the orc as a fantasy figure and notes with amusement that "for a while, 'orcing' became slang for SFF fans of color getting pissed off at authors' racefails . . . but there's a reason that slang caught on, and there's a reason it was as painful as it was funny when we used it." Orcs, she concludes, "are fruit of the poison vine that is *human fear of 'the Other'*."

David Brin's 2010 essay takes a similar approach. Brin points out that the "urge to crush some demonized enemy" is old and deep, and satisfied too easily by Tolkien. Of particular concern are the orcs. Brin laments: "the vicarious thrill we feel over the slaughter of orc foot soldiers at Helm's Deep. Then again as Ents flatten even more goblin grunts at Saruman's citadel, taking no prisoners, never sparing a thought for all the orphaned orclings and grieving widorcs. And again at Minas Tirith, and again at the Gondor Docks and again . . . Well, they're only orcs, after all" (35).

Brin, tongue firmly in cheek, calls for "empathy" for the Orcs, a task that could be complicated by two facts: (1) they're supposed to be entirely alien from us; and (2) they don't exist. The cultivation of empathy is one of the many uses of fiction, particularly when readers and viewers find themselves empathizing with characters who are, in some way or another, alien to them.[5]

Such empathy can also be problematic, in that audiences might be manipulated into empathizing with characters whose actions and values remain repellent even when the story is over, by the simple virtue of the characters being either the protagonists, the narrator, or both (see *American Psycho* or *Dexter*). But what happens when the most alien, most "othered" characters—by virtue of plot, description, and world building—provide an unexpectedly easy platform for identification by those who are not part of the initial target audience?

The story of Russia's Orcs has roots both deep and shallow: deep, in that they stretch back almost to the beginning of Russian Tolkien fandom; and shallow, because Tolkien's work arrived in the former USSR with a significant delay. Although there were nine translations of Tolkien in circulation by 2004, this was the result of a decades-long process.[6]

The famed F&SF translator Zinaida Bobyr' tried to get her abridged Russian version published throughout the Khrushchev years, with the result that three typed and bound copies of it circulated as samizdat in the mid-1960s (Markova, 163–64). It would only be in the last days of perestroika that an abridged version was published, with a full edition brought out a year after the Soviet collapse.

As a result, Tolkien's reception in Russia is distinguished by two important features. First, in a country with a history of distrust of "subcultures," Tolkien fans (*Tolkinisty*) were greeted with suspicion by the media and the Russian Orthodox Church, with Tolkienists treated as yet another "foreign sect" that threatened Russian traditions. Second, and more important for our purposes, the timing of Tolkien's Russian fame facilitated political readings of *The Lord of the Rings*. In a 1997 article in *Nezavaisimaia gazeta*, Ivan Sleptsov wrote, "*The Lord of the Rings* is—among other things—a political pamphlet in which Tolkien included an encoded description of the conflict of the political darkness of the East and the freedom of the West, and a prediction of the inevitable fall of Mordor and its analog on the real earth, the Soviet Union" (Sleptsov, quoted in Markova, 165). More recently, on the "Law in Russia" web portal associated with the online journal *Politicheskoe obrazovanie* (Political education), a user identifying himself as "Egorov" (http://lawinrussia.ru/content/russkie-orki) developed this idea in greater detail:

> Hidden and unhidden chains of association have their effect on the subconscious. Let's take, for example, good old fantasy, in particular the fundamental world of Middle Earth by the great author John Tolkien. And let's look at it through the prison of the geopolitical circumstances at the time this work was written. And so there are four main races: elves, humans, gnomes, and force. Let us break them down according to their associations with nations in the atmosphere of the middle of the last century. "Of course," the elves are Anglo-Saxons, a higher race, immortals who can always run back to their island if need be. The human alliance is most of Europe at the time. The gnomes are the residents of Belgium, Switzerland, and other mountainous areas of Europe. What's left are the orcs. Here there is disagreement as to whether they are Chinese or Russian. At times they are presented as yellow-skinned people, a direct reference to the Chinese. At other times their skin is

green. But let's not be racist. After all, we also live in Asia. But the land of the orcs was most likely the Soviet Union. And if we take a look at our character, then we obviously fit the role of orcs. The Russian character: simplicity, a tendency toward risk-taking and heroic deeds, an expansive soul, tenacity, group thinking. We are directly associated with orcs not only through our character; our historic path over a great deal of time is connected with the horde, from the Tatar-Mongol Horde to the communist system. And it's no surprise that for the elves and the European alliance we were and remain a horde; if you like, it's a matter of genetic memory reinforced by "authorial opinions." Recall that this world was created on the verge of World War II. Then Europe feared a union of Sauron and Nazgul—which one was Hitler and which one was Stalin hardly matters. The orc army is a direct association with the Soviet army and the peoples of the Union, that was the message for lovers of John Tolkien's work.

While such a reading is not unknown in the West, it does run into several obvious problems. First, Tolkien himself was adamantly against political or allegorical interpretations of his work. This, however, is not a serious objection for most literary scholars, who, for a variety of critical and theoretical reasons, dismiss the idea that a meaning's work is equal to the author's intent.

The more serious problem is that it is anachronistic. *The Lord of the Rings* was written between 1937 and 1949; if we assume that contemporary concerns could have crept into the manuscript against the author's will, a British citizen writing during this period has a much more obvious model for the embodiment of evil than Stalin's Soviet Union. Thus the equation of Sauron with Hitler and his dark hordes with the Nazis seems far more likely, if still reductive, and it is a comparison that is easy to find in English-language writings about Tolkien's trilogy.

There are specific linguistic reasons for Russian readers to find a Soviet subtext in *Lord of the Rings*, depending on the book's translation. Mark T. Hooker devotes an entire chapter to the subject in *Tolkien through Russian Eyes*: "One Day in the Life of Frodo Drogovich: Stalin and Yezhov in the Shire." In particular, the translation of Tolkien's trilogy by Mariia Kamenkovich and Valerii Karrik, numerous editions of which were brought out by the noted F&SF publishers Azbuka and Amfora, weaves a Stalinist thread throughout the entire text. Their annotations inform the reader that "The Scouring of the Shire" is a parody of socialism: "Tolkien never had any doubts as to the true face of the socialist utopia, which Lotho Sackville-Baggins tries to introduce into the Shire" (Kamenkovich and Karrik, as cited by Hooker, 185).[7]

This is an interpretation that is much easier to dismiss thousands of miles from Moscow, with the self-satisfied assurance that comes from reading Tolkien in its more or less native, quasi-Anglo-Saxon linguistic and cultural milieu. But we should not be so quick to discount the "Russia as Mordor" idea, if only because Russian culture during the perestroika years and the decades that followed cannot be understood without the creative anachronism that came with the return of both Western and prerevolutionary culture after the removal of censorship.

Sigmund Freud, Oswald Spengler, Otto Weininger, Cesaro Lombroso, Nikolai Fyodorov, and Andrei Platonov were all contemporaries of the last Soviet generation and its children, taking on a relevance that they might arguably lack without Russia's twentieth-century experience of rupture and return. Why, then, shouldn't Tolkien be equally timeless?

How to Read Like an Orc

We cannot dismiss popular reading strategies simply because of their faulty grasp of history. Misreading is a crucial part of the fantasy experience. Even when the worldview is simplistic, the allegorical potential of fantasy, the fantasists' tendency to extrapolate their secondary worlds based on recognizable cultures and historical events, and the intensity of the emotional and imaginative investment by fan communities mean that these fictional worlds are serious business.

Moreover, their heroes and plots often recapitulate commonly accepted values in the cultures that produce them: the freedom-fighting of *Star Wars*, the emphasis on diversity and tolerance in the Harry Potter books, and the crusading yet restrained liberalism of the original *Star Trek* may not be particularly appealing to other cultures, even when the stories themselves are popular.

The real-world parallels to events and situations in secondary worlds can, once again thanks to fan identification, take on political and ideological baggage that may not have been intentionally packed by the stories' creators. If, for example, the greed and cowardice of *Star Trek's* diminutive, big-nosed Ferengi are reminiscent of antisemitic stereotypes but are in no way actually identified with Jews, is there reason for Jews to take offense? Is the planet Bajor, once occupied by the morally suspect Cardassians, a stand-in for Palestine, or maybe even Israel? If these questions strike you as trivial or absurd, then you clearly have not been spending enough time in the appropriate subreddits or comment sections.

What many Russian fans are recognizing is something akin to the experience of minority readers and viewers in the West: a limit to the possibilities for identification provided by a work of mainstream (or majority) entertainment. The heroes do not "look" like them, whether it is a matter of physical appearance (and really, how many of us want to admit a resemblance to hobbits?) or of culture and values.

Tolkien insisted that his location of the villains in the "East" of Middle Earth was nothing more than a matter of geographical convenience, but intent aside, today such a claim seems naive. Think of the visceral shock many liberal and minority viewers felt at the end of the third season of *Game of Thrones*, when Daenerys Targaryen (perhaps the whitest White Savior we have ever seen) is so beloved by the throngs of recently liberated brown slaves that they pass her from hand to hand in a bizarre scene of faux-medieval crowd surfing.

The minority or liberal subject position here is not a neutral interpretive strategy; for the reader who feels un- or misrepresented, the result can be a sense of empowerment or reclamation. For the majority reader, who is used to seeing himself (properly) represented wherever he looks, this can seem like a politicized misreading; see, for example, the crusade in right-wing science fiction circles against so-called Social Justice Warriors, a crusade that nearly ruined the 2015 Hugo Awards, as detailed by Kehe (2017). In the cases of both Tolkien's evil East and Daenerys's White Goddesshood, we are more than likely dealing with the unintended consequences of underexamined cultural bias. But what is noteworthy about the case of Russian reactions to Tolkien is the persistent claim of Tolkien's Russophobic intent. The equation of Orcs with Russians is an example of paranoid reading.

The Hobbit Menace

The paranoid reading of Tolkien begins as playful, revisionist fan fiction. Throughout the 1990s, Natalia Vasilieva and Natalia Nekrasova produced a multivolume reinterpretation of *Lord of the Rings* online: *Chernaia kniga Ardy* (The black book of Arda). Here the point was not so much that the Orcs were good, but that Tolkien's dualism was too simplistic. A similar claim can be made for Nik Perumov's revisionist Tolkien sequel series, *Kol'tso t'my* (The ring of darkness).

But the true moment in the sun for Russian Orcdom was the 1999 release of Kirill Yeskov's *Poslednii kol'tsenosets* (The last ringbearer). Yeskov, a professional biologist and avowedly amateur novelist, exposes Tolkien's account as a work of elvish propaganda. Mordor, it turns out, is a beacon of rationality and enlightenment besieged by the dying and decadent forces of magic.[8] Here the Orcs (who are now simply another human ethnic group) are the good guys, Gandalf is a spell-casting Hitler looking for the "final solution to the Mordor problem," and Saruman is the only wizard smart enough to realize he's been on the wrong side.[9]

Inverting the classics is nothing new; while *The Last Ringbearer* is a well-conceived semisequel to Tolkien, Gregory Maguire (*Wicked*), Jean Rhys (*Wide Sargasso Sea*), and John Gardner (*Grendel*) have done this sort of thing much better. Not only do these three novels work brilliantly as freestanding literary works, none of them has, to my knowledge, produced *ressentiment*-infused subcultures (though Maguire, in providing the inspiration for the shlock anthem "Defying Gravity," is guilty of much worse).

Yet if the political overtones of *The Last Ringbearer* are relatively restrained ("final solution" references excluded), the novel reinforces a political reading that some in the West might find baffling. Baffling, but brilliant: Internet users in the orbit of the "liberpunk" subgenre of Russian science fiction (dystopias in which the world has gone to hell thanks to the triumph of liberalism and tolerance), have reappropriated not just Tolkien but the simplistic, pop-culture-inspired metaphysics of American exceptionalism as articulated by Ronald Reagan and extended by George W. Bush. Fine, they say, we'll be your evil empire. But we'll do it with an irony and pride that you'll never entirely comprehend.

The ironic reappropriation of alien evil reaches its apotheosis in the third book of Maksim Kalashnikov's and Yuri Krupnov's four-volume paranoid rant, *Amerika protiv Rossii* (America versus Russia), to which they give the title *Gnev orka* (The rage of the orc). Kalashnikov and Krupnov dismiss the "common perception" that the Orcs are supposed to represent Muslims: "Remember that the orcs are 'Easterners' in Tolkien's Western consciousness": "The time has come to understand that, for the West, we have always been and will always be—unless the best people in the West change their consciousness—those revolting, savage orcs, those barbarians for whom the earth has no place" (26). After excerpting several pages of descriptions of Orcs from *The Lord of the Rings*, they simply assert that the connection is obvious: "Can you feel it? Tolkien's somnolent mysticism is about us. The hundreds of years of slavery, the pathological, animal cruelty, the disdain for death, and the clinical incapacity for the market and democracy. It's all there. . . . The time has come to understand that, for the West, we have always been and will always be—unless the best people in the West change their consciousness—those revolting, savage orcs, those barbarians for whom the earth has no place" (26).

Kalashnikov's and Krupnov's miniature Orc manifesto is breathtaking in the scope of its projections. If Tolkien's depiction of the Orcs resembles the authors' imagined slanderous depiction of Russians, then Tolkien is speaking about Russians. When they boldly take on the Orc mantle as an act of subversive appropriation, the objects of their rebellion start to lose focus: they assume the identity of a famous group of villains in order to spite the authors of this Russophobic calumny, but those authors are the same as the authors of the entire book: Kalashnikov and

Krupnov. The equation between Russians and Orcs is all but unknown in the West, but it spreads in Russia largely due to the efforts of those who claim to be offended by it. This isn't just self-colonization; it's self-orientalizing.

Kalashnikov and Krupnov complete this process when they proclaim that they, like Aleksandr Blok, are willing to say:

> And if not—we have nothing to lose,
> And we are capable of betrayal! . . .
>
> We, too, can burn buildings, and drive herds into the church,
> And fry up the meat of white people!

Yes, Orc-ism turns into a variation of idiosyncratic Eurasianism through the quotation of Blok's famous poem "The Scythians" almost in its entirety (a move that is frequently repeated by later "Orcs" online). Later in the book, the authors justly condemn George W. Bush for his Manichaean world view, yet their critique suits *The Rage of the Orc* even better: any plot structure with two sides, one of which is said to be civilized and the other barbaric, becomes available as a mode of Russian self-representation. (The authors also compare contemporary Russia to Isaac Asimov's fallen, now barbaric Galactic Empire from the *Foundation* series).

If the appeal to literary fantasy might seem to cheapen ideological discourse, then, from my point of view, this is a job well done. While the comparison of a classic poem by Blok to *Lord of the Ring* fan fiction is troubling on aesthetic grounds, it exposes the fantasy inherent in ideological claims of primordialism. After all, how much did Aleksandr Blok know about the actual Scythians when he wrote this poem? How much does anyone? What starts out as popular ethnography ends up as ideological cosplay.

Orcs Online

Published in 2003, Kalashnikov and Krupnov's *The Rage of the Orc* could be the inspiration for the Russian Orc Runet (*Ru*ssian Inter*net*) meme, but the search for a point of origin might be as much an exercise in fantasy as the primordialism I have just condemned.

Like all Internet memes, it spreads digitally, with no need of an original. It lurks in the comment sections of right-wing and SF-related *LiveJournal* pages; in spirit if not in frequency, this borrowing from Tolkien is comparable to the invocation of the "red pill" throughout the antifeminist manosphere (an appropriation of a term from *The Matrix* that has become gloriously, unintentionally ironic, since we now know the film series was created by a pair of transgender sisters initially known as cisgender brothers). While there are numerous essays and blogposts about the hidden Russophobia in Tolkien's Orcs, it took one notorious *LiveJournal* personality to make Orc-ism a key part of one of his many manifestos: Vladimir Georgievich Frolkov, the Aryan nationalist most famous first as "Yarovrat," then as "heideg."

After a long and tortured explanation about the difference between the "Rus" (the powerful, hypermasculine wolf man responsible for all of Russia's victories and for the very nature of the Soviet Union) and the "russkii" (a slave, that which belongs to the Rus), an explanation that rejects Europe in favor of "Northwest Asia" and Eurasia in favor of "Sakharaziia," Yarovrat/heideg declares that the "true Russian ideology" is Orc-ism. This is the best of three possible paths for Russians:

> U russkikh tri puti: libo pizdoboliia, libo selfkheit, libo orkizm.
> Pizdoboliia: "my ne orki, my el'fy!"
> Selfkheit: "my orki, nado stat' el'fami!"
> Orkizm: "my orki, i slava B-gu Mokoshi!"
>
> Russians have three paths: bullshit, self-hatred, or orc-ism.
> Bullshit: "We're not orcs, we're elves!"
> Self-hatred: "We're orcs, and we must become elves!"
> Orc-ism, "We're orcs, thank God Mokosh!"

Yarovrat's protestations to the contrary, I would submit that the line between Orc-ism and self-hatred is somewhere between thin and nonexistent. If we keep in mind the frequent use of "Orc" as sarcastic self-reference in comment sections, usually referring to the West's disdain for the "savage" and "unrefined" Russians, then the Orc's true identity becomes clear: the Orc is the latest incarnation of the sovok, the Soviet yokel whose lack of civilized habits of thought and behavior was a source of simultaneous embarrassment, humor, and even pride. But the Orc is not merely a fantasy-inflected, post-Soviet update of the sovok; the Orc is the sovok weaponized.

The Orc Song of Mikhail Y. Elizarov

The Orc, like the right-wing ideology behind him, has needed time to move from the margins to the mainstream. The best of his earliest champions, such as Yeskov (*The Last Ringbearer*), rehabilitated him with the light touch of authors more concerned with plot and aesthetics than with explicit ideology. Yarovrat and the online community that interacts with him are relatively self-contained;

if Yarovrat's ideas migrated beyond his circle of interlocutors, they most likely did so without any attribution to Yarovrat himself or to his wider project. Given time, however, the Orc would be taken up by writers and performers with a much broader appeal, all of whom would facilitate the appropriation of the "Orc" epithet after Russia's seizure of Crimea. This brings us to Mikhail Elizarov.

Of all the nationalist, right-wing authors discussed in this book so far, it is Elizarov who has been most successful at tempering ideology with talent. Although his 2003 novel, *Pasternak*, caused a minor scandal for its reinterpretation of the (ethnically Jewish) Russian poet as a demon, much of his later work imposes fewer ideological requirements on his readers. For example, his 2007 novel, *The Librarian* (translated into English by Andrew Bromfield in 2015), in which the nearly forgotten books of a tedious but prolific socialist realist writer are revealed to grant magical powers to anyone who reads them in one sitting, manages to turn the theme of Soviet nostalgia into something of a magical treasure hunt, like Harry Potter searching for horcruxes.

Structurally, the novel transforms the familiar post-Soviet gang war plot into a battle among libraries desperate to accumulate as many original copies of the book as possible. While Elizarov's nationalist views are well known, the novel's contents contain enough ambiguity about the role of Soviet relics to facilitate readings that might run counter to the author's ideology.

But Elizarov is also a musician, working in a style he calls "bard/punk/*chanson*." His songs, though clever and playful, are ideologically something of a blunt instrument. His 2014 "Orkskaia" (Orc song) is no exception. The full Russian text is easily available online, as is a video of Elizarov performing the song on YouTube. I'm quoting it here in English in my own translation, with the caveat that Elizarov's original rhymes, scans, and is generally clever, while my version is blunt and prosaic. Elizarov reminds his listeners of the time they "crushed the Elven scum," sending them fleeing to the West. Their swords struck down "the Gandalf Youth," and soon they had triumphed. A "Mordor Tribunal" sent most of the fallen enemies to Kolyma but sentenced Gandalf and Aragorn to death, "mostly for taking part in faggot porn." Only after "General Secretary Sauronich" got "fucked up" and fell into a volcano did things get really bad:

> That was when a Zionist Silmarillion named Tolkien
> Threw together his unprincipled talmud.
> Historical truth vanished that day.
>
> Since then we have lost the ridges, plateaus, and shelves
> And now unbeatable Mordor
> Is conquered by Rohanites, Jews, and Elves. . . .

> We've read *The Lord of the Rings* from cover to cover,
> With baited breath while we learned all the lies.
> Of course, our Mordor is totally fucked
> Because we are no longer Orcs!

Recall our earlier discussion of the competing geopolitical readings of *The Lord of the Rings*: the anachronistic equation of the Orcs with the Soviets/Russians and the more historically grounded connection between *Lord of the Rings* and World War II (not to mention Tolkien's own disdain for all political interpretations of his work). Ingeniously, Elizarov is having it both ways: the Orcs are the Russians/Soviets, but the initial conflict appears to be World War II (the Elves speak German, for instance).

By the end of the poem, the humiliated post-Soviet Russia is the victim of a fascist restoration, in which the NATO powers are the heirs apparent to the Nazis. But that is not all. The real villains of the piece appear to be the Jews and Zionists (including Tolkien himself), while the European Elves are, of course, decadent and effeminate ("faggot porn").

The song is an implicit call for the renewal of Orc pride; that is, Russia has lost its way by trying to please the "Rohanites, Jews, and Elves" who have conquered it. In *The Librarian*, Soviet nostalgia was a force of nature, granting power to anyone regardless of ideology. In this song, Elizarov appropriates the Orc meme to root that nostalgia in strength, violence, and savagery.

Off the Reservation

Macho posturing aside, the Russian Orc still faces one more challenge: he may not even be Russian. The reasons, however, make sense only in Russian. Back in 2002, the always inventive Goblin Studios released their own version of Peter Jackson's *The Lord of the Rings: The Fellowship of the Ring* (2001), replacing *bratstvo*, the Russian term used here for "Fellowship" with *bratva*, a slang term for a band of criminals. Offering up an irreverent "translation" from the English that functioned as a cross between *What's Up, Tiger Lily?* and *Mystery Science Theater 3000*, Goblin had the fellowship fighting not Orcs (*orki*), but "urks" (*urki*), slang for professional criminals that happens to be only one vowel away from Tolkien's prominent villains.

Almost a decade later, Victor Pelevin picked up on this phonetic resemblance in his novel *S.N.U.F.F.* Pelevin, who generally overestimates the cleverness of his precious bilingual wordplay, made the *orki/urki* parallel the foundation of the novel's media-besotted dystopian future. After a series of wars and disasters, the "civilized" population of humanity has moved to floating cityglobes called *ofshary*.[10] The novel's protagonist, Damian-Landolo Damilola Karpov, lives in Big Byz ("big business" crossed with "Byzantium") and pilots a camera/weapon drone that films "snuffs" (ultraviolent propagandistic newsreels) while cavorting with his sentient, synthetic sex doll, Kaya.

The snuffs are primarily about the Orcs (spelled "Orks" in Andrew Bromfield's 2014 translation), the population that lives on the ground. Damilola somehow anticipates his readers' surprise and quickly offers an explanation about their name:

> Why are they called that? It's not at all that we despise them and regard them as racially inferior—we don't have any prejudices like that in our society. They're people, the same as we are. At least physically. The fact that the word is formally identical to the ancient word "ork" (or "orc") is purely coincidental (although, let me remark in an undertone, there's really no such thing as a coincidence).
>
> It's all a matter of their official language, which is called Upper Mid-Siberian. (25)

Upper Mid-Siberian turns out to be an invented language, based on "Ukrainian, larded with yiddishisms." When its creators turned their attention to phonetics, "they threw in an aberrant vowel reduction from 'o' to 'u'—apparently they couldn't think of anything better." To make matters more complicated:

> Upper Mid-Siberian has made virtually no inroads into colloquial speech. The only exception is the name of their country. They call it the Urkainian Urkaganate, or Urkaine, and they call themselves Urks (apparently this was a hasty revamping of the word "ukry"—a High Russian name for an ancient Slavic tribe—although there are other philological hypotheses). In everyday speech the word "Urk" is unpopular—it belongs to high-flown, pompous style and is regarded as fusty, bureaucratic and old-fashioned. But it was the origin of the Church English "Orkland" and "Orks." (25)

Pelevin's narrator marshals a great deal of fake linguistics to justify this conceit, which seems to be in the service of multiple authorial agendas, the most apparent of which is the linkage of "orc" to "Ukraine." But Ukraine itself does not seem to be the primary target of Pelevin's satire; if anything, the only real anti-Ukrainian element of his use of this toponym as a convenient link to Tolkienist vocabulary is the conflation of Ukraine with Russia. For the split between Big Byz and the Orcs dramatizes a different set of international and intranational conflicts.

On the international level, *S.N.U.F.F.* is a straightforward satire of the relationship between imperialist, Westernized powers and the Second- and Third-World objects of their manipulation, condescension, and aggression. The snuffs serve to entertain a rich and jaded populace while simultaneously demonizing the Orcs as the primitive enemy of Big Byz "democracy." In December 2011, Mikhail Boiko asserted that the filming and bombing by drones are "obviously" animated by the civil war in Libya. The sad truth is, of course, that Pelevin's drone satire always seems current—only the names of the battle zones change.

In addition, the Big Byz/Orcs split facilitates a bit of liberpunk-lite on Pelevin's part: thanks to the triumph of political correctness, feminists in Big Byz have raised the age of consent to forty-five, the rights of "faggots" must never be denied, and adult heterosexual males have developed their own "perverted" sexual subculture, based on their love of synthetic, surrogate women.

The Orc question becomes much more provocative when seen in terms of internal cultural dynamics. For one thing, there is no actual ethnic distinction between the population of Big Byz and the people who live below. And the condescension toward Orcs turns out to replicate the age-old Russian split between the elites and the common people, with the Orcs at times appearing to be just another variation on the snobbish Russian epithet *bydlo*. The rank-and-file Orcs are scorned by their own elites, who call themselves "Global Orcs."

To the contemporary Russian reader, the object of satire is obvious: the short-lived, online movement of cosmopolitan Russian-speakers throughout the world who called themselves "Global Russians" (a project associated, appropriately enough, with a journal named *Snob*). Global Orcs flock to anything foreign and do their best to distance themselves from the yokels who share their ethnicity.

In *S.N.U.F.F.*, as in Elizarov's "Orc Song" and Kalashnikov and Krupnov's *Rage of the Orc*, Russia is the Orcish motherland. But Pelevin complicates their jingoistic vision of Orc Pride, placing it squarely back within its native context: the inferiority complex that insists on turning the substance of Russian critique into a point of pride.

The Tank Drivers of Mordor

The canon of noncanonical Russian Orc fiction continues to grow, although without much fanfare. Even hard-core fans of Russian fantasy and science fiction could be excused for missing the phenomenon, because, unlike the ever-popular tales of *popadantsy* (accidental travelers to other times and dimensions), it has yet to cohere into a recognizable subgenre.

These books constitute a small handful of texts with a few key elements in common: post-Tolkien revisionism, to be sure, but almost always in the service of the aggressive, nationalist, and militaristic ideology we have already seen in Elizarov's "Orc Song," albeit without its playfulness and wit. In 2014, Sergei Shkenev published a novel called *Krasnyi vlastelin* (Red lord), whose blurb is delightful:

> There's never been a book like it! The most unexpected twist in the eternal *popadanets* plot. After his death in our reality, J. V. Stalin is reborn in a parallel Swords and Sorcery world.
>
> The people's Power (Derzhava) versus the aristocratic Empire! The Red Army versus cannibal dragon warriors! Can the Red Lord in his white jacket with a single Gold Star transform a magical war into a Patriotic War and once again lead his people to a Great Victory?

Has there really never been a book like it? Yes, in that the combination of Stalin and Tolkien (the word for "Lord" here is the same as in the Russian translation of *Lord of the Rings*) is certainly novel, but no, in that it is otherwise a mash-up of two very familiar narratives.

The readers' comments on the Fantasy Worlds website (https://fantasy-worlds.org/lib/id21689/) are certainly edifying. A reader with the Internet handle Araviel complains that Stalin is absent for most of the novel (a critique I want to adopt now for every novel I read, from *The Color Purple* to *David Copperfield*), which is admittedly a useful data point. Otherwise, the comments quickly devolve into arguments about Russian patriotism and insults lobbed at Ukraine and its supporters.

Pavel Mochalov's 2017 *Tankist Mordora* (The tank driver of Mordor) is exactly what it sounds like. A student at a Soviet tank drivers' school finds himself in Mordor. The novel's big selling point is that the hero is not a hypercompetent warrior, as is usually the case in the popadantsy genre, but an ordinary guy. In Mordor. Mochalov's book looks like a typical "chosen one" story, except the chosen one here seems to be the tank itself. The hero, Sergei Popov, starts the novel in a twenty-first-century mental hospital, where no one believes that he has spent thirty-three years in Middle Earth thanks to a spell cast by the wizard Myron. Poor Popov has been transported to unknown lands twice in the course of the novel: first to Mordor, then to post-Soviet Russia. Myron brought him to his world in order to defend Mordor, "a model of statehood for all of Middle Earth": "We represent ideal organization and order. Wherever we come to power, we put an end to the arbitrary rule of the little people who imagine themselves kings. Yes, sometimes our methods are harsh, but you can't plant wheat without pulling up a few weeds, can you? . . . Unified power and unified order are the ideals of Mordor. We have brought the light of truth to the far east and south. But the west . . ." Among the peoples he encounters are Orcs, who are clearly inferior, but the leaders of Mordor hope that he will join in their eugenics plan and mate with Orc women to produce a stronger breed.

Leonid Meshalkin's 2014 short novel, *Orki i russkie—brat'ia navek!* (Orcs and Russians are brothers forever!), is a particularly odd specimen. A work of fan fiction (fic) set in the universe of the multiplayer online role-playing game (MMORPG) EVE Online, it is also both an example and parody of a smaller subsection of neural-network-themed EVE Online fan fiction called *khortiatina*, named after Igor Khort, who wrote a fic called *Shakhter* (The miner) that inspired numerous imitators.

Orcs and Russians tries to be all things to all fic readers. It somehow combines the space opera of EVE Online with the tropes of epic fantasy (largely thanks to the main character's habit of whimsically naming the types of creatures he encounters after species found in *Lord of the Rings* and *World of Warcraft*), peppering this stew with frequent self-conscious, apparently humorous asides about the clichés of the popadantsy and *khortiatina* genres, all in the service of none-too-subtle nationalist geopolitical satire.

The hero, a popadanets named Vladimir Vol'fovich Shirokovskii, is an obvious stand-in for the neofascist parliamentarian Vladimir Vol'fovich Zhirinovsky. He insists on naming his goblin aide-de-camp Chubais (after the architect of post-Soviet privatization); dreams of verbal jousting with the enemy of humanity, a thinly veiled analog of the human-rights activist Valeriia Novodvorskaia, here named Starokhatskaia; and pranks the idiots from Pindosiia (a version of a Russian slur for America) by teaching them Russian names for their weapons that actually mean "combat homo" and "combat lesbo," as revenge against the Americans who dared refer to the Russian Empire by the derogatory term "Rashka."[11]

Finally, though it is not an Orc book, there is one more novel worth mentioning here: Viktor Dubchek's *Krasnyi padavan* (Red padawan). As we have seen, the "evil empire" meme in Russia depends not just on *Lord of the Rings* fandom but on the universe of *Star Wars*, suggesting that there may be *Star Wars*-inflected fiction that serves the same function as pro-Orc nationalist F&SF. *Red Padawan* is yet another popadantsy story, but with a twist. Here Darth Vader and his armies are the accidental travelers who find themselves orbiting Earth in 1941. Naturally, Vader forms an alliance with Stalin in order to fight World War II.

Surprisingly, this book gets a positive blurb from the best-known Russian F&SF writer alive today: Sergei Lukyanenko, author of the *Night Watch* series. Lukyanenko admits that everything about this plot suggests that the book should be terrible, "yet the most surprising thing is that at some point this joyful, ironic burlesque balanced on the edge of trash and farce becomes something greater than just a parody—and the author, without changing his facial expression, starts to speak of serious things."

This is precisely what turns off one fan reviewer (https://fantasy-worlds.org/lib/id17882/Viktor_Dubchek_Krasnyiy_padavan), who expected ironic parody (*styob*) but was disappointed to find that the book was "socialist realist, hurrah-patriotic war fiction with all its ideological cliches." In other words, perfect grist for our mill.

Orknash: Supporting the Home Team

Like many a reclaimed epithet, the identification of Russians with Orcs shifts its valence depending on the speaker. That is, when a patriotically inclined Russian such as Kalashnikov or Elizarov claims the Orc mantle for his people, the term is, overall, positive—even if it also contains multiple layers of irony. Out of the mouths of non-Russians, or of Russian liberal critics of Putinist politics, "Orc" remains a fighting word. And, as Pelevin's wordplay suggests, the "Orc/hobbit" paradigm is not merely a metaphor for bilateral East/West tensions; Orc-ism has taken on a new life since the annexation of Crimea and the fighting in Ukraine.

Earlier I compared the Orc with the sovok, the yokel who embodied stereotypes of Soviet backwardness. Both terms are negative projections that can nonetheless overcome their origins in abjection: the savagery of the Orc is transformed into a primal strength, while the ridiculousness of the sovok can still be tinged with an ironic affection. Unlike the sovok, however, the Orc is not a symbol of a multinational Soviet state. Thus its true identity is up for grabs.

Since the outbreak of hostilities in Ukraine, "Orc" has evolved further: now the Ukrainians are *ukropy*, while the presumably savage, warlike Russian invaders are, of course, Orcs. In the aftermath of the Eye of Sauron fiasco, Leonid Bershidsky recalled that, as far back as 2012, his colleagues in Kyiv joked that Ukraine was "much like [the] Shire, the hobbits' home country, while Putin's Russia was Mordor, working its evil magic on the bucolic land." He inevitably compares Putin to Sauron and notes that the Russian president's "repressive machine is run by orcs."[12]

Not to be outdone, Ukrainian hackers hijacked Google Translate in the early days of 2016, adding a distinctively Orcish twist to the Ukrainian-to-Russian translation function. The Ukrainian words for "Russian Federation" became "Mordor" in Russian, while Foreign Minster Sergei Lavrov's last name became "sad little horsie" ("Google ob"iasniaet"). Google promptly fixed these "errors," but if there was damage to be done, it had been done already. On the scale of

Russian/Ukrainian conflict, this is small potatoes, but it is appropriately Tolkienist: *The Lord of the Rings* was just as much an exercise in philological imagination as it was in faux medieval mortal combat.[13]

The connection between the Russian Orc identity and the war in Ukraine inevitably colored both the outrage and the schadenfreude associated with the Eye of Sauron fiasco in Moscow. Aleksandr Nevzorov, the former nationalist Soviet television broadcaster turned anticlerical gadfly, invoked the Eye of Sauron in his 2014 review of the new *Hobbit* as an opportunity for pointed political commentary:

> Of course, Jackson's Tolkienist epic is yet another blow to the whole ideology of the "Russian world's" "unique" essence. Phenomena of such a scale as *The Lord of the Rings: The Hobbit,* having accumulated and partly cultivated the examples of European aesthetics is, as a rule, merciless toward the accomplishments of the natives. They simply squeeze them out and successfully replace them.
>
> Russia and its "great culture" once again had nothing with which to resist Tolkien's gnomes....
>
> The appearance of *The Hobbit* in Russia contains only one riddle: why did the priests, Black Hundreds, and other commissars of official spirituality make such a scandal out of the Eye of Sauron over Moscow?...
>
> The patriots should have overcome their culturological timidity, taken the reins of the situation, and used the image of the Orcs for the successful propaganda of their ideology.
>
> After all, it is the Orcs who, like no others, have demonstrated their capacity to give their all in the service of the military industrial complex. They are ready to die on the field of battle by the thousands, unthinkingly and joyfully. No doubt their portraits would be the best visual aids for military-patriotic preparation classes.
>
> Moreover, it is the Orcs who embody politeness in the sense that the Russian Federation now understands the word.

The tale of the Russian Orc is more than simply a chronicle of the Russification of a Tolkien meme. It is the tale of a national, ideological emplotment based on a set of resistant, paranoid reading strategies: *The Lord of the Rings* becomes available at a key historical moment, and it is such a powerful narrative that Russian audiences find their own story encoded within it. The outlines of this story are, by the 1990s, sadly familiar: an evil empire has been thwarted by the forces of good. A Russocentric reading of *Lord of the Rings* would have to be self-hating, at least in the initial stages, but a resistant interpretation of the book gained popularity at the same time as resentment of the so-called forces of good (the United States and Europe) increased.

Just as the once-earnest perestroika refrain, *Zapad nam pomozhet* (The West will help us), could be uttered only with bitter irony, *The Lord of the Rings* showed some Russian readers just how devastating Western help could be. But the greatest irony is the one that always surrounds Russian ideological rejections of the West: the Orc identity imagines rejection by the West, only to turn the Orc into an imaginary weapon against the West. But the vocabulary employed was nonetheless developed by an eccentric European, dreaming his Elvish dreams in a study in Oxford.

Salting the Earth

As the Orc meme has developed over the course of the 2014 war in Ukraine, back in Russia it has come to occupy a space that is not just contested but bifurcated. With the Orc identity simultaneously reclaimed as a demonic yet positive image in some Russian circles and used as an anti-Russian epithet among supporters of Maidan, it cannot be fully and comfortably assimilated by either side. Here Pelevin's "Urkaina" becomes more apt than he could possibly have intended when *S.N.U.F.F.* was published back in 2011: the definition of "Orc" is now dependent on the speaker's attitudes toward separatist movements in Eastern Ukraine. Discursively, Donbas has become the homeland of the Orcs; the question is whether the Orcs are the heroes or the villains.

Just three years after Elizarov's song about fascist Gandalf Youth undermining Mordor, the Orc question would get the musical treatment once again. In late 2017, the ultrapatriotic Russian Orthodox rap group Sol' zemli (Salt of the earth), a group formed in the suburbs of Moscow in 2005, released a track called "Varkraft" (Warcraft). Its main target is liberals, but the group's polemic centers on Russia's historic mission and the noble crusade to liberate Donbas from its Ukrainian oppressors. As with Elizarov, all of the song's poetry has been brutally stripped away by my literal translation. "Warcraft" laments the rise of the "half-elves" who "hold court" in cafes in the capitals, support gay rights, buy Apple products, and go crazy over anything "indie." These half-elves have disdain for the Donbas, worship the West, and consider everyone else simply Orcs. The singer of the song is different, however:

> I'm an ugly little guy with yellow teeth,
> Like half of Russia, I'm covered with scars, my lips are chapped . . .
> I'm your nightmare, like a prole, like a Cossack,
> The whole bestiary stuffed into a paddy wagon . . .

The singer is a proud Orc, whose values are, of course, traditionally Russian. His people are:

> Those who walk around the church at Easter with a candle,
> Who believe in the holiness of the word "mama" and don't live in Rashka.
> Who in Rus had all their children baptized,
> Without even posting the pics to Instagram.

In the song's chorus, which is repeated six times, the Orc is identified with the Russian Donbas fighters who mourn the 2016 assassination of the Donetsk military leader nicknamed "Motorola." They proudly wear uniforms with a Novorossiia patch. As the singer repeatedly proclaims, "Yes, we're Orcs. Not from Tolkien, but from Warcraft."

Andrei Korobov-Latyntsev, a philosopher and scholar of Russian rap at the University of Voronezh, provided a close, polemical reading of the song not long after its release (in 2017). Drawing a comparison with Blok's "The Scythians," Korobov-Latyntsev identifies the song's Orcs as "traditionalists and patriots," the sort of people who "defend their brothers in the Donbas and fight for their brother Christians in Syria." The elves, of course, are the liberals who betray Russia with their every breath. All of this is clear from the song's text, and it also differentiates the Salt of the Earth track from Elizarov's "Orc Song," which is the expression of a general stance, while "Warcraft" is much more closely aligned not just with current events but with the current policies of the Russian government.

Despite these minor variations in politics, the actual text of "Warcraft" continues the redemptive interpretation of the Orc identity championed by Elizarov. Where Elizarov warns that Mordor (Russia) is doomed if Orcs (real Russians) abandon their Orcish ways, "Warcraft" does not even entertain the possibility that real Russians (Orcs) could ever betray their true nature. Their steadfastness is, in fact, one of their defining features (consistent with the common Russian nationalist slogan that "Russian's don't surrender" (*russkie ne sdaiutsia*).

Korobov-Latyntsev expands on the central claim of the chorus of "Warcraft" in order to extend the song's antiliberal sentiment even further. What, after all, is the difference between the Orcs in *Lord of the Rings* and their counterparts in the *Warcraft* game?

Although in complete agreement with Salt of the Earth's characterization of today's Orcs in "Warcraft," Korobov-Latyntsev takes issue with the category of "elves" (he dispenses with the "half-" used consistently in the song). He reminds the reader that Tolkien's Orcs are Elves whose long-ago turn to the dark side rendered them ugly both inside and out. These liberals resemble neither the Elves of Tolkien nor those of *Warcraft*. In fact, it is the liberals who are the true Orcs—but from Tolkien, not from *Warcraft*. There is no longer any common language with liberals, who are unable to understand such important words as "Motherland," "Soil," "Duty," "People," or "God":

> They have their own motivations: a new iPhone, or the latest pre-election clip by the latest clown styling himself as a fighter against corruption, or a stylish selfie on Instagram and the number of likes it gets.... Look on in horror at how everything with them is identical, how it has all become so uniform! That can't happen to such a large mass of people of their own free will. This is a matter of some kind of black magic. These people's will has been enslaved, they are under the command of dark forces. That's why they have so much aggression and hubris. They are incapable of explaining this hubris and this aggression. The Dark Lord has enslaved them and maimed them, like the Orcs in Tolkien's novel. And we face the question that the popular fantasy writer George R. R. Martin posed to Professor Tolkien: after the triumph of the forces of Light, what is to be done with the servant of the Dark Lord, that is, the Orcs? Will there be special concentration camps for them? Or will they somehow be reeducated and socialized? Or tried and executed? ... This is a very topical question, you must admit. If truth will, indeed, triumph. If it does not triumph, and the Orcs win, then ... Well, it's clear what Tolkien's Orcs will do if they win.

The distinction between the two kinds of Orcs is a perennial topic in fan communities throughout the world, with the general consensus that Tolkien's more bestial Orcs win battles thanks to their overwhelming numbers, while smarter, better trained, and slightly less monstrous *Warcraft* Orcs are more individuated and capable of strategic thinking. By recasting the conflict in Salt of the Earth's song as a struggle between two kinds of Orcs, Korobov-Latyntsev manages to maintain the most flattering aspects of the equation between Russians and Orcs while projecting the more troubling Orcish traits onto anti-Russian liberals (Tolkien's Orcs). The origin story of the *Lord of the Rings*' Orcs is a key point, because it allows Korobov-Latyntsev to contrast true Russian steadfastness with liberal (anti-)Russian treachery and inconstancy.

Even the worst mass violence is attributed to the liberals as the heirs to Tolkien's Orcs: somehow, the next step in the conflict between the two Orcish tribes is going to end with liberals putting Russian patriots in concentration camps. Korobov-Latyntsev's reading is the apotheosis of aggressive Russian nationalist victimhood, reveling in the threat of antiliberal and anti-Ukrainian violence while maintaining that it is the true Russians who are threatened with Western-inspired genocide.

This is still fantasy, but it is that of neither Tolkien nor *Warcraft*. It is the fantasy of Freud, Jacques Lacan, and Slavoj Žižek: imaginary projections onto a demonized other in the service of an aggressive, wounded ego. Treatment would require the services of both the psychoanalyst and the literary critic, perhaps in the form of a *Game of Thrones* book club facilitated by a therapist. The humanities provided so much of the source material for this particular nationalist narrative. It would be nice to think the humanities could help provide a remedy.

A Song of Orcs and Trolls

Should we really be surprised that the Russian Orc, though born in late-Soviet misreadings of Tolkien, has found its natural habitat on the Internet? The Internet has been a bestiary of creatures real and mythological since its foundation: haunted by daemons and (mail)chimps, providing an alternative to snail mail and a pool for both phishing and cat fishing, while serving as a haunted house for ghosting, the Internet is home to species predatory and mild. Its most infamous resident shares some crucial cultural DNA with the Orc: I speak, of course, of the troll.

Internet trolls, like Orcs, are creatures defined by aggression. They don't just seek out conflict; they create it. As individual independent actors, trolls spend their time online baiting their victims. If they make you angry or start an argument, they have already won. But the past decade has shown the power trolls can have when they band together (as a "troll army"), harassing their targets with death threats, doxing, swatting, and photoshopped porn images. It took the wider world some time to recognize the effect trolls can have, in part because the stories covered in the media involved communities that, though large, are almost invisible to outsiders: gamers, science fiction fans, comics fans. Not to mention the inevitable downplaying of the threat when its most visible targets were women.

Or at least that was the case in the West. As far back as 2003, Anna Polyanskaya, Andrei Krivov, and Ivan Lomko alleged that a radical shift in the political content on the Russian Internet after 2000 may have been the result of state security interventions. In 2013, a report for the *St. Petersburg Times* wrote that the St. Petersburg-based Internet Research Agency was employing people to write pro-regime comments on blogs and other websites (Chernov). By the time the Internet Research Agency was profiled by Adrian Chen in the *New York Times* just two years later, the agency and organizations were known widely as "troll farms."

At this point, I wish I could say that the rest is history, but, sadly, it's current events. The run-up to the 2016 US election saw a series of reports on the activities of paid Russian trolls fanning the flames of White nationalist fear in social media under false names, spreading conspiracy theories, demonizing Democrats and migrants, and making sure that the words "Benghazi" and "Hillary's email" would never disappear from the news feed.

The success of Russian trolling within the US informational ecosystem is unparalleled, but not necessarily because of the effects of any particular troll campaign. Russian trolling in the United States is a boss-level victory, upping the ante from trolling to metatrolling by spawning intense paranoia *about Russian trolling*. When people on the American Left, so traumatized by this MAGA nightmare, start looking for Russian trolls under every bridge they cross, they have fallen into a Foucauldian trap. Like the denizens of the panopticon who get into the habit of surveilling themselves because they never know if they are actually under surveillance, Americans who are paranoid about Russian trolls are trolling themselves.

Whether by design or by accident, Russian trolls have fulfilled a fantasy whose roots lie not in Tolkien but in pre-Newtonian physics. They have turned trolling into a perpetual motion machine, one that no longer actually needs them in order to function. Like the deistic conception of a God as First Cause, creating the universe and then stepping back, Russian trolls, should they choose, have the luxury of simply sitting back and enjoying their handiwork as spectators. It works because the nature of this machine is virtual and informational, a triumph of memes over matter. While the jury is still out as to whether the fictional troll should be considered a mammal or a reptile, the Russian troll is oviparous, a cuckoo bird laying its eggs in the minds of anxious Westerners who will raise its offspring as their own.

What does this have to do with Russian Orcs? If the American victims of Russian trolls are self-trolling, the Russian Orcs are, to use an Internet term of art, self-owning. In each case, we have a complicated problem of self and other.

On the Internet, the Orc can be seen as a particular variety of troll. Both Orcs and trolls have broad, abstract targets in their sites: liberals, snowflakes, Social Justice Warriors (SJWs), feminists, and so on. The troll wages war against the abstract enemy by focusing on specific targets and engaging in coordinated campaigns. The Orc is comfortable remaining at a high level of abstraction. Though the metaphor doesn't fit their respective mythologies, trolls are ground troops, engaging their enemy in hand-to-hand combat; Orcs are masters of ideological drone warfare.

But the Orc will never be as successful as the troll. This is not just because the definition of the Orc is so easily hijacked by the enemy, but because the very notion of the Russian Orc is based on a faulty premise about self and other. The Russian Orc is a reappropriation of an anti-Russian meme for pro-Russian purposes, yet, before the war in Ukraine, the equation of Russian and Orc existed almost entirely within Russian-language cultures, based on a reading of Tolkien that few in the West were inclined to make. The Russian Orc is a double projection: projecting onto Westerners the projection of Orcs onto Russians. Proponents of the Russian Orc are defiant, but defiant in the face of nothing, since no one was calling Russians Orcs except for Russians themselves.

This does not render the Russian Orc idea ineffective, just intramural. It makes sense that the Russian Orc stands at the intersection of nationalism and F&SF fandom, because both nationalists and fans display an enthusiasm and defensiveness about cultural phenomena that, to outsiders, can look trivial. Here we should recall the opposition between the two types of fandom: affirmational (rigidly orthodox and closed) and transformational (improvisational and open), because the Russian Orc occupies both ends of the affirmational/transformational spectrum at once. On the level of historical metanarrative, the Orc is as affirmational as they come. In terms of traditional fandom, however, the Russian Orc is a clear example of the transformational approach, reclaiming Tolkien for the fans' own purposes. The Russian Orc stands at the intersection of two different fandoms, *Lord of the Rings* and the Russian nationalist metanarrative, transforming the former for the greater glory of the latter.

Russia, then, can be Mordor and Motherland at the same time. If affirmational Tolkienists find such a reading mistaken, and if opponents of Russian nationalism or state policy consider it a slur, this hardly bothers the Russian Orc. The Russian Orc laughs at his enemies' outrage, and Mordor does not believe in tears.

Conclusion
RUSSIAN SELF-HATRED

On October 30, 1998, just two months after the Russian Federation's economy went into a tailspin, the director Nikita Mikhalkov released *Sibirskii tsiriul'nik* (The barber of Siberia), an overambitious failure that was the cinematic equivalent of the ruble's collapse. Not that its viewers at the star-studded Kremlin premiere were unimpressed by what was then the most expensive film in the country's history. By most accounts, Russian audiences loved the film (Beumers, 77, 120; Norris, chapter 2); indeed, from what I could tell from my own, somewhat less glamorous screening in downtown Moscow, my (American) wife and I were the only ones in the theater stifling groans rather than bursting with laughter at the film's comic moments.

The film's release followed an intensive advertising campaign, from billboards to television spots to a limited-edition eau de cologne (*Iunkerskii* [Cadet])—Mikhalkov wanted it to combine the "smell of a shaven cheek, saddle leather, a recently downed shot of vodka, and the first drag on a *papirosa*" (Maslova). The story of the late-nineteenth-century doomed love affair between a Russian military cadet with the unlikely name of Andrei Tolstoy (Oleg Menshikov) and an American woman (Julia Ormond) representing the interests of a rapacious American inventor (his "Barber of Siberia" is a machine that will chop down Russia's precious woods with inhuman efficiency), Mikhalkov's film had the ambition to match its imperial setting. Not content with winning an Oscar for best foreign picture in 1995 for his *Burnt by the Sun*, Mikhalkov apparently wanted to nab the great white whale of American cinematic acclaim: best picture, full stop ("Mikhalkova vydvinuli").

Hence the odd contrivance that nearly everyone the Americans encounter in 1885 speaks English, and the resulting 70 percent of the dialogue spoken in what for the Russian audience was a foreign language. Whatever Oscar hopes Mikhalkov had for this tactic, it could have been seen as an insult to Russian audiences, who experienced the film the way they always do when the movie is foreign rather than domestic: with a single voice talking over the foreign dialogue in Russian. Granted, this overdubbing was by Mikhalkov himself, an accomplished actor with a soothing and mellifluous voice. But this only reinforces the director's maniacal control of the finished product.

The Barber of Siberia was a curious intervention in the debate over Russia's past, its future, and, most important, its identity. Authored by a man so thoroughly invested in his own fantasies of Orthodox, monarchic traditionalism that he cast himself in the role of Tsar Alexander III, the film unsuccessfully negotiated the geopolitics of global cinema.[1] Everything about *Barber* itself was designed to portray a positive image of Russia and Russians: the cadet core is filled with honest, earnest young men, the tsar himself is good, the nobility and common people even better, while the greatest threat to the country is an overreaching, blundering United States that wants to turn Russia's natural resources and natural beauty into fodder for a global capitalist mill.[2] The film tries to pander to everyone: flattering to Russian viewers, it nonetheless revels in stereotypes about the Russian soul that verge on minstrelsy—most notoriously, in the Maslenitsa (pre-Lenten festival) scene, when a Russian officer starts drinking only to go on an epic spree. Russians often complain that Westerners think their country is nothing but vodka and dancing bears, and this is, quite literally, what *The Barber of Siberia* supplies. Had a foreigner made this movie, it would have been offensive.

The irony of this film about two generations of men training with guns is that it misfires: aimed at a Western audience, the only target it hits is domestic. For an avowedly patriotic director, that should be enough, and yet it clearly was not. Among the many reasons that the film flopped in the West is that the very question of Russian identity is primarily a Russian concern. In his attempts to make a film for export, Mikhalkov distorts his characters for an imagined foreign gaze that will never be turned on them. The film's tag line—"He's Russian. That explains a lot"—comes from an exchange between an exhausted American drill sergeant and the mother of the recruit whose stubbornness has driven the officer to distraction. But what, exactly, does it explain? And to whom?

Perhaps the oddest, yet almost appropriate, thing about this formulation is that it is an answer standing in for a question.

On the most superficial level, the tag line is supposed to elucidate the main conflict in the two scenes that, framing the movie proper, take place twenty years after the main story. The young recruit is Andrei Tolstoy's son, and his

Russianness is meant to justify his almost idolatrous dedication to a portrait of Mozart. He would rather suffer unending punishment at the drill sergeant's hands than simply repeat the phrase demanded of him: "I don't give a shit about Mozart." Mozart, of course, is even less Russian than his half-American admirer, but in addition to showing a presumably Russian steadfast devotion to high ideals, this episode also prefigures the strategy that would be later adopted by Alexander Sokurov in his 2002 film, *Russian Ark*, which suggests that the European heritage collected in the Hermitage is housed and saved specifically by Russia (de Khegel, 85; Shlikhar, 168).

Yet despite the Eurocentric cast it gives to Russian culture, *The Barber of Siberia* stands out as a remarkable work of self-orientalization. The overreliance on Russian stereotypes and national culture in the Maslenitsa scene has all the subtlety of Disneyland's "It's a Small World" ride, with animatronic Russians dancing in their colorful national garb. The Russian audience's pleasure is that of both direct recognition ("this is us!") and mediated or alienated pleasure ("this is us, showing those Westerners who we truly are"), even if the West greeted the film with resounding indifference.

This self-orientalization on screen is performative by definition, but it is a performance that is hardly naturalistic. Mikhalkov is no David Mamet, inventing hyperrealistic dialogue to show the very specific, and very problematic, underside of his country's culture. *The Barber of Siberia* performs identity in such broad, exaggerated strokes that one hardly needs the writings of a Judith Butler to identify what makes it performative as opposed to "natural." Indeed, the characters of *The Barber of Siberia* are so mannered, so artificial that they resemble nothing more than . . . a drag show.

Consider: Oleg Menshikov is a talented and popular actor, so it is no surprise that Mikhalkov would want him in his film. But casting him as a member of the Cadet Corps strained credibility: when *Barber* was released, Menshikov was already thirty-eight, and he spent most of the first half of the film contorting his features into a wide-eyed impression of naïveté as a way to look younger. His mother is played by another acclaimed actress, Marina Neyolova, who at the time was only fifty-one. The role of the American femme fatale is filled by the British Julia Ormond (who, to be fair, manages a convincing American accent). And, of course, all of the English dialogue is overdubbed in Russian by Mikhalkov himself when he is not too busy playing the film's literal and figurative tsar. If Mikhalkov were of a less conservative bent, one might be inclined to think of *The Barber of Siberia* as an exercise in nontraditional casting, akin to having Bob Dylan played by six different actors of various genders and races in Todd Haynes's *I'm Not There*. Instead, Mikhalkov's aesthetic of excess points us back to an unconscious replication of drag. The performances are all over-the-top, with the main actors saddled with roles they can embody only through campy exaggeration, and Mikhalkov turning all of them into Russian cinematic Lypsinkas.

It may have been the most expensive drag show in history. Mikhalkov himself has stated repeatedly that the film cost more than $46 million to make, with a quarter of the funds coming from Russian state coffers. One source places *The Barber of Siberia* as number seventy-six on a list of the top hundred money-losing films in the Russian Federation, grossing only $1.6 million (Karsanova). On a financial level, *Barber* was a spectacularly bad investment, but the lost money must not obscure the fascinating role the film plays in the drama of post-Soviet Russian mass culture's renegotiation of Russian identity. On one hand, the film was clearly an occasion for the country's elites to celebrate themselves. Mikhalkov's lack of artistic subtlety was outdone only by the pomp occasioned by the premiere: fireworks, the ringing of the Kremlin's fabled chimes, and a four-course "tsar's" banquet ("Desperate Siberian Gamble"). On the other hand, its failure in the international arena recapitulated the film's performance of Russian soulfulness in the face of a combination of capitalist cynicism and the West's inability to understand Russia's "authentic self."

Mikhalkov had insisted that *Barber* would restore Russia's national pride while reviving the domestic film industry ("Desperate Siberian Gamble"); the man who cast himself as Russia's second-to-last tsar saw little distinction between his ambitions for himself (international critical acclaim) and for his country (a return to glory).[3] No amount of *Cadet* eau de cologne could hide the stench of this flop at Cannes or the Academy Awards, but it was still granted a special (consolation?) prize by the Russian state in 2000. From a distance of two decades, *The Barber of Siberia* appears to have succeeded at only one thing: being the perfect symptom. Mikhalkov's film, in no small part thanks to its aesthetic of unrelenting excess, is a snapshot of the post-Soviet, pre-millennial national preoccupation with national identity. Such a preoccupation should not be surprising, given the circumstances. As an independent state, the Russian Federation was only seven years old, and the trauma of the Soviet collapse has not been resolved to this day. What *Barber* shows, however, is how much this concern with identity depends on the imagined gaze of the other. If the debate on national identity happens, and no one outside the national borders pays attention, does it really matter?

"He's Russian. That explains a lot" is a substitute for an explanation, or perhaps a pointer in the explanation's direction. Its placement toward the end of the film suggests that the explanation has already been provided by the film itself. Its deployment is humorous, since there is little chance that the drill sergeant actually has any idea about Russia beyond a few stereotypes. In contrast, it is precisely stereotyping that the film so gleefully provides. And as an advertising slogan in Russia, and in Russian, it was a peculiar choice, since the majority of people reading it would be Russians, and therefore should be unlikely to see a fellow Russian's Russianness as a persuasive explanation for anything they might otherwise find confusing. Only the imagined other justifies the need for such a gloss, and yet the content of the film (the explanation) was far more satisfying to Russian audiences than to any outside the country's borders. Earlier I called the film's stereotypes "self-orientalization," a process that only works as part of the audience's self-alienation: imagining how this looks to outsiders.

When Mikhalkov deflects accusations that the film was made for Hollywood, not Moscow, he portrays his cinematic project as messianic, precisely because the distinction between the foreign and the domestic is threatened with total erasure. Russians themselves are so alienated from their own culture that they need to be educated like foreigners:

> The substantive questions always amounted to the same thing. Why did he cover Red Square with salt and turn off the Kremlin star lights? Why are they speaking English in the film? Why such a large budget, and what was the money spent on? And, finally, most important: why did Mikhalkov come up with a Russia that never was [*Rossiiu, kotoroi ne bylo*]? . . .
>
> Was Russia the way it looks in the film or wasn't it—it's the Russia I see and love. . . . And the conversation about "Russian clichés" [*kliukva*], about Mikhalkov making this picture for foreigners. . . . Yes, for foreigners. For the hundred million foreigners living in my country. Who don't know its culture, it's history, and—most important—don't love it. (quoted in Arkus)

Though based very much on post-Soviet realities, Mikhalkov's sentiment is nothing new. Indeed, he appears to be channeling Pyotr Chaadaev, whose *Philosophical Letters* (1829–1836) led to him being declared a madman (rather than, in Mikhalkov's case, a cinematic national treasure). In his first letter, Chaadaev wrote, "Our memories reach back no further than yesterday; we are, as it were, strangers to ourselves." Chaadaev's quote is, of course, translated from the original . . . French, as if heralding Mikhalkov's musings on the Russian soul in English. When Mikhalkov responds to criticism about language and audience, he sees no contradiction. His recreation of Russia is an exercise in sympathetic magic, meant to transform the de-Russified masses from de facto foreigners into the Russians they are meant to be.

Mikhalkov's recreation of his favorite imaginary iteration of Russia is a project very much of its time, but also pointing to the way that the discourse of Russianness would develop beyond the models examined elsewhere in this book. Rather than separate out a subgroup of Russian citizens, whether for praise or stigmatization, Mikhalkov longs to define Russia and Russians in their totality. Ultimately, this is the direction in which Putinist culture would go: repeatedly appealing to an ideal of "Russians" while refraining from imbuing the concept with any real specificity.

The tag line from *The Barber of Siberia* alludes to wisdom while remaining defiantly content-free. By assuming that the definition of "Russian" is common knowledge, Mikhalkov reaps the benefits of a flattering patriotic marketing strategy without having to commit to anything. Or rather, the film itself becomes the thesis, and if it does its job correctly, it positions the viewers to accept this thesis as confirmation of something they already know rather than as a polemical stance they can choose to adopt or reject.

As a contribution to Russian identity discourses, *The Barber of Siberia* was a tonic for an old malady: the self-hatred that has been an integral part of unofficial Soviet and Russian identities. But this is a remedy that is more homeopathic than medical, as self-aggrandizement and self-hatred are not so much binary opposites as they are overlapping categories, based on the same habit of anxious self-assessment through the eyes of an imagined other.

In terms of its content, *The Barber of Siberia* contributes little of substance to actual debates about Russian identity. Structurally, however, it is a powerful rebuke of all the phenomena discussed in the previous chapter. At the turn of the millennium, Mikhalkov used the tsarist 1880s to make a statement about Russianness that was meant to be valid and compelling over one hundred years later. Implicit in *The Barber of Siberia* is an argument for a static, eternal Russian identity that withstands the forces of history rather than being shaped by them. Though Mikhalkov's late nineteenth century is more a reflection of his concerns about the twentieth and twenty-first (hence the American antagonists at a time when the United States was irrelevant), the goal of the film is, in fan terms, decidedly affirmational rather than transformational: there is a core of Russianness that must be emphasized and preserved.

Bombing Kyiv

Twenty-four years after the premiere of *The Barber of Siberia*, Russia once again faces financial collapse, but this time entirely of its own making. Breaking with any rational analysis of costs and benefits, Putin sent the Russian army into Ukraine on February 24, 2022, starting a full-scale war on its neighbor. The human and economic toll of this invasion have yet to be calculated, because, as of this writing (April 2022), there is no end in sight to this bloody, criminal war. This is not a book on Ukraine; nor am I a specialist in that country. But even though the war is taking place in Ukraine, and it is Ukrainian citizens who are its primary victims, the conflict itself says far more about Russia. It was Russia, after all, that crossed the border to invade. So in keeping with the themes of this book, and in full recognition that the killings, kidnappings, and torture of Ukrainians at the hands of the Russian military must be recognized and condemned, I want to consider what this conflict means for Russia.

To do so, let us recall where this book began: with the pervasive meme about bombing Voronezh. The idea behind it was that the only way to induce Russia to allocate resources to its ailing provinces would be to turn them into victims of Russian military campaigns that now must be rebuilt. The meme is a satirical comment on the Russian state's priorities as well as a portrait of perversion: self-improvement through self-harm.

Throughout March 2022, the Russian military was bombing Kyiv (along with several other Ukrainian cities), with little prospect of a postwar Russian economic bailout. But the Ukrainian war on the country that started it strangely inverts the logic of bombing Voronezh. The longer Russia's assault continues, the greater the Western resolve to punish the aggressor with crippling economic sanctions. The Russian military is physically destroying Ukraine, but at an increasingly enormous cost to the Russian Federation. In a weird variation on the logic of the Voodoo doll, Russia is flattening Ukraine but destroying itself.

Russia's war on Ukraine is an act of self-destruction, as well as a particularly complex form of self-hatred. As I previously wrote in *Plots against Russia*, the anti-Ukrainian sentiment within the Russian Federation is based on a refusal to admit the difference between self and other (210–17). Ukraine cannot be allowed to be seen as an entity, nation, or culture that is distinct from Russia. Here the entangled linguistic and historical ties play their role, of course. Both modern-day Russia and Ukraine trace their roots to medieval Kyiv. The languages still maintain a high degree of mutual intelligibility (although in general, because of centuries of subordination, Ukrainians understand Russian better than Russians understand Ukrainian). And the very language of empire in pre-1917 Russia defined both Belarus and Ukraine as variations on a Russian standard—Belorussia (White Russia) and Malorossiia (Little Russia). Many Russians retained an imperial attitude of condescension toward Ukraine, aided by the ability of Russian speakers to dismiss Ukrainian as a kind of amusing, substandard Russian. Just using Ukrainian words in Russian has become a way to mock Ukrainianness, such as describing Ukrainian with the Ukrainian word for language (*mova*) or constantly using the Ukrainian word for "independent" (*nezalezhnyi*) in reference to the neighboring state.

Putinist historiography is a kind of state-sponsored affirmational fandom, built on a traditional Russian imperialist notion of legitimacy; no competing narratives are allowed. Even before this latest invasion, Putin repeatedly stated that Ukraine was "not a real country" (Remnick 2014). From the point of view of international law, not to mention a number of agreements signed by the leaders of the Russian Federation itself, such a statement is nonsense. What is at work here is an extralegal notion of legitimacy based on historical longevity: a country that has been around for centuries is real, while one that has existed for only a few years or decades is merely a consensual fantasy. The idea of primordial nationhood has taken a firm hold of the Russian educational system in recent years, spurred on by a revived interest in Lev Gumilev's crackpot theory of ethnogenesis, in which nations are like living organisms, fueled by a charisma-like quality called "passionarity" derived from cosmic rays. Intentionally or not, such approaches serve to transform the imperialist past into a fact of nature; if your country wasn't a "real country" two hundred years ago, then it had no reason to be. Therefore, Ukraine is not real.

Demonizing the Ukrainian enemy is a complex problem: how do you condemn the evil of a people you claim do not even exist? Even before the 2014 invasion, the Russian media roundly condemned the "Kiev junta" that they claimed had been installed by the US State Department after the Euromaidan protests while pointing to every instance of right-wing extremism in Ukraine to dismiss all anti-Russian or pro-Western sentiment as the resurgence of World War II-era fascism. The presidency of Volodymyr Zelensky, a popular entertainer and star of a comedy series about an ordinary schoolteacher who becomes president of Ukraine, brought the anti-Ukrainian rhetoric to new heights. Not only was Zelensky young, good-looking, and obviously talented (as a quick visit to YouTube will show), he was a Jewish comedian whose irreverence and wit had far more in common with the Russian protest movement than with any regime in Russian memory. To top it all off, he was a native Russian speaker who committed to serious study of the Ukrainian language in order to make the linguistic switch, ultimately winning majorities among Ukrainian- and Russian-speakers alike.

Less than three years after Zelensky's election, the Russian president would have us believe that the "Kiev junta" is not merely fascist but a nest of neo-Nazis. The distinction may be subtle, but it is one worth making. Until recently, "Nazi" was an uncommon word in Russian; during and after World War II, Hitler's armies were usually referred to as "fascists." As Brandon Schechter points out, the more generic term "fascism" fit better within Soviet ideological discourse, since it was framed as an inevitable stage in the decline of capitalism. The term persisted long after the Soviet collapse and was still used to describe the alleged extreme right-wing forces in Ukraine in 2014. Schechter argues that Putin's adoption of the term "Nazi" is meant to resonate more strongly with audiences in the West. I would add that it also helps Putin continue to maintain his embrace of right-wing Western populists, for whom Antifa (short, of course, for "antifascist") has become a useful bogeyman. Moreover, it gives a more specific name to an enemy that the Putinist media would prefer to define as anything other than "Ukrainian." On April 4, 2022, the columnist Timofei Sergeitsev argued on the state-owned RIA.novosti site that "denazification will inevitably include de-ukrainization," because "Ukrainism is an artificial anti-Russian construct that has no civilizational substance of its own, a subordinate element of an extraneous and alien civilization" (Smith-Peter). "De-ukrainization" implies Ukraine's reversion back into "Little Russia"—that is, merely a variation on a Russian theme.

By insisting on Ukraine's inherent Russianness, Putinism implicitly redefines this war of aggression on a sovereign country as something even more perverse than a fratricidal conflict: it is a war to expunge an evil that hides within the self. In the first chapter of his book of essays *The Russian Intelligentsia*, Andrei Sinyavsky (a non-Jewish dissident who published samizdat fiction under the Jewish name Abram Tertz) made an argument about antisemitism that could easily be applied to the current anti-Ukrainian campaign: "Russian anti-Semitism represents a kind of alienation of evil. It is a popular, mythic, almost fairy-tale notion that the people cannot be bad. Our people are good. They are our people. But some outsiders have wormed their way into the government, and they are to blame for everything" (13–14).

Ukraine here functions both as the people (who are good) and the outsiders (who are bad). "Ukrainism" is an alien cancer on the Russian body, but the Ukrainians who suffer from it are actually Russians who have been duped by Western propaganda and agents of influence. Ukraine now serves as its own "alienation of evil," and the atrocities committed by Russian forces are the apotheosis of a particular perverse form of self-hatred. Russia is locked into a dyad with the perceived enemy, displacing actions attributed initially to one party as a shared characteristic of both. This sharing is not simultaneous but rather a time-share: the accusation is passed back and forth like a football. This is why a reasonable response to the Kremlin's conspiratorial blather about Western-backed chemical and biological weapons labs is to worry that Russia is planning to use chemical weapons in Ukraine.

This is also the logic implicit in the insistence on Ukrainian "Nazism." Russia is rounding up protesters, crushing dissent, and banning news outlets at home while slaughtering civilians and bombing indiscriminately in Ukraine. The Russian Federation's anti-Nazi rhetoric is the perfect corollary to its Nazi-style behavior. Russia commits the crimes that match the label it uses to condemn Ukraine, all in the name of national greatness.

Like Russia and Ukraine, grandiosity and self-hatred share a common border. Sadly, it is now Ukrainians who are more likely to agree with the tagline from *The Barber of Siberia*: "He's Russian. That explains a lot."

Notes

INTRODUCTION

1. On nationalism, imperialism, and Eurasianism, see chapter 8 of Bassin, *Gumilev Mystique*; Bassin and Pozo, eds., *Politics of Eurasianism*; Bodin, "Russian Geopolitical Discourse"; Clover, *Black Wind, White Snow*; and three works by Marlene Laruelle—*In the Name of the Nation*; "Larger, Higher, Farther North"; and *Russian Eurasianism*. On Russian Orthodoxy and the state, see Engstrom, "Contemporary Russian Messianism and New Russian Foreign Policy"; and Sidorov, "Post-Imperial Third Romes: Resurrections of a Russian Orthodox Geopolitical Metaphor." Mikhail Suslov has published a fascinating monograph on these topics, *Geopolitical Imagination*.

2. On shame in the first post-Soviet decade, see Sharafutdinova, *Red Mirror*, 88–96.

3. On aphasia and despair, see Oushakine, "In the State of Post-Soviet Aphasia"; and Oushakine, *Patriotism of Despair*. On trauma, see Noordenbos, *Post-Soviet Literature and the Search for Russian Identity*; and Wakamiya, "Post-Soviet Context and Trauma Studies." On nostalgia, see Boym, *Future of Nostalgia*; and Kalinin, "Nostalgic Modernization." See also Lipovetsky, "Post-Sots."

4. Eng and Hann's subsequent book on the subject, *Racial Melancholia, Racial Dissociation: On the Social and Psychic Lives of Asian Americans*, came out in 2019.

5. In *Mastering the Art of Soviet Cooking: A Memoir of Food and Longing*, Anya von Bremzen devotes an entire chapter to the centrality of the Olivier salad: "Piling potato, carrot, and pickle fragments into a bowl, I think that Olivier could be a metaphor for a Soviet émigré's memory: urban legends and totalitarian myths, collective narratives and biographical facts, journeys home both real and imaginary—all loosely cemented with mayo" (177).

6. Martin Muller makes this point in "Goodbye, Postsocialism!"

7. In *Neoliberalism, Personhood, and Postsocialism*, Nicolette Makovicky contends that "postsocialism continues to be bandied about for lack of a better alternative," which Muller in "Goodbye, Postsocialism!" sees as an imperative if we are to develop alternatives. Muller's argument makes sense, but we are all still waiting.

8. See my *Plots against Russia* (53–98) and Yablokov, *Fortress Russia* (50–78).

9. Putin, "Postsovetskii period," as quoted in TASS, April 11, 2012.

10. Kirill Kobrin also proclaimed the death of the post-Soviet in 2016, in both Russian and English: "What has changed? The public agenda. The hierarchy of what's important and what's not for Russian society. What is appropriate and desirable. And, most importantly, the project of the present and the past. The old post-Soviet project, once relevant back in 1991, is over. It has achieved its aims. It's just that nobody's rushing to pronounce what has happened as the 'natural, logical results' of this process" ("Death of the Post-Soviet Project in Russia").

11. As detailed in Gordon, "Post-Communist Russia Plumbs Its Soul."

12. For an early post-Soviet analysis of this terminological shift, see Freidin ("Romans into Italians"). Irina Souch and Mark Steinberg have separately noted Putin's shift from *rossiiskii* back to *russkii* in the aftermath of the seizure of Crimea.

13. Souch writes, "I consistently refer to the 'post-Soviet' era and do not divide the period after 1991 into separate decades. The term 'post-Soviet' is treated here not as indicative of a static situation but as a dynamic category" (*Popular Tropes of Identity*, 9).

14. The choice of the male pronoun here is deliberate. And the etymological and historical connections between "fan" and "fanatic" are long established.

15. It was issue 171, and I'm ashamed to say that I did not have to look this up.

16. For a thorough overview of nationalist and imperialist science fiction and its influence, see chapter 4 of Suslov, *Geopolitical Imagination*.

1. ZOMBIE SOVIETICUS

1. By the time the sequel (sorry, "subsequent moviefilm") came out in 2020, the Kazakhstan government had given up its outrage in favor of cashing in, advertising Kazakhstan tourism with Borat's catchphrase, "Very Nice!"

2. See Isenberg, *White Trash*; Newitz and Wray, eds., *White Trash*; and Wray, *Not Quite White*.

3. As Jill Lepore writes in "A New Americanism" (2019):

> The United States is different from other nations—every nation is different from every other—and its nationalism is different, too. To review: a nation is a people with common origins, and a state is a political community governed by laws. A nation-state is a political community governed by laws that unites a people with a supposedly common ancestry. When nation-states arose out of city-states and kingdoms and empires, they explained themselves by telling stories about their origins—stories meant to suggest that everyone in, say, "the French nation" had common ancestors, when they of course did not. As I wrote in my book *These Truths*, "Very often, histories of nation-states are little more than myths that hide the seams that stitch the nation to the state. But in the American case, the origins of the nation can be found in those seams. When the United States declared its independence, in 1776, it became a state, but what made it a nation?"

4. See the introduction to my *Men without Women*.

5. Maja Soboleva, looking at the material from a different angle, proposes a periodization that basically agrees with Krylova's: theoretical (1900s–1930s), the development of norms of Soviet morality (1930s–1950s), and moral theory and Marxist ethics (starting in the 1960s).

6. A fuller version of this argument can be found in my "Defying Interpretation."

7. The gendered implications of Babichev's role are discussed in *Men without Women*.

2. THE RISE AND FALL OF SOVOK

1. The most comprehensive compilation of sovok origin stories can be found in a footnote to Konstantin Bogdanov's *Vox populi*.

2. "Aleksandr Gradskii" (2009).

3. For more on the *anekdot*, see Graham, *Resonant Dissonance*; Draitser, *Taking Penguins to the Movies*; and Draitser, *Making War, Not Love*.

4. For more on *meshchanstvo*, see Dunham, *In Stalin's Time*, 19–23, 87–109.

5. For more on MMM, see my "Public Offerings: MMM and the Marketing of Melodrama."

6. On the importance of Paris in Russian culture, see Gilburd, *To See Paris and Die*.

7. Mamin himself wrestled with this conundrum, ultimately emigrating to the United States in 2019 (Ponomareva, "'Zdes' stalo nechem dyshat'").

3. JUST A GUY NAMED VASYA

1. In addition, the phrase "Vasya was here" is the generic stand-in for graffiti, like "Kilroy was here."

2. Sometimes Vasya gets a last name: for years, Russians have used the name "Vasya Pupkin" as shorthand for the virtually nameless average person, the equivalent of "John Doe" or "Joe Blow."

3. I am tempted to say "genes," but the legacy of Lysenkoism makes the term problematic here.

4. In *Plots against Russia,* I examined the way in which charges of Russophobia enable a conspiratorial and defensive stance on behalf of the Russian state. For approaches that take Russophobia more seriously as a real phenomenon, see Basulto, *Russophobia*; Mettan, *Creating Russophobia*; Robin, *Making of the Cold War Enemy*; Shafarevich, *Rusofobiia*; and Tsygankov, *Russophobia.*

5. Yes, I'm aware that the same could be said of the United States, but the contours of the debate in a country whose national myth rests on the cult of opportunity, success, and self-reinvention are different.

6. The title *ZhD* is also a pun on the novel's ethnic and religious themes; it sounds suspiciously similar to the plural form of the most common Russian antisemitic slur (*zhidy*).

7. Here Bykov is playing with the fringe theory that Ashkenazi Jews are actually descendants of the vanished Khazars, popularized first by Arthur Koestler.

8. I am adapting the English translation, replacing "Joe" with "Vaska" in all the quotes from the text.

9. "Anka still didn't understand. Sometimes at the dacha she would look through old magazines—children's ones no longer interested her—and would come across the mysterious word 'bomzh,' the old name for them, meaning 'of no fixed abode.' Bomzh! Like the strike of a deep bass gong, ending in a long buzzing echo. It was only under the new humane programme for them that they were called Vaskas and were sent treated and sterilized from the shelters to stay in people's homes. There weren't only Vaskas in the shelters, of course. Sometimes an old granny with nothing to eat would apply to live there, or a runaway with nowhere to live. They would have to pay for a doctor's certificate saying they were Vaskas (the proper medical term was 'Vasilenko Syndrome'), and without one they wouldn't get in. Several illegal deals had been exposed, and the scandal was discussed at length on television; her father said it was only the tip of the iceberg" (204–5).

10. Seth Graham provides a thorough analysis of the Chapaev joke cycle in *Resonant Dissonance* (105–13).

11. At one point, one of the characters even jokes that Vasily Ivanovich's last name is Chapaev.

12. Yuliya Minkova, in "The Squid and the Whale *a la Russe*," contrasts *Living Souls* with the "wearying struggles between interchangeable political factions in fantastic or futuristic settings." Instead, she sees the novel's inventive approach to history and nationality as evidence of a desire to show "why the Russian nation still has not been formed" (286).

13. For more on bydlo, see Anne Marie Devlin's excellent "Lard-Eaters, Gay-ropeans, Sheeple, and Prepositions."

14. In the same year, S. G. Bochkarev called bydlo the "key word" on the Russian Internet, citing a sharp rise in its use in the years prior to the publication of his article, "'Bydlo' kak kliuchevoe slovo runeta."

4. WHATEVER HAPPENED TO THE NEW RUSSIANS?

1. Williams need not have worried; it turns out that the wealthy elites are the forgiving types, at least when their business interests are not threatened.

2. Those trendy shoes were also featured in that year's hit song "Exhibit" by Leningrad, which Williams may not have known.

3. The burgeoning field of Russian romance fiction has been the subject of several fascinating articles by Julie Cassiday and Emily D. Johnson, who also coedited a special issue on international romance fiction in the *Journal of Popular Romance Studies* (2020). In her contribution to the issue, "Exploring His/Her Library," Johnson argues that the booming market for Russian-language romance novels has not been accompanied by the kinds of professional networks and readers' communities that characterize the Anglo-American romance world.

4. The same holds true for science fiction. The simple fact that H. G. Wells called his novel *The Time Machine* tells the uninformed reader that it comes at the beginning of the SF time travel subgenre.

5. My only memory of it from everyday Soviet life was as the name of one of the three kinds of cheese I could count on finding in the store.

6. Galina Lindqist, for example, argues in her "Spirits and Souls of Business" that "New Russians are in many ways a 'phantasm' (Agamben, 1993), an imagined cultural entity, known to most culture bearers, as well as to observers, by representations alone." Mark Lipovetsky writes in his "New Russians as a Cultural Myth": "Whether New Russians are real is an open question. For a literary critic, they are real insofar as they are reflected in literary and cultural texts."

7. Nor would a New Russian be likely to call himself a "New Russian," as Iuliia Idlis notes in a roundtable about the New Russian phenomenon recorded by Radio Svoboda on November 14, 2010: "I never met a single person who would say with complete sincerity, absolutely honestly while looking you in the eye: 'I'm a New Russian.' . . . The closest he might come would be 'I probably was one of those New Russians.' . . . That is, no one is ready to take on the full burden of the cultural symbols the term carries" (https://www.svoboda.org/a/2218403.html).

8. As Seth Graham notes, there were numerous famous, wealthy Russian citizens who could have provided fodder for the jokes about New Russians, but they are rarely mentioned (2009, 135).

9. As Graham puts it, "The *anekdot*-al New Russian is a type defined by a cluster of behaviors and accessories associated with a single demographic category: the rich. Other standard attributes of the type—stupidity, violence, drunkenness, amorality—are important (but secondary, even optional), but material wealth is de rigueur" (2009, 132).

5. RICH MAN'S BURDEN

1. Unless otherwise indicated, all the New Russian jokes come from https://anekdoty.ru/pro-novyh-russkih/ and were translated by me.

2. As Seth Graham puts it in *Resonant Dissonance*: "The Chukchi are unlike most other ethnicities conscripted into joke-lore in that their history, ethnography, and especially their relations with the Russians are largely irrelevant to the functions and content of the jokes" (115).

3. Justin Cronin toys with a similar trick at the end of his *Passage* trilogy, only to reveal that the story is not entirely over.

4. This naming convention is maintained in the seven volumes of fan fiction that have been released online since the project began, with the exception of an anthology called *Bitva rasskazov* (Battle of the Short Stories).

5. The *Ethnogenesis* series is as much an e-book phenomenon as a print one, if not more so. I have been unable to get copies of the print editions; as a result, the quotations here are from the unpaginated e-book editions of the *Billionaire* novels. The translations are mine.

6. In real life, Lev Gumilev had no children.

7. In Russian, referring to Russia as "this country" (*eta strana*) rather than the "motherland" or "fatherland" has come to be construed as dismissive and unpatriotic.

8. Later in the first book, Gumilev says to another character, "Why are you looking at me like I'm Roman Abramovich?"

9. The first novel begins at the same time as Russia's armed conflict with Georgia in 2008. Gumilev's wife, Eva, begs him to find a way to help the poor people suffering at Georgian (not Russian) hands. He arranges to invest in the rebuilding of the town of Tsinkhval when the fighting is over, telling Eva, "I think that's enough for now. . . . You know I've always held the principle that if you want to feed a hungry man, don't give him a fish, but teach him how to fish."

10. "Self-made man" is in English in the original Russian text.

11. The very process of moving from superrich amorality to respectable, responsible citizenship is enacted over the three seasons of the hit television series *Mazhor* (Silver spoon, 2014–). The main character is a spoiled young rich man named Igor, whose father, desperate to find a means to force his son to mend his ways, forces him to join the police force. He surprises everyone, himself included, by rising to the challenge.

6. RUSSIAN ORC

1. The first letter of the word "Orc" is capitalized by some writers and left lower-case by others. Tolkien himself was inconsistent, although in his private correspondence he argued for capitalization. (See the discussion about this on the Science Fiction & Fantasy Stack Exchange, "Tolkien's Capitalisation of Races, i.e, Elf, Dwarf, Orc," https://scifi.stackexchange.com/questions/176914/tolkiens-capitalisation-of-races-i-e-elf-dwarf-orc.) I have chosen to capitalize the noun in English throughout the book, except when the original writers do not.

2. In his discussion of the paradoxes of Russian paleoconservatism in *Russia's Postcolonial Identity*, Viacheslav Morozov notes the double bind enforced by the movement's binary framework: "By grounding its every move in the Eurocentric normative order, Russian paleoconservatism abuses and inverts the hegemonic vocabulary but makes no attempt at transcending or abandoning it" (122).

3. Miéville is notorious in fantasy circles for calling Tolkien "the wen on the arse of fantasy literature." For a slightly more polite elaboration of his views, see her "Tolkien— Middle Earth." Scholarly opinions on the alleged racism of Tolkien's depiction of the Orcs varies, though even his defenders register some level of discomfort. In "Let Us Now Praise Famous Orcs," Robert T. Tally Jr. argues against the common assumption that Tolkien's Orcs are inherently evil; while Orcs "are presented with surprising uniformity as loathsome, ugly, cruel, feared, and especially terminable . . . Tolkien could not resist the urge to flesh out and 'humanize' these inhuman creatures from time to time" (17). Richard Angelo Bergen concludes that "one gets the sense from his essays and letters that Tolkien is uncomfortable with stating that orcs are altogether irredeemable, and this is probably because of his commitment to an Augustinian understanding of evil, and orcs' close association with corrupted humanity. However, orcs in *The Lord of the Rings* certainly do appear unredeemable" (116). In a blogpost, James Mendez Hodes asserts, "Tolkien explicitly and purposefully crafted orcs as a detrimental depiction of Asian people specifically." See also Robin Anne Reid's comprehensive bibliographic essay

on the topic, as well as chapter 4 of Helen Young's *Race and Popular Fantasy Literature: Habits of Whiteness*.

4. See Paul B. Sturtevant's blog post on *The Public Medievalist* (2017), as well as his *Middle Ages in Popular Imagination*.

5. Brin's call for a more sympathetic treatment of Orcs was primarily political, but it has implicitly been answered by many within the F&SF community. Or rather, it was answered before Brin even raised the issue. In 1999, the British writer Stan Nicholls began a series of novels where the protagonists are Orcs. Here the Orcs are not exactly paragons of virtue, but their plight is compelling. Humans, in bringing agriculture and industry to the Orcs' enchanted world, have caused environmental devastation and an ever-worsening shortage of magic. The series, which consists of two trilogies to date, is unsurprisingly called Orcs.

6. Most of my information about Tolkien's translation and circulation in the Soviet Union comes from Mark T. Hooker's exhaustive *Tolkien through Russian Eyes*.

7. Hooker also shows how fraught certain English terms have been when rendered into Russian, and not just by Kamenkovich and Karrik. Depending on the translation, the term "Chief" in *Return of the King* ends up as "Generalissimo," "Boss" (Nachal'nik), "Predvoditel'" and "Pravitel'." Vladimir Murav'ev made the obvious but daring choice rejected by all the other translators: *Vozhd'*, a word that cannot be dissociated from Stalin.

8. For more on Yeskov in English, see Miller.

9. Orc revisionism is not exclusively a post-Soviet phenomenon. In 2017, Netflix released *Bright*, a Will Smith vehicle that takes place in a world just like our own, except that Orcs and Elves share our world after a Last Battle with the Dark Lord a couple of thousand years ago. The idea had potential, but all of it was squandered. The world building makes absolutely no sense—somehow, everything else about twenty-first-century Los Angeles is more or less the same, despite the long-term presence of magical creatures. There is an earnest but poorly developed attempt to use Orcs and humans as a metaphor for race relations, but the result never rises above painfully recognizable racial stereotypes (Orcs in street gangs sound like Hollywood Latinos in street gangs). The filmmakers use what could have been an intriguing premise as the setup for one of the most overplayed genres: the buddy-cop tale (Will Smith is partnered with an Orc, played by Joel Edgerton). Netflix claims the film was popular, but given its notorious reticence to share actual data, we are asked to accept it at its word, admittedly reinforced by its otherwise inexplicable decision to go forward with a sequel (Spangler). Critics have been almost uniformly unkind to *Bright*, trashing it as one of the worst movies of the century. As an example David Ehrlich titled his review on *Indiewire* "'Bright' Review: Netflix's First Blockbuster is the Worst Movie of 2017."

10. See, it sounds like "offshore," and it's literally floating above ground! Who comes up with this stuff?

11. Never mind the fact that this term does not exist in English and therefore is used a slur against Russia only by speakers of Russian.

12. The longtime dissident, Valeriia Novodvorskaia, in a statement on Russia's invasion of Ukraine made not long before her death, addresses the Donbas separatists: "Do you know who Putin is? He is a beast, he is a Stalinist, he was spawned from gloom, he is from Mordor, he is the real Sauron!" (quoted in Davidzon).

13. Other online examples include a 2016 *LiveJournal* post titled "Va vsem vinovatye russkie orki, i lichno VV, razbor golubogo breda (Russian Orcs are to blame for everything [deceptors]), referring to "Orcs from the neofascist Putin's reich"; a 2106 *LiveJournal* post called "Russkie orki unichtozhili pamiatnyi znak nevinnym zhertvam NKVD" (Russian Orcs have destroyed a memorial display to the innocent victims of the NKVD" [Leusenko]); and a pro-Putinist open letter to an ethnic Georgian Russian media figure

accusing her of Russophobia: "Putin = Voldemort, Sauron, and Darth Vader in one convenient package?? (I'm copyrighting that)" (sensei-yoda), as well as "Ukraina Tolkina protiv Ukrainy Martina" (Tolkien's Ukraine vs. Martin's Ukraine [Kazarin]). The references to Orcs and Mordor continued after the 2022 invasion. After the execution-style killings of Ukrainian civilians in Bucha, the Russian liberal journalist Andrei Loshak wrote on Facebook: "These really are Orcs. Under their president's leadership, they have declared war on civilization and are marching their way to a new barbarism."

CONCLUSION

1. Stephen Norris (chap. 2) notes that "Mikhalkov's decision to play Alexander III, tsar of Russia, led many observers to conclude that the director was making a play at becoming the leader of Russia."

2. Susan Larsen sums up the film's affirmative messages best: "Mikhalkov is summoning his viewers to return to the three codes embodied in his hero's life: the Russian officer's code of honor, the Mozart lover's allegiance to high culture, and the patriot's loyalty to the traditional 'folk' (*narodnyi*) way of life that Andrei adopts in his Siberian exile as a village barber living humbly with his wife—and his family's former maid—the loyal Dunia (Anna Mikhalkova) in a wooden cottage filled with apples (emblems of paradise regained, perhaps) and small children" (501). Kirill Razlogov notes that, despite the film's attempt to dramatize a "clash of civilizations," the ideological messages are a mismatch with the film's emotional drama: "The contrast between 'us' and 'them,' the West and Russia explains almost all of the plot's twists and turns," but does not reflect the individual scenes, nor one's conclusive feelings about the film as a whole. It appears that the rational and emotional principles . . . exist and develop independently of each other" (24).

3. Chapter 2 of Stephen Norris's *Blockbuster History in the New Russia* includes a short but thorough discussion of Mikhalkov's role in the revitalization of the Russian film industry.

Works Cited

Adams, John Joseph, and David Barr Kirtley. *The Geeks' Guide to the Galaxy* [podcast], episode 336. November 22, 2018. https://geeksguideshow.com/2018/11/16/ggg336-andy-duncan/.
Agamben, Giorgio. *Homo Sacer: Sovereign Power and Bare Life*, translated by Daniel Heller-Roazen. Stanford, CA: Stanford University Press, 1998.
Ahmed, Sara. *The Cultural Politics of Emotion*. Edinburgh: Edinburgh University Press, 2004.
Akunin, Boris. *Altyn-Tolobas*. St. Petersburg: Neva, 2000.
"Aleksandr Gradskii: Mne seichas interesna bolee slozhnaia muzyka, chem rok." RIA-Novosti. March 3, 2009. https://ria.ru/20091103/191732613.html.
"Andrei Lukin: Ia Vatnik!" Read by Iurii Vladimirovich Nazarov. March 17, 2018. https://www.youtube.com/watch?v=O-TG_5A3EpI.
"Anekdoty pro sovok." http://www.vysokovskiy.ru/anekdot/sovok/.
Arkus, Liubov'. "Ia sdelal kartinu dlia sta millionov inostrantsev, zhivushchikh v moei strane." *Seans*. December 7, 2011. https://seance.ru/films/sibirskij-tsirjulnik/?ap=numeric.
Artamonova, Aleksandra. "Vnuk 'sovka': Anton Chadskii o iavlenii i poiavlenii 'Vatnika.'" November 25, 2014. https://www.newkaliningrad.ru/news/politics/4821328-vnuk-sovka-anton-chadskiy-o-yavlenii-i-poyavlenii-vatnika.html.
Attwood, Margaret. *The Handmaid's Tale*. New York: Knopf, 1998.
Atwood, Lynn. *The New Soviet Man and Woman: Sex Role Socialization in the USSR*. New York: Palgrave, 1990.
Bassin, Mark. *The Gumilev Mystique: Biopolitics, Eurasianism, and the Construction of Community in Modern Russia*. Ithaca, NY: Cornell University Press, 2016.
Bassin, Mark, and Gonzalo Pozo, eds. *The Politics of Eurasianism: Identity, Popular Culture, and Russia's Foreign Policy*. Lanham, MD: Rowman and Littlefield, 2017.
Basulto, Dominic. *Russophobia: How Western Media Turns Russia into the Enemy*. S.l.: The Druzhba Project, 2015.
Bellamy, Edward. *Looking Backward*. Mineola, NY: Dover Publications, 1996.
Belostotskii, Gennady. "Lennon i Karenina." *Kul'tura*. March 5, 2009. https://dlib.eastview.com/browse/doc/19703537.
Benediktov, Kirill. *Milliarder 3: Konets igry*. Moscow: Populiarnaia literatura, 2011.
Berdiaev, Nikolai. *Novoe srednevekov'e*. Moscow: T8, 2018.
Bergen, Richard Angelo. "'A Warp of Horror': J. R. R. Tolkien's Sub-Creations of Evil." *Mythlore* 36, no. 1 (2017): 103–22.
Bershidsky, Leonid. "Putin's Russia, Tolkien's Mordor: What's the Difference." *Bloomberg*. December 11, 2014. https://www.bloomberg.com/opinion/articles/2014-12-11/putins-russia-tolkiens-mordor-whats-the-difference.
Beumers, Birgit. *Nikita Mikhalkov: Between Nostalgia and Nationalism*. New York: I. B. Tauris, 2005.

Beumers, Birgit, and Mark Lipovetsky. *Performing Violence: Literary and Theatrical Experiments of New Russian Drama*. Bristol: Intellect Books, 2009.
Bitard671. "Ia Vatnik." https://www.youtube.com/watch?v=vKr8jRutWrw.
Blok, Aleksandr. "The People and the Intelligentsia." In *Russian Intellectual History: An Anthology*, edited by Marc Raeff, 359–63. New York: Harcourt, Brace, and World, 1966.
———. "The Scythians." In *Selected Poems*, translated by Jon Stallworthy and Peter France, 111–14. Manchester: Carcanet Press, 2000.
Bochkarev, S. G. "'Bydlo' kak kliuchevoe slovo runeta." *Politicheskaia lingvistika* 3, no. 41 (2012): 17–26. https://gist.github.com/demidovakatya/35645a547643ba9 1a9d2089674526501.
Bodin, Per-Arne. "Russian Geopolitical Discourse: On Pseudomorphism, Phantom Pains, and Simulacra." In *Eurasia 2.0: Russian Geopolitics in the Age of New Media*, edited by Mark Bassin and Mikhail Suslov, 167–84. Lanham, MD: Lexington Books, 2016.
Bogdanov, Konstantin A. *Vox populi: Fol'klornye zhanry sovetskoi kul'tury*. Moscow: Novoe literaturnoe obozrenie, 2009.
Boiko, Mikhail. "Viktor Pelevin: Bor'ba orkov za svobodu obrechena." December 2011. http://www.centrasia.ru/newsA.php?st=1324094880.
Borenstein, Eliot. "Defying Interpretation: Allegory and Ideology in Yuri Olesha's *Envy*." *Russian Literature* 49 (2001): 25–42.
———. *Men without Women: Masculinity and Revolution in Russian Fiction, 1917–1929*. Durham, NC: Duke University Press, 2000.
———. "Our Borats, Our Selves: Yokels and Cosmopolitans on the Global Stage." *Slavic Review* 67, no. 1 (2008): 1–7.
———. *Overkill: Sex and Violence in Contemporary Russian Popular Culture*. Ithaca, NY: Cornell University Press, 2008.
———. *Plots against Russia: Conspiracy and Fantasy after Socialism*. Ithaca, NY: Cornell University Press, 2019.
———. "Public Offerings: MMM and the Marketing of Melodrama." In *Consuming Russia*, edited by Adele Marie Barker, 49–75. Durham, NC: Duke University Press, 1999.
Bourdieu, Pierre. *Distinction: A Social Critique of the Judgement of Taste*, translated by Richard Nice. Cambridge, MA: Harvard University Press, 1987.
Boym, Svetlana. *The Future of Nostalgia*. New York: Basic Books, 2002.
Bozovic, Marijeta. "Party Like a Russian." *All the Russias*. October 3, 2016. http://jordanrussiacenter.org/news/party-like-russian/.
Brin, David. "The Lord of the Rings: J. R. R. Tolkien vs. the Modern Age." In his *Through Stranger Eyes: Reviews, Introductions, Tributes and Iconoclasitc Essays*. Ann Arbor, MI: Nimble Books, 2010.
Bulgakov, Mikhail. *Heart of a Dog*, translated by Mirra Ginsburg. New York: Grove Press, 1994.
Bykov, Dmitrii. *Living Souls*, translated by Cathy Porter. Richmond: Alma Books, 2010.
———. "Sovetskoe—znachit shampanskoe!" *Moskovskaia pravda*. September 9, 2005.
———. "Vatnik i nenavist'." RuFabula.com. January 6, 2015. https://rufabula.com/author/anton-chadsky/264.
———. "Vnuk 'sovka': Anton Chadskii o iavlenii i poiavlenii 'Vatnika'." November 25, 2014. https://www.newkaliningrad.ru/news/politics/4821328-vnuk-sovka-anton-chadskiy-o-yavlenii-i-poyavlenii-vatnika.html.
Cassiday, Julie, and Emily D. Johnson. "A World Without Safe-Words: Fifty Shades of Russian Grey." *Journal of Popular Romance*

Studies 9 (March 30, 2020). http://www.jprstudies.org/2020/03/a-world-without-safe-words-fifty-shades-of-russian-grey/.

Chelcea, Liviu, and Oana Drujta. "Zombie Socialism and the Rise of Neoliberalism in Post-Socialist Central and Eastern Europe." *Eurasian Geography and Economics* 57, nos. 4–5 (2016): 521–44.

Chen, Adrian. "The Agency." *New York Times Magazine*. June 7, 2015. https://www.nytimes.com/2015/06/07/magazine/the-agency.html.

Chernov, Sergei. "Internet Troll Operation Uncovered in St. Petersburg." *St. Petersburg Times*. September 18, 2013. https://web.archive.org/web/20130922072019/http://www.sptimes.ru/story/38052.

Chernyshova, Natalya. *Soviet Consumer Culture in the Brezhnev Era*. New York: Routledge, 2013.

Chess, K. *Famous Men Who Never Lived*. Portland, OR: Tin House Books, 2019.

Clark, Katerina. *The Soviet Novel: History as Ritual*, 3rd ed. Bloomington: Indiana University Press, 2000.

Clover, Charles. *Black Wind, White Snow: The Rise of Russia's New Nationalism*. New Haven: Yale University Press, 2016.

Creative Association of Orthodox Writers, Tula (Tvorcheskoe ob"edinenie pravoslavnykh pisatelei). "Ia Vatnik avtor A. Lukin, chit. V. Aleshin." https://www.youtube.com/watch?v=a5iQYuLqKLA.

Cronin, Justin. *The Passage*. New York: Ballantine, 2011.

Davidzon, Vladislav. "A Requiem for Russia's Last Great Dissident, Valeriya Novodvorskaya." *Tablet*. October 14, 2014. https://www.tabletmag.com/jewish-news-and-politics/186205/valeriya-novodvorskaya.

Dazhunts, El'vira. "Okno v Parizh skoro opiat' otkroetsia." *Nevskoe vremia*. March 18, 2020. https://nvspb.ru/2014/11/14/okno-v-parij-skoro-opyat-otkroetsya-55965.

De Khegel, Isabelle. "Sokurov's *Russian Ark*: Reflections on the Russia/Europe Theme." In *Russia and Its Other(s) on Film: Screening Intercultural Dialogue*, edited by Stephen Hutchings, 77–94. New York: Palgrave, 2008.

deceptors. "Va vsem vinovatye russkie orki, i lichno VV, razbor golubogo breda." *LiveJournal*. June 13, 2016. https://urb-a.livejournal.com/12371043.html.

"A Desperate Siberian Gamble." *Telegraph*. March 6, 1999. https://www.telegraph.co.uk/culture/4716975/A-desperate-Siberian-gamble.html.

Devlin, Anne Marie. "Lard-Eaters, Gay-ropeans, Sheeple, and Prepositions: Lexical and Syntactical Devices Employed to Position the Other in Russian Online Political Forums." *Russian Journal of Communication* 9, no. 1 (2017): 53–70.

Draitser, Emil. *Making War, Not Love: Gender and Sexuality in Russian Humor*. New York: Palgrave, 1999.

———. "The New Russians' Jokelore: Genesis and Sociological Interpretations." *Demokratizatsiya* 9, no. 3 (2001): 446–60.

———. *Taking Penguins to the Movies: Ethnic Humor in Russia*. Detroit: Wayne State University Press, 1998.

Dubchek, Viktor. *Krasnyi padavan*. Moscow: Yauza-Press, 2012.

Dubogrei, Vitalii. "'Zvezdnye voiny' v SSSR: Obzor sovetskoi pressy." *LiveJournal*. December 17, 2016. https://dubikvit.livejournal.com/502707.html.

Dubov, Iulii. *Bol'shaia paika*. Moscow: Vagrius, 2002.

Dudukina, Lena. "Kto i zachem reshil 'bombit Voronezh,' ili pochemu prizhilsia etot mem." *Radio Svoboda*. September 8, 2018. https://www.svoboda.org/a/29463330.html.

Dunham, Vera S. *In Stalin's Time: Middleclass Values in Soviet Fiction*. Enlarged and updated ed. Durham, NC: Duke University Press, 1990.

Dunn, Elizabeth Cullen, and Katherine Verdery. "Postsocialism." In *Emerging Trends in the Social and Behavioral Sciences: An Interdisciplinary, Searchable, and Linkable Resource*. Hoboken: Wiley Online Library, 2015. https://doi.org/10.1002/9781118900772.etrds0261.

Elizarov, Mikhail. *The Librarian*, translated by Andrew Bromfield. London: Pushkin Press, 2015.

———. "Orkskaia." *LiveJournal*. https://ru-elizarov.livejournal.com/326546.html.

———. *Pasternak*. Moscow: Ad Marginem, 2008.

Ellis, Bret Easton. *American Psycho*. New York: Knopf, 1991.

Eng, David L., and Shinhee Han. "A Dialogue on Racial Melancholia." *Psychoanalytic Dialogues* 10, no. 4 (2000): 667–700.

———. *Racial Melancholia, Racial Dissociation: On the Social and Psychic Lives of Asian Americans*. Durham, NC: Duke University Press, 2019.

Englund, Will. "Russian TV Channel Takes Flak Just for Asking: 'Should Leningrad Have Surrendered?'" *Washington Post*. January 30, 2014. https://www.washingtonpost.com/world/europe/russian-tv-channel-takes-flak-just-for-asking-should-leningrad-have-surrendered/2014/01/30/c1455812-89c0-11e3-833c-33098f9e5267_story.html.

Engstrom, Maria. "Contemporary Russian Messianism and New Russian Foreign Policy." *Contemporary Security Policy* 35, no. 3 (2014): 356–79.

Epshtein, Mikhail N. "Sovki i drugie: K istorii i znacheniiu slova 'sovka.'" *Topos*. October 8, 2008. https://www.topos.ru/article/6455.

———. *Velikaia sov'*. Samara: Bakhrakh-M, 2006.

Epstein [Epshtein], Mikhail N. *After the Future: The Paradoxes of Postmodernism and Contemporary Russian Culture*, translated by Anessa Miller-Pogacar. Amherst: University of Massachusetts Press, 1995.

Erlich, David. "'Bright' Review: Netflix's First Blockbuster Is the Worst Movie of 2017." *IndieWire*. December 10, 2017. https://www.indiewire.com/2017/12/bright-review-netflix-will-smith-max-landis-david-ayer-worst-movie-2017-1201909960/.

Etkind, Alexander. "Magical Historicism." In *Russian Literature since 1991*, edited by Evgeny Dobrenko and Mark Lipovetsky, 104–19. Cambridge: Cambridge University Press, 2017.

———. *Warped Mourning: Stories of the Undead in the Land of the Unburied*. Stanford, CA: Stanford University Press, 2013.

Frankfurt, Harry. *On Bullshit*. Princeton, NJ: Princeton University Press, 2005.

Freidin, Gregory. "Romans into Italians: Russian National Identity in Transition." *Stanford Slavic Studies* 7 (1993): 241–74.

Furmanov, Dmitrii. *Chapaev*. Moscow: Eksmo, 2013.

Gardner, John. *Grendel*. New York: Vintage, 1989.

Genis, Aleksandr. "Sovki i vatniki." *Radio Svoboda*. June 30, 2014. https://www.svoboda.org/a/25438392.html.

Gilburd, Eleonory. *To See Paris and Die: The Soviet Lives of Western Culture*. Cambridge, MA: Belknap, 2018.

Gilman, Sander L. *Jewish Self-Hatred: Anti-Semitism and the Hidden Language of Jews*. Baltimore: Johns Hopkins University Press, 1990.

"Google ob"iasniaet perevod Rossii kak 'Mordor' sboem v algoritmakh." BBC.com. January 4, 2016. https://www.bbc.com/russian/news/2016/01/160105_google_translate_russia_mordor.

Gordon, Michael R. "Post-Communist Russia Plumbs Its Soul, in Vain, for New Vision." *New York Times*. March 31, 1998. https://www.nytimes.

com/1998/03/31/world/post-communist-russia-plumbs-its-soul-in-vain-for-new-vision.html.

Goscilo, Helena. "Popular Image of the New Russians: Seen through Class, Darkly." Washington, DC: National Council for Eurasian and East European Research. November 16, 1998.

Govrin. "Russkie—orki." March 1, 2009. https://govrin.diary.ru/p62909272.htm?oam#form.

Graham, Seth. *Resonant Dissonance: The Russian Joke in Cultural Context*. Evanston, IL: Northwestern University Press, 2009.

———. "The Wages of Syncretism: Folkloric New Russians and Post-Soviet Popular Culture." *Russian Review* 62, no. 1 (2003): 37–53. https://doi.org/10.1111/1467-9434.00262.

Gudkov, Lev. *Negativnaia identichnost': Stat'i 1997–2002*. Moscow: Novoe literaturnoe obozrenie, 2004.

Halford, Macy. "Harry Potter and Religion." *New Yorker*. November 4, 2010. https://www.newyorker.com/books/page-turner/harry-potter-and-religion.

Hayek, F. A. *The Road to Serfdom: Text and Documents. The Definitive Edition*. Chicago: University of Chicago Press, 2007.

heideg (Yarovrat). "Orkizm." *LiveJournal*. November 18, 2011. http://heideg.livejournal.com/6845.html?thread=2412989.

Heldt, Barbara. *Terrible Perfection: Women and Russian Literature*. Bloomington: Indiana University Press, 1987.

Heller, Mikhail. *Cogs in the Soviet Wheel: The Formation of Soviet Man*. London: Collins Harvill, 1988.

Hodes, James Mendez. "Orcs, Britons, and the Martial Race Myth. Part I: A Species Built for Racial Terror." January 14, 2019. https://jamesmendezhodes.com/blog/2019/1/13/orcs-britons-and-the-martial-race-myth-part-i-a-species-built-for-racial-terror.

Hooker, Mark T. *Tolkien through Russian Eyes*. Zollikofen, Switzerland: Walking Tree Publishers, 2003.

Ilf, Alexandra. "Foreword." In Ilya Ilf and Evgeny Petrov, *The Twelve Chairs*, translated by Anne O. Fisher. Evanston, IL: Northwestern University Press, 2011.

Isenberg, Nancy. *White Trash: The 400-Year Untold History of Class in America*. New York: Penguin, 2017.

Jefferson, Ed. "'Lord of the Rings Is Racist about Orcs' Is Not an Important New Front in the Culture War." *New Statesman*. November 27, 2018. https://www.newstatesman.com/culture/books/2018/11/lord-rings-racist-about-orcs-not-important-new-front-culture-war.

Jemisin, N. K. "From the Mailbag: The Unbearable Baggage of Orcing." NKJemisin.com. February 13, 2013. http://nkjemisin.com/2013/02/from-the-mailbag-the-unbearable-baggage-of-orcing/.

Jenkins, Henry, with Ravi Purushotma, Margaret Weigel, Katie Clinton, and Alice J. Robison. *Confronting the Challenges of Participatory Culture: Media Education for the 21st Century*. Cambridge, MA: MIT Press, 2009.

Jigoulov, Vadim. *A Record of Interesting Choices: Tales of a Post-Soviet Man in the West*. Self-published via Lulu.com, 2014.

Johnson, Emily D. "Exploring His/Her Library: Reading and Books in Russian Romance." *Journal of Popular Romance Studies* 9 (2020). https://www.jprstudies.org/2020/03/exploring-his-her-library-reading-and-books-in-russian-romance/.

Jovic, Dejan. "Fear of Becoming Minority as a Motivator of Conflict in the Former Yugoslavia." *Balkonologie* 5, no. 1–2 (December 2001). https://journals.openedition.org/balkanologie/674#text.

Kalashnikov, Maksim, and Iurii Krupnov. *Gnev orka: Amerika protiv Rossii*. Moscow: AST, 2003.

Kalinin, Ilya. "Nostalgic Modernization: The Soviet Past as a 'Historical Horizon.'" *Slavonica* 17, no. 2 (2011): 156–66.

Karpova, Anna. "Sozdatel' 'Vatnika' Anton Chadskii: Kak ia stal rusofobom." *Snob*. October 14, 2014. https://snob.ru/selected/entry/82278.

Karsanova, Ekaterina. "Bednyi platit dvazhdy: U rossiskikh nalogoplatel'shchikov zabrali den'gi za udovol'stvie uvidet' fil'm Nikity Mikhalkova 'Sibirskii tsiriul'nik." *Moskovskie novosti*. January 3, 2000. http://www.compromat.ru/page_10483.htm.

Kartseva, Elena. *Gollivud 70-kh*. Moscow: Iskusstvo, 1987.

Kazarin, Pavel. "Ukraina Tolkina protiv Ukrainy Martina." *Snob*. July 28, 2014. https://snob.ru/profile/27147/blog/79017.

Kehe, Jason. "The Hidden, Wildly NSFW Scandal of the Hugo Nominations." *Wired*. April 6, 2017. https://www.wired.com/2017/04/hugo-nominations-who-is-stix-hiscock/.

Khort, Igor' Anatolevich. *Shakhter*. Electronic text, current URL unavailable.

Kobrin, Kirill. "The Death of the Post-Soviet Project in Russia." Open Democracy. October 19, 2016. https://www.opendemocracy.net/en/odr/death-of-post-soviet-project-in-russia/.

———. "Smert' postsovetskogo proekta. Chast' 2. Nostalgiia atomov po molekulam." Colta.ru. December 21, 2016. https://www.colta.ru/articles/society/13458-smert-postsovetskogo-proekta-chast-2-nostalgiya-atomov-po-molekulam.

Kolina, Elena. *Dnevniki novoi russkoi*. Moscow: AST, 2010.

Kondrat'eva, Elena. *Milliarder 1: Ledovaia lovushka*. Moscow: Populiarnaia literatura, 2010.

Korobov-Latyntsev, Andrei. "Kto takie russkie orki?" Syg.ma. December 30, 2017. https://syg.ma/@atpernat8/kto-takiie-russkiie-orki.

Krylova, Anna. "Imagining Socialism in the Soviet Century." *Social History* 42, no. 3 (2017): 315–41.

"Kuda delis' novye russkie?" *Kommersant vlast'*, no. 34. September 2, 2002. https://www.kommersant.ru/doc/338863.

Kurii, Sergei. "Kak gruppa BRAVO sozdala svoi khity pro Vasiu, koroliam Oranzhevoe leto, i Oranzhevyi galstuk? Ko dniu rozhdeniia Evgeniia Khavtana." *Shkola zhizni*. October 16, 2014. https://shkolazhizni.ru/culture/articles/69428/.

Larsen, Susan. "National Identity, Cultural Authority, and the Post-Soviet Blockbuster: Nikita Mikhalkov and Aleksei Balabanov." *Slavic Review* 62, no. 3 (2003): 491–511.

Laruelle, Marlene. *In the Name of the Nation: Nationalism and Politics in Contemporary Russia*. New York: Palgrave, 2009.

———. "Larger, Higher, Farther North . . . : Geographical Metanarratives of the Nation in Russia." *Eurasian Geography and Economics* 53, no. 5 (2012): 557–74.

———. *Russian Eurasianism: An Ideology of Empire*. Baltimore: Johns Hopkins University Press, 2012.

Lemon, Alaina. *Technologies for Intuition: Cold War Circles and Telepathic Rays*. Berkeley: University of California Press, 2017.

Lepore, Jill. "A New Americanism: Why a Nation Needs a National Story." *Foreign Affairs*. March–April 2019. https://www.foreignaffairs.com/articles/united-states/2019-02-05/new-americanism-nationalism-jill-lepore.
Leusenko, Oleg. "Russie orki unichtozhili pamiatnyi znak nevinnym zhertvam NKVD." *LiveJournal*. May 31, 2016.
Levada, Iurii. "'Chelovek sovetskii': Problema rekonstruktsii iskhodnykh form." *Monitoring obshchestvennogo mneniia: Ekonomicheskie i sotsial'nye peremeny* 52, no. 2 (2001): 7–16.
Lindquist, Galina. "Spirits and Souls of Business: New Russians, Magic, and the Esthetics of Kitsch." *Journal of Material Culture* 7, no. 3 (2002): 329–43.
Lipovetsky, Mark. "New Russians as a Cultural Myth." *Russian Review* 62, no. 1 (2003): 54–71.
———. "Post-Sots: Transformations of Socialist Realism in the Popular Culture of the Recent Period." *Slavic and East European Journal* 48, no. 3 (2004): 356–77.
Liu, Hailong. "Love Your Nation the Way You Love an Idol: New Media and the Emergence of Fandom Nationalism." In *From Cyber-Nationalism to Fandom Nationalism: The Case of Diba Expedition in China*, edited by Hailong Liu, 125–47. New York: Routledge, 2019.
LordByronic. "Note: The Following Has Hella Generalizations. If You Feel Like This Doesn't Apply to You, Congratulations, Let Me Slow Clap It Out." 2015. https://np.reddit.com/r/gallifrey/comments/2u73cg/tumblrbashing_why_or_why_not/co5ucsk/.
Loshak, Andrei. Facebook post. April 5, 2022. https://www.facebook.com/andrey.loshak.
Lukin, Andrei. "Ia Vatnik." https://www.stihi.ru/2015/04/28/1439.
Maguire, Gregory. *Wicked: The Life and Times of the Wicked Witch of the West*. New York: William Morrow, 2000.
Makovicky, Nicolette. *Neoliberalism, Personhood, and Postsocialism*. New York: Routledge, 2016.
Markova, Olga. "When Philology Becomes Ideology: The Russian Perspective of J. R. R. Tolkien," translated by Mark. T. Hooker. *Tolkien Studies* 1 (2004): 163–70.
Maslova, Lidiia. "'Sibirskii tsiriul'nik' budet pakhnut' seldom." *Kommersant*. February 9, 1999. https://www.kommersant.ru/doc/212657.
Mayakovsky, Vladimir. *The Bedbug*. In *Plays*, translated by Guy Daniels. Evanston, IL: Northwestern University Press, 1968.
Medvedev, Sergei. "Fenomenologiia bydla." *Iskusstvo kino*, no. 3 (March 2012). https://old.kinoart.ru/archive/2012/03/fenomenologiya-bydla.
Meshalkin, Leonid. *Orki i russkie—brat'ia navek!* Self-published e-book. 2014.
Mettan, Guy. *Creating Russophobia: From the Great Religious Schism to the Anti-Putin Hysteria*. New York: Clarity Press, 2017.
Miéville, China. "Tolkien—Middle Earth Meets Middle England." *Socialist Review*. January 2002. http://www.socialistreview.org.uk/article.php?articlenumber=7813.
"Mikhalkova vydvinuli na 'Oskar.'" *Kommersant*. November 4, 1998. https://www.kommersant.ru/doc/208176.
Miller, Laura. "Middle-Earth according to Mordor." Salon.com. February 15, 2011. https://www.salon.com/2011/02/15/last_ringbearer/.
Minkova, Yuliya. "The Squid and the Whale *a la Russe*: Navigating the 'Uncanny' in Dmitry Bykov's *ZhD*." *Russian Review* 72, no. 2 (2013): 285–302.
Mochalov, Pavel. *Tankist Mordora*. Moscow: Eksmo, 2017.

Molchanova, Mariia. "'Novye russkie' v detaliakh." *Diletant*. September 7, 2016. https://diletant.media/articles/30746058/.

Moorcock, Michael. *Wizardry and Wild Romance: A Study of Epic Fantasy*. London: Victor Gollancz, 1987.

Morimoto, Lori Hitchcock, and Bertha Chin. "Reimaging the Imagined Community: Online Media Fandoms in the Age of Global Convergence." In *Fandom: Identities and Communities in a Mediated World*, 2nd ed., edited by Jonathan Gray, Cornel Sandvoss, and C. Lee Harrington, 174–88. New York: New York University Press, 2017.

Morozov, Viacheslav. *Russia's Postcolonial Identity: A Subaltern Empire in a Eurocentric World*. New York: Palgrave Macmillan, 2015.

Muller, Martin. "Goodbye, Postsocialism!" *Europe-Asia Studies* 71, no. 4 (2019): 533–50.

Naydenova, Kristiana. "Squatting Slavs: A Culture, a Stereotype, or Just a Meme?" *Diggit Magazine*. https://www.diggitmagazine.com/articles/squatting-slavs-culture-stereotype-or-just-meme.

Nevzorov, Aleksandr. "Vezhlivye orki." *Snob*. December 22, 2014. https://snob.ru/selected/entry/85572/.

Newitz, Annalee, and Matt Wray, eds. *White Trash: Race and Class in America*. New York: Routledge, 1997.

Nicholls, Stan. *Orcs*. New York: Orbit, 2008.

Niedowski, Erika. "'Borat'? Russia and Kazakhstan Are Not Amused." *Baltimore Sun*. November 10, 2006.

Noordenbos, Boris. *Post-Soviet Literature and the Search for Russian Identity*. New York: Palgrave, 2015.

Norris, Stephen M. *Blockbuster History in the New Russia: Movies, Memory, and Patriotism*. Bloomington: Indiana University Press, 2012.

Novak, Joseph. *Homo sowjeticus: Der Mensch unter Hammer und Sichel*. Bern: Alfred Shertz, 1962.

obsession_inc. "Affirmational Fandom vs. Transformational Fandom." June 1, 2009. https://obsession-inc.dreamwidth.org/82589.html.

Olesha, Yuri. *Envy*, translated by Marian Schwartz. New York: NYRB Classics, 2004.

Orwell, George. *1984*. New York: Signet, 1961.

Osminkin, Roman. Facebook post, December 27, 2019. https://www.facebook.com/profile.php?id=100000332535250.

Oushakine, Serguei Alex. "The Fatal Splitting: Symbolic Anxiety in Post-Soviet Russia." *Ethnos: Journal of Anthropology* 66, no. 3 (2001): 291–319.

———. "In the State of Post-Soviet Aphasia: Symbolic Development in Contemporary Russia." *Europe-Asia Studies* 52, no. 6 (2000): 991–1016.

———. *The Patriotism of Despair: Nation, War, and Loss in Russia*. Ithaca, NY: Cornell University Press, 2009.

———. "The Quantity of Style: Imaginary Consumption in the New Russia." *Theory, Culture, and Society* 17, no. 5 (2000): 97–120.

"'Party Like a Russian'": Robbi Uil'iams vypustil kip o vessel'e po-russki." *Vesti*. September 30, 2016. https://www.youtube.com/watch?v=geuYtygbIn0.

"Pchela iz 'Brigady' nazval serial prestupleniem protiv Rossii." Lenta.ru. January 30, 2018. https://lenta.ru/news/2018/01/30/mi_s_pervogo_klassa_vmeste/.

Pelevin, Victor [Viktor]. *Buddha's Little Finger*, translated by Andrew Bromfield. New York: Penguin, 2001.

———. *Homo Zapiens*, translated by Andrew Bromfield. New York: Penguin, 2002.

———. *S.N.U.F.F.*, translated by Andrew Bromfield. London: Gollancz, 2015.

Pelevin, Viktor. "Dzhon Faulz i tragediia russkogo liberalizma." 1993. http://pelevin.nov.ru/rass/pe-jon/1.html.
Perumov, Nik. *Kol'tso t'my*. 3 vols. St. Petersburg: Azbuka, 1996.
Pilkington, Hilary. *Russia's Youth and Its Culture: A Nation's Constructors and Constructed*. London: Routledge, 1994.
Pilkington, Hilary, Elena Omel'chenko, Moya Flynn, and Uliana Bliudina. *Looking West? Cultural Globalization and Russian Youth Cultures*. University Park: Pennsylvania State University Press, 2012.
Platt, Kevin M. F. "The Post-Soviet Is Over: On Reading the Ruins." *Republic of Letters* 1, no. 1. December 19, 2008. https://arcade.stanford.edu/rofl/post-soviet-over-reading-ruins.
———. "Zachem izuchat' antropologiiu? Vzgliad gumanitariia. Vmesto manifesta," translated by A. Markov. *Novoe literaturnoe obozrenie*, no. 106 (2010): 13–26.
"Pochemu novye russkie nosili imenno malinovye pidzhaki?" Factroom. October 27, 2018. https://www.factroom.ru/rossiya/pochemu-novye-russkie-nosili-imenno-malinovye-pidzhaki.
Polyanskaya, Anna, Andrei Krivov, and Ivan Lomko. "Commissars of the Internet: The FSB at the Computer." *La Russophobe*. September 16, 2006. http://lrtranslations.blogspot.com/2007/02/commissars-of-internet.html.
Ponomareva, Alia. "'Zdes' stalo nechem dyshat': Rezhisser Iurii Mamin emigriroval v SShA." *Radio Svoboda*. March 25, 2019. https://www.svoboda.org/a/29840747.html.
Prilepin, Zakhar. Facebook post. February 26, 2016. https://www.facebook.com/zaharprilepin/posts/1097238960320424.
Putin, Vladimir. "Postsovetskii period v zhizni Rossii zavershen, vperedi novyi etap razvitiia strany." ITAR-TASS, April 11, 2012. http://itar-tass.com/arhiv/542941.
Quilligan, Maureen. *The Language of Allegory: Defining the Genre*. Ithaca, NY: Cornell University Press, 1992.
Razlogov, Kirill. *Konveier grez i psikhologicheskaia voina*. Moscow: Politicheskaia literatura, 1986.
Rann, Jamie. "How to Make a Russian Salad: Food, Art and Patriotism on the Russian Internet." *Digital Icons*, no. 16 (2016): 51–78.
Reid, Robin Anne. "Race in Tolkien Studies: A Bibliographic Essay." In *Tolkien and Alterity*, edited by Christopher Vaccaro and Yvette Kisor, 33–74. New York: Palgrave, 2017.
Reitter, Paul. *On the Origins of Jewish Self-Hatred*. Princeton, NJ: Princeton University Press, 2012.
Remnick, David. *Lenin's Tomb: The Last Days of the Soviet Empire*. New York: Vintage, 1994.
———. "Putin's Pique." *New Yorker*. March 10, 2014. https://www.newyorker.com/magazine/2014/03/17/putins-pique.
Rhys, Jean. *Wide Sargasso Sea*. New York: W. W. Norton, 2016.
Rich, Joshua. "Is No. 1! 'Borat' Breaks Records." *Entertainment Weekly*. November 3, 2006. https://ew.com/article/2006/11/03/no-1-borat-breaks-records/.
Rivituso, Chris. "For Artist, Leaving Lenin Behind Is a Piece of Cake." *Moscow Times*. April 2, 1998. https://www.themoscowtimes.com/archive/for-artist-leaving-lenin-behind-is-a-piece-of-cake.
"Robbi Uil'iams ob"iasnil 'Vestiam,' zachem snial klip pro russkikh." *Vesti*. October 27, 2016. https://www.youtube.com/watch?v=oNM8mJlzZEk.
Robin, Ron Theodore. *The Making of the Cold War Enemy: Culture and Politics in the Military-Intellectual Complex*. Princeton, NJ: Princeton University Press, 2003.

Rogers, Douglas. "Postsocialisms Unbound: Connections, Critiques, Comparisons." *Slavic Review* 69, no. 1 (2010): 1–15.
Saprykin, Iurii. "20 let Putina: Transformatsiia obshchestva." *Vedomosti*. August 12, 2019. https://www.vedomosti.ru/opinion/articles/2019/08/13/808649-20-let-putina.
Saprykin, Yury [Iurii]. "20 Years of Vladimir Putin: How Russian Society Has Changed." *Moscow Times*. August 20, 2019. https://www.themoscowtimes.com/2019/08/20/20-years-of-vladimir-putin-how-russian-society-has-changed-a66930.
Saunders, Robert A. *The Many Faces of Sacha Baron Cohen: Politics, Parody, and the Battle over Borat*. Lanham, MD: Lexington Books, 2009.
Schechter, Brandon. "What Russians Really Think When They Hear the Word 'Nazi.'" *All the Russias*. March 29, 2022. https://jordanrussiacenter.org/news/what-russians-think-when-they-hear-the-word-nazi/#.Yl7LgC-B3s1.
Schimpfössl, Elisabeth. *Rich Russians: From Oligarchs to Bourgeoisie*. Oxford: Oxford University Press, 2018.
sensei-yoda. "Nikogda takogo ne bylo—i vot opiat' . . . Otkrytoe pis'mo Tine Kandelaki." *LiveJournal*. June 22, 2019. http://sensei-yoda.blogspot.com/2019/06/blog-post_1486.html.
Shafarevich, Igor. *Rusofobiia*. Algoritm, 2011.
Sharafutdinova, Gulnaz. *The Red Mirror: Putin's Leadership and Russia's Insecure Identity*. Oxford: Oxford University Press, 2020.
———. "R.I.P. 'Soviet Man': Scrapping Homo Sovieticus in the Spirit of Yuri Levada." Washington, DC: Wilson Center. April 29, 2019. https://www.wilsoncenter.org/blog-post/rip-soviet-man-scrapping-homo-sovieticus-the-spirit-yuri-levada.
———. "Was There a 'Simple Soviet' Person? Debating the Politics and Sociology of 'Homo Sovieticus.'" *Slavic Review* 78, no. 1 (2019): 173–95.
Shkenev, Sergei. *Krasnyi vlastelin*. Moscow: Eksmo, 2014.
Shlikhar, Tetyana. "Russia on the Margins?" In *Cinemasaurus: Russian Film in Contemporary Context*, edited by Nancy Condee, Alexander Prokhorov, and Elena Prokhorova, 156–89. Boston: Academic Studies Press, 2020.
Sidorov, Dmitri. "Post-Imperial Third Romes: Resurrections of a Russian Orthodox Geopolitical Metaphor." *Geopolitics* 11, no. 2 (2006): 317–47.
Sinyavsky, Andrei. *The Russian Intelligentsia*, translated by Lynn Visson. New York: Columbia University Press, 1997.
Skvirskaja, Vera. "'Information Turned Entertainment': Images of the Enemy and Conspicuous Patriotic Consumption in Russia." *Studies in Russian, Eurasian, and Central European New Media* 16 (2016): 9–29.
Sleptsov, Ivan. "Kosmos Tolkina." *Nezavisimaia gazeta*. January 30, 1997.
Smith, Hedrick. *The New Russians*. New York: Random House, 2012.
———. *The Russians*. New York: Times Books, 1978.
Smith-Peter, Susan. "A Russian Plan for the Genocide of the Ukrainian People." *Medium*. April 5, 2022. https://medium.com/@jkmuf1861/a-russian-plan-for-the-genocide-of-the-ukrainian-people-8c866bed9c63.
Smolkin, Victoria. *A Sacred Space Is Never Empty: A History of Soviet Atheism*. Princeton, NJ: Princeton University Press, 2018.
Soboleva, Maja. "The Concept of the 'New Soviet Man' and Its Short History." *Canadian-American Slavic Studies* 51, no. 1 (2017): 64–85.
Sol' zemli. "Varkfraft." https://vk.com/wall-1104113_53526.
Sorokin, Vladimir. *Day of the Oprichnik*, translated by Jamey Gambrell. New York: Farrar, Straus, and Giroux, 2006.

———. *Sakharnyi Kreml'*. Moscow: AST, 2008.
Souch, Irina. *Popular Tropes of Identity in Contemporary Russian Television and Film*. London: Bloomsbury, 2017.
Spangler, Todd. "Netflix's 'Bright' Lands 11 Million U.S. Streaming Viewers over First Three Days." *Variety*. December 28, 2017. https://variety.com/2017/digital/news/netflix-bright-ratings-viewers-nielsen-1202649332/.
Steinberg, Mark. "Putin: Man of Mystery? Hardly." *History News Network*. April 13, 2014. http://hnn.us/article/155232.
Strauss, Neil. "Sacha Baron Cohen: The Man behind the Mustache." *Rolling Stone*. November 30, 2006. https://www.rollingstone.com/movies/movie-news/sacha-baron-cohen-the-man-behind-the-mustache-249539/.
Sturtevant, Paul B. *The Middle Ages in Popular Imagination: Memory, Film and Medievalism*. London: Bloomsbury, 2018.
———. "Race: The Original Sin of the Fantasy Genre." *Public Medievalist*. December 5, 2017. https://www.publicmedievalist.com/race-fantasy-genre/.
Suslov, Mikhail. *Geopolitical Imagination: Ideology and Utopia in Post-Soviet Russia*. Stuttgart: ibidem, 2020.
Tally, Robert T., Jr. "Let Us Now Praise Famous Orcs: Simple Humanity in Tolkien's Inhuman Creatures." *Mythlore* 29, no. 1–2 (2010): 17–28.
Timpf, Katherine. "Lord of the Rings Slammed for Perpetuating Racism through Depiction of Orcs." *National Review*. November 27, 2018. https://www.nationalreview.com/2018/11/lord-of-the-rings-slammed-for-perpetuating-racism-through-depiction-of-orcs/.
"Tolkien Was 'Racist' to Orcs? Sci-fi Author Echoes Dank Memes, Totally Unironically." rt.com. November 27, 2018. https://www.rt.com/news/445016-tolkien-racist-orcs-fantasy/.
Tolkin, Dzhon [J. R. R. Tolkien]. *Sodruzhestvo kol'tsa*, translated by Mariia Kamenkovich and Valerii Karrik. St. Petersburg: Terra/Azbuka, 1994.
Tolstaya, Tatyana. *The Slynx*, translated by Jamey Gambrell. New York: New York Review Books, 2000.
Tsygankov, Andrei. *Russophobia: The Anti-Russian Lobby and American Foreign Policy*. New York: Palgrave, 2009.
Tuchkov, Vladimir. *Smert' prikhodit po Internetu*. Moscow: Novoe literaturnoe obozrenie, 2001.
"V Kieve razrezali torta v vide russkogo mladentsa." January 14, 2015. https://www.youtube.com/watch?v=gwBO22yDg94.
Vasilieva, Natalia, and Natalia Nekrasova. *Chernaia kniga Ardy*. Published multiple times in five different editions, ranging from two to eighteen volumes.
Verdery, Katherine. *What Was Socialism, and What Comes Next?* Princeton, NJ: Princeton University Press, 1996.
Vodolazkin, Eugene. *The Aviator*, translated by Lisa C. Hayden. New York: Oneworld Publications, 2018.
Volkov, Vadim. *Violent Entrepreneurs: The Use of Force in the Making of Russian Capitalism*. Ithaca, NY: Cornell University Press, 2002.
Von Bremzen, Anya. *Mastering the Art of Soviet Cooking: A Memoir of Food and Longing*. New York: Random House, 2013.
Wakamiya, Lisa Ryoko. "Post-Soviet Context and Trauma Studies." *Slavonica* 17, no. 2 (2011): 134–44.
Walker, Shaun. "Russia Scraps Plan for Eye of Sauron Art Installation." *The Guardian*. December 10, 2014. https://www.theguardian.com/world/2014/dec/10/russia-scraps-eye-of-sauron-art-installation.

———. "Russian War Film Set to Open Amid Controversy over Accuracy of Events." *The Guardian*. November 23, 2016. https://www.theguardian.com/film/2016/nov/23/russian-war-film-set-to-open-against-controversy-over-accuracy-of-events.

Weinhold, Florian. *Path of Blood: The Post-Soviet Gangster, His Mistress, and Their Others in Aleksei Balabanov's Genre Films*. North Charleston, SC: Reverlands Books, 2013.

Williams, Robbie. "Party Like a Russian." September 30, 2016. https://www.youtube.com/watch?v=MdYGQ7B0Vew.

Winters, Joseph R. *Hope Draped in Black: Race, Melancholy, and the Agony of Progress*. Durham, NC: Duke University Press, 2016.

Wray, Matt. *Not Quite White: White Trash and the Boundaries of Whiteness*. Durham, NC: Duke University Press, 2006.

Yablokov, Ilya. *Fortress Russia: Conspiracy Theories in the Post-Soviet World*. New York: Polity, 2018.

Yang, Gene. *American Born Chinese*. New York: First Second, 2006.

Yeskov, Kirill. *The Last Ringbearer*, translated by Yisroel Markov. *LiveJournal*, 2011. https://ymarkov.livejournal.com/280578.html.

Young, Helen. *Race and Popular Fantasy: Habits of Whiteness*. New York: Routledge, 2015.

Zamlelova, Svetlana. "Nam amerikantsy ob"iavili sanktsii." *Sovetskaia Rossiia*. December 30, 2014.

Zhogov, Dmitrii. "Otets Vatnika perebiraetsia v Odessu: Vkusen li russkoiazychnyi mladenets?" March 15, 2018. https://dumskaya.net/news/otetc-vatnika-perebiraetsya-v-odessu-ili-vkusnyy-083173/.

Zinoviev, Alexander. *Homo Sovieticus*, translated by Charles Johnson. New York: Paladin, 1986.

Zorich, Aleksandr. *Somnambula (1): Zvezda po imeni Solntse*. Moscow: Populiarnaia literatura, 2010.

Zubok, Vladislav. "Russia's Identity Quest." *Orbis* 49, no. 1 (2005): 183–93.

Index

1984 (Orwell), 109

access: money and, 117; role in post-Soviet era, 97; Soviet system and, 95, 96
Ackroyd, Dan, 25
affect theory, and concept of self-hatred, 4
affirmational fandom, 22; and reactionary defense of Tolkien, 131; and Russian Orc, 153; state-sponsored, Russian historiography under Putin as, 160–61; war in Ukraine as extreme real-life expression of, 23
African Americans, and racial melancholia, 6
Agamben, Giorgio, 35, 37
Ahmed, Sara, 4–6
Akhmatova, Anna, 114, 115
Akunin, Boris, 28
alienation: between elites and common people, Russia's history of, 68–69; of evil, Russian antisemitism as, 62; negative identities and process of, 16, 63, 67; *sovok*'s, from post-Soviet trends, 69
American Born Chinese (Yang), 26–27
American exceptionalism, and self-proclaimed Russian Orcs, 17, 137
American Psycho, New Russian compared to, 102
America protiv Rossii (Kalashnikov and Krupnov), 137–38
Anderson, Benedict, 20
Andropov, Yuri, 32
anekdoty (jokes): about Chukchi, 107, 166n2; about New Russians, 103–8, 166n9; characters populating, 48; political, in Soviet era, 103
anime fan culture, 21
Anninsky, Lev, 41
antisemitism, Russian: explanation for, 62; slur used in, 165n6; and war on Ukraine, 162
Asian Americans: anxieties of, 26–27; and racial melancholia, 6–7
Asimov, Isaac, 138
Atwood, Lynn, 27
Atwood, Margaret, 109

Balabanov, Aleksei, 105, 108
The Barber of Siberia (film), 154–59; affirmative messages of, 169n2; casting of, 155, 156, 169n1; cost of, 157; and Russian identity, renegotiation of, 156, 157–59; tagline from, 155, 157–58, 162
Baron Cohen, Sacha, 24–26, 80, 81
The Bedbug (Mayakovsky), 29–30, 98
Bellamy, Edward, 24, 25
Belostotsky, Gennady, 50
Bender, Ostap, 92–93
Benediktov, Kirill, 115
Berdiaev, Nikolai, 98
Berezovsky, Boris, 89
Bershidsky, Leonid, 146
Bezrukov, Sergei, 112
Bilbo, Theodore G., 131
Billionaire trilogy, 114–18, 119
Bimmer (film), 112
The Black Book of Arda (Vasilieva and Nekrasova), 136
Blok, Aleksandr: "The People and the Intelligentsia," 68; "The Scythians," 138, 149
Bobyr', Zinaida, 133
Bodrov, Sergei, Jr., 18
Bogdanov, Konstantin, 34
Boiko, Mikhail, 143
Bolshevism: approach to feminism, 27–28; and New Man, idea of, 28
Bond, James, Cold War plots in movies about, 123
Borat character, 24–26, 80, 81; Kazakhstan government's response to, 25, 26, 164n1; post-Soviet shame exemplified by, 26
Bozovic, Marijeta, 80–82
Bravo (band), 60–61, 66, 79
Brezhnev, Leonid, 32, 71
Brigada (film), 112–13, 114, 119
Bright (film), 168n9
Brin, David, 130, 132, 168n5
Bromfield, Andrew, 140, 142
The Bronze Horseman (Pushkin), 55
Brother (film), 105, 108
Buber, Martin, 103
Buddha's Little Finger (Pelevin), 66

INDEX

Bulgakov, Mikhail: *Heart of a Dog*, 29, 30; *The Master and Margarita*, 52
Bumer (film), 112
Burnt by the Sun (film), 56, 154
Bush, George W., 17, 137
Buslov, Pyotr, 112
Butler, Judith, 156
bydlo, 16, 63, 67–69; connection to self-hatred, 62, 69; Internet and, 165n14; national and global, 69; Orcs compared to, 143; as proxy for socioeconomic class, 79; television and, 69–72; as tool for alienation, 67
Bykov, Dmitrii, 23, 52, 53; *Justification*, 66; *Living Souls*, 16, 63, 64–67, 165n12; popularity of, 53; on *sovok*, 52, 69

capitalism: accumulation of wealth in, assumed rationality of, 88; management of scarcity in, 95; Marxist perspective on, 108
capitalism, Russian: criminality and, 108–9; injustice and deceit characterizing, 88, 97; New Russian as face of, 88, 98
Cassiday, Julie, 166n3
Chaadaev, Pyotr, 158
Chadsky, Anton, 77; public art action in Ukraine, 77–78; and Vatnik Internet meme, 72, 73–74, 75
Chapaev: jokes about, 48, 66; literary works about, 65–66
Chapaev (film), 66
Chapaev (Furmanov), 65
Chapaev and the Void (Pelevin), 66
Chaplin, Vsevolod, 121
Chekhov, Anton: *The Cherry Orchard*, 52, 53, 108; *The Three Sisters*, 108
Chen, Adrian, 151
chern' (term), 68
Chernaia kniga Ardy (Vasilieva and Nekrasova), 136
The Cherry Orchard (Chekhov), 52, 53, 108
Chess, K., 58
Chin, Bertha, 20
Chukchi, jokes about, 107, 166n2
Clark, Katerina, 110
class. *See* socioeconomic class
Clinton, Bill, 129
Colbert, Stephen, 75
Cold War, 122; dualistic storytelling popularized during, 122–23; politics of, entanglement with Western mass fantasy, 124–25; reversal of binaries of, Russian Orc and, 130; in Western popular culture, 122–23
common people: alienation between elites and, Russia's history of, 68–69; as *bydlo*, 67; as category under Soviet ideology, 61, 63; infatuation with, in 19th-century Russia, 68; post-Soviet types embodying disdain for, 61–63; as Vasyas/Vaskas, 61, 63, 64–67, 165n2
conservative nationalists, 22–23, 42–43
conspiracy theories: about Soviet collapse, 11; Russophobia as tool in, 62, 129, 165n4; and US elections of 2016, 151–52; and war in Ukraine, 162
consumer culture/consumption: negative identities defined in relation to, 51; New Russian and, 95, 103–6; *sovok* and, 17, 45, 49, 50, 51
Crimea, Russian annexation of, 12; appropriation of "Orc" epithet after, 140, 146; nationalists supporting, 16, 76
criminality: imaginary post-Soviet identities and, 16–17, 79; New Russian and, 17, 52, 79, 83, 106, 108–9, 112–13, 114; privatization in 1990s and, 94
Cronin, Justin, 166n3
culture: imaginary post-Soviet identities and, 16–17, 79; New Russian and, 100, 102, 106–7; Russian Orc and, 17; *sovok* and, 17, 69
curatorial fandom, 22. *See also* affirmational fandom

The Daily Show, right-wing person in, 75
The Day of the Oprichnik (Sorokin), 98
Dead Man's Bluff (film), 105, 108–9
Dead Souls (Gogol), 64, 68
Death by Internet (Tuchkov), 99–102, 118
DeLillo, Don, 82
Dilbert (comic strip), 25
dissidents, Brezhnev-era, 43
Donbas: as live-action-role-playing game (LARP), 23; as Orc homeland, 148, 149
Dontsov, Sergei, 55
Dostoevsky, Fyodor, 28
Dozhd TV, 22
Draitser, Emil, 103, 107
Dreiden, Sergei, 55
Dubchek, Viktor, 145–46
Dubin, Boris, 38
Dubov, Yuli, 89
Duncan, Andy, 131
Dunn, Elizabeth, 10–11
dystopia, New Man as product of, 29–32

effectiveness, imaginary post-Soviet identities and, 16–17, 79
egalitarianism, Soviet, 97; vs. access, 96; vs. elitism of educated urbanites, 61, 63; vs. post-Soviet capitalism, 97
Elizarov, Mikhail, 140–41; *The Librarian*, 140, 141; "Orkskaia" ("Orc Song"), 140–41, 143, 144, 146, 148, 149; *Pasternak*, 140

Eng, David L., 6, 7
Envy (Olesha), 30–32
Epstein, Mikhail, 41–42
Erofeev, Venedikt, 94
Erofeyev, Viktor, 37
Estingeev, Denis, 112
Ethnogenesis (literary project), 114–18, 167n5
ethnogenesis, theory of, 102, 114, 161
Etkind, Alexander, 7
EVE online fan fiction, 145
Everything Is Illuminated (film), 25
Eye of Sauron: as basilisk, 127; planned art installation in Moscow, 121–22, 128–29, 147

Famous Men Who Never Lived (Chess), 58
fandom, 20–21; nationalism compared to, 20, 21, 153; types of, 21–22, 153. *See also* affirmational fandom; transformational fandom
fantasy: allegorical potential of, 135; Cold War dualism and, 123; ideology as form of, 125, 138; politics compared to, 129; *Star Wars* (film series) as, 130
Fantasy Worlds website, 144
fascism: *The Lord of the Rings* (Tolkien) and connections to, 128, 134, 141; online trolls and espousal of, 127; Soviet use of term, 161
feminism, Bolshevik approach to, 27–28
feudalism: fantasies of New Russian and, 98–102; nostalgic, *The Lord of the Rings* (Tolkien) and, 130
Foer, Jonathan Safran, 25
Forster, E. M., 58
The Forsyth Saga (Galsworthy), 128
Foundation (Asimov), 138
Frankfurt, Harry, 91
Freud, Sigmund: on conflicts between ethnicities/nations, 21; on hatred as libidinal attachment, 4; impact on Russian audiences, 135; Russian revisionist reading of *The Lord of the Rings* (Tolkien) and, 151
Frolkov, Vladimir Georgievich ("Yarovrat"), 139–40
Fukuyama, Francis, 24
Furmanov, Dmitry, 65
Fyodorov, Nikolai, 135

Galsworthy, John, 128
Game of Thrones (TV series): ethical compromises of, 125; racial undertones of, 136
Gardner, John, 137
Gates, Bill, 88
gay propaganda law (2013), 19
Geller, Mikhail, 33

gender: of New Man, 27; of New Russian, 83–84; and post-Soviet identity constructs, 17–19. *See also* masculinity; women
Generation P (Pelevin), 127
Genis, Alexander, 41
Georgia, Russia's 2008 invasion of: and post-Soviet, declaration of end of, 12; and Voronezh bombing meme, 1
Gilman, Sander, 3, 4, 5
Global Orcs, 143
global unity, predictions regarding, 24
Gnev orca (Kalashnikov and Krupnov), 137–38
Goblin Studios, 141
Gogol, Nikolai: *Dead Souls*, 64, 68; influence on Tuchkov, 99
Goscilo, Helena, 107
Gradsky, Alexander, 40–41
Graham, Seth, 103, 107, 166n2, 166nn8–9
Griboyedov, Alexander, 77, 101
Gudkov, Lev, 6, 38, 63
Gulag, vatnik associated with, 72, 74
Gumilev, Lev, 167n6; in *Billionaire* trilogy, 114–18; ethnogenesis theory of, 102, 114, 161
Gumilev, Nikolai, 114

Han, Shinhee, 6, 7
The Handmaid's Tale (Atwood), 109
Harry Potter (Rowling): Anglo-Saxon values in, 124, 126, 135; fundamentalist US Protestants' objections to, 121; Russian audiences' response to, 124, 126, 128
hatred: complicated dynamic between self and other in, 4; role in conspiracy theories, 62; toward New Russians, 111; Vatnik associated with, 74, 75. *See also* self-hatred
Hayek, F. A., 98
Haynes, Todd, 156
Heart of a Dog (Bulgakov), 29
Heldt, Barbara, 31
"hereditary proletarian," category of, 61
heterotopia, political fantasies and, 129
Hitler, Adolf: in *Ethnogenesis* series, 115; representation in *The Lord of the Rings* (Tolkien), 134; in revisionist *Lord of the Rings* fan fiction, 136
The Hobbit (film series): Eye of Sauron art installation in honor of, 121–22, 128–29, 147; Russian nationalist review of, 147
homelessness crisis, post-Soviet, 16, 64
Homo sacer, 35, 37; vs. Homosos, 38
Homosos, 17, 34–38, 39; origins of term, 34, 40; *sovok* compared to, 34, 37, 40
Homo Sovieticus, 33–35; as Homosos, 17, 34–38; ideological function of, 39

INDEX

Homo Sovieticus (Zinoviev), 17, 34–37, 38, 94
Homo Zapiens (Pelevin), 127
Hooker, Mark T., 134
humanism, New Russians' reflexive rejection of, 104
humor: American, Russian *anekdoty* compared to, 48; centered on *sovok*, 45–48. *See also anekdoty; styob*

"I Am a Vatnik" (Lukin), 75–77
identity: imaginative formation of, 2, 19; Soviet collapse and crisis of, 2–3, 7, 157–58; Soviet experiment with, 27. *See also* identity constructs; negative identity
identity constructs, post-Soviet, 16, 19; axes for evaluation of, 16–17, 79; *The Barber of Siberia* (film) and, 156, 157–59; gender and, 17–19; as masks/performances, 8; melancholy and, 7; negative, 6, 63; pride and shame and, 3, 8, 15, 67; self-hatred and, 7, 15, 159
identity constructs, Soviet: degradation of, 33–39; development of, 27–33
ideology, as form of fantasy, 125, 138
Ilf, Ilya, 92–93
imagined community, notion of, 20
immigrant experience: Soviet collapse compared to, 50; *sovok* compared to, 50; yokel as reflection of, 26–27
I'm Not There (film), 156
intelligentsia: late Soviet, *sovok* as typical member of, 51–53, 57, 69, 108; in rich Russians' origin story, 119–20
Intergirl (film), 112
Internet: Bill Gates and, 88; *bydlo* on, 165n14; Russian Orc on, 138–39, 151; Sovok of the Week on, 45–48
Internet meme(s): Russian Orc Runet, 138, 139; Vatnik, 63, 72, 73, 75; Voronezh bombing, 1–2, 160
Internet Research Agency, St. Petersburg, 151
Internet trolls: and fascist tropes, 127; Orcs compared to, 151–52
Irony of Fate (film), 8–9

Jackson, Peter, 124, 127, 128, 147. *See also The Hobbit* (film series); *The Lord of the Rings* (film series)
Jameson, Frederic, 129
Jemisin, N. K., 131–32
Jenkins, Henry, 20
Jew(s): as descendants of Khazars, theory of, 66–67, 165n7; designation on Soviet internal identity papers, 86; *Lord of the Rings* revisionism and, 140–41

Jewish anxiety: Borat character as variation of, 26; self-hatred as variation of, 3–4, 5
Jewison, Norman, 124
Jigoulov, Vadim, 45
Jobs, Steve, 99
Joel, Billy, 82
Justification (Bykov), 66

Kalashnikov, Maksim, 137–38, 143, 146
Kamenkovich, Mariia, 134
Karlsson-on-the-Roof (Lindgren), 128
Karrik, Valerii, 134
Kartseva, Elena, 126
Kasta (band), 60, 61, 66, 79
Kaufman, Andy, 25
Kazakhstan, Borat films and, 25, 26, 164n1
Khavtan, Evgeny, 60, 61
Khazars, 64, 66–67, 165n7
Khort, Igor, 145
Kibirov, Timur, 12–13
Kobrin, Kirill, 163n10
Koestler, Arthur, 66, 165n7
Kolina, Elena, 84
kolorady, as ethnic slur, 73
Kol'tso t'my (Perumov), 136
Konchalovsky, Andrei, 56
Kondrateva, Elena, 115
Korobov-Latyntsev, Andrei, 149–51
Kostya Gumankov's Paris Love (film), 50
Krasnyi padavan (Dubchek), 145–46
Krasnyi vlastelin (Shkenev), 144
Krivov, Andrei, 151
Krupnov, Yuri, 137–38, 143
Krylova, Anna, 28, 32

Lacan, Jacques, 125, 151
Lapin, Sergei, 61
The Last Ringbearer (Yeskov), 136–37, 139
Law of the Lawless (film). *See Brigada*
Levada, Yuri, 38–39
Leviathan (film), 111
LGBTQI community, demonization of, 19
liberals: anti-Russian, projecting Orc traits onto, 149–50; patriotic, 22, 23; post-Soviet, negative identity constructs employed by, 16, 67, 74–75
"liberpunk" science fiction, 137
The Librarian (Elizarov), 140, 141
Limita (film), 112
Lindgren, Astrid, 128
Lipovetsky, Mark, 3, 92, 99, 101, 166n6
Liu, Hailong, 20
Liubit' po-russki (film), 110–11
live-action-role-playing game (LARP), Donbas as, 23

LiveJournal, and Russian Orc Runet meme, 138, 139
Living Souls (Bykov), 16, 64–67, 165n12
Lombroso, Cesare, 135
Lomko, Ivan, 151
Looking Backward (Bellamy), 24, 25
The Lord of the Rings (film series): first installment of, 124, 127; Goblin Studios version of, 141
The Lord of the Rings (Tolkien): Anglo-Saxon values in, 124, 126, 130; dualistic cosmology of, 125, 130; "evil empire" in, 17, 122, 128, 136; racist undertones in, 128, 130–32, 133–34, 167n3; resonance in Russian culture, 122, 127–29; revisionist fiction based on, 136–38, 139–45, 168n5; Russian audiences' response to, 124, 126, 130, 133, 136, 147–48; Russian nationalist reading of, 149–51; Russian translations of, Soviet subtext in, 134–35; Russophobic intent of, accusations of, 133–34, 136, 137–38, 139; and Soviet collapse, prediction of, 133; unofficial circulation in Soviet Union, 129, 133; war in Ukraine and references to, 146–47; World War II and, 128, 134, 141. *See also* Orc(s)
"Lord of the Steppe" (Tuchkov), 100–101, 102
Love, Russian Style (film), 110–11
Lucas, George, 124
Lukin, Andrei Iurevich, 75–77
Lukyanenko, Sergei, 145
Lungin, Pavel, 89–93

MAGA hat, *vatnik* compared to, 75, 79
Maguire, Gregory, 137
Maikov, Pavel, 112
Mamet, David, 156
Mamin, Yuri, 164n7; *Window to Paris* (film), 50, 55–59
Mamleev, Yuri, 37
Martin, Steve, 25
Marxism: on capitalism, 108; on class, 51, 97; on common people, 68; and labor as cult, 94; and nurture vs. nature, 35; and utopianism, 27, 28
masculinity: and affirmational fandom, 22; of New Man, 27; of New Russian, 83; and post-Soviet identity constructs, 17–19; of yokel figure, 25
mass culture: categories of, as interpretive framework, 20; dualistic Western, and Cold War imaginary, 122–23; and post-Soviet identity constructs, 16, 18, 157; Soviet, 122; Westernized, anxieties about, 3, 69
The Master and Margarita (Bulgakov), 52
The Matrix (film), 138–39

Matveev, Yevgeny, 110, 111
Mavrodi, Sergei, 105
Mayakovsky, Vladimir, 29–30, 98
McFarlane, Seth, 72
medievalism: alt-right and, 131; faux, Tolkien and, 131; new, 98–102
Medinsky, Vladimir, 22
Medvedev, Dmitri, 114
Medvedev, Sergei, 67–68
melancholy: and contemporary Russian identity, 7; racial, 6–7
meme(s). *See* Internet meme(s)
Menshikov, Oleg, 154, 156
Meshalkin, Leonid, 145
meshchanstvo, Soviet struggle against, 49
Miéville, China, 130, 167n3
Mikhalkov, Nikita: *The Barber of Siberia* (film), 154–59; *Burnt by the Sun* (film), 56, 154; Oscar hopes of, 154–55; in role of Tsar Alexander III, 155, 169n1
Milošević, Slobodan, 129
minorities: identity studies regarding, 3–4; parallels with Russian fans' experience, 135–36; in Soviet Union, 85
Mironenko, Sergei, 22
MMM pyramid scheme, 94–95; ad campaign for, 53–54; founder of, 105
Mochalov, Pavel, 144–45
money: New Russian and, 79, 84, 87, 95, 97, 102–3, 117, 166n9; after reforms of 1990, 95; rich Russian and, 117; in Soviet society, 95, 96
Moorcock, Michael, 128, 130
Morimoto, Lori Hitchcock, 20
Moscow-Petushki (Erofeev), 94
moskali, as ethnic slur, 73
Muller, Martin, 15, 163n7

Narbikova, Valeria, 37
nationalism: fandom compared to, 20, 21, 153; Swift's satire of, 21; transformational/affirmational binary in, 22–23
nationalism, Russian: and annexation of Crimea, 16, 76; and Orc phenomenon, 19–20, 147–49, 153; Putin-era, Vatnik as representative of, 16, 72, 73, 75, 76–77; and revisionist *Lord of the Rings* interpretations, 144–45, 149–51; and *Star Wars* fan fiction, 145–46
nation building, shame as form of, 5
Navalny, Alexei, 114
Nazarov, Yuri, 75–76
Nazis: Orcs modeled on, 134; in Soviet binary storytelling, 123; victory over, pride in, 42–43; war in Ukraine framed as battle against, 161–62

Nebesa obetovannye (film), 55
negative identity, 6, 63; process of alienation and, 16, 63, 67; reclaiming as point of pride, 17, 63, 67
Nekrasova, Natalia, 136
NEPman, 29–30
Nevzorov, Aleksandr, 147
New Economic Policy (NEP), 29
New Man: dystopian representations of, 29–32; limitations of term, 32; masculinity associated with, 27; NEPman as rival of, 29–30; New Russian compared to, 28, 98; New Soviet Man replacing, 28, 32; paradox of, 43; Soviet Man compared to, 35; utopian roots of, 28–29, 35
new medievalism, 98–102
New Russian(s), 16, 79, 82; American Psycho compared to, 102; business model of, 114; characteristics of, 84, 95, 102–3; as concept, 87–88; and consumer culture, 95, 103–6; and criminality, 17, 52, 79, 83, 106, 108–9, 112–13, 114; and culture, 100, 102, 106–7; decline of, resurgence of state power and, 109–10; as economic pseudophenomenon, 93–94; as face of Russian capitalism, 88; and feudalist fantasies, 98–102; as figure of urban folklore, 87; in film, 89–93, 108–9, 111; financial collapse of 1998 and, 113–14; gender of, 83–84; hint at masculine inadequacy in, 18–19; jokes *(anekdoty)* about, 103–8, 166n9; literary depictions of, 99–102; New (Soviet) Man compared to, 28, 98; North American robber barons compared to, 97; oligarchs as version of, 89, 93, 95; origins of term, 84–86; Putin-era successors to, 82, 95; rich Russian distinguished from, 117, 118, 120; romance novels and features of, 82–84; *sovok* compared to, 16, 17, 49, 52, 87, 95, 106; and taste, 95, 105–7; temporalities suggested by, 97–98; transformation into rich Russian, 110, 112–13, 119–20; and wealth, 79, 84, 87, 95, 97, 166n9
The New Russians (Smith), 85, 86, 98
New Soviet Man: New Man replaced by, 28, 32; New Russian as parodic counterpart to, 98; as political aspiration, 38
Neyolova, Marina, 156
Night Watch series (Lukyanenko), 145
Novak, Joseph, 34
Novodvorskaia, Valeriia, 145, 168n12
Novoe srednevekov'e (Berdiaev), 98

Okno v Parizh (film), 50, 55–59
Olesha, Yuri, 30–32

oligarch(s): as New Russians, 89, 93, 95; Putin and, 109–10, 114
Oligarkh (film). See *Tycoon* (film)
Olivier salad, 8, 9, 163n5
Orc(s)/Orc identity, 136–38; Internet trolls compared to, 151–52; mass culture and, 18; online, 138–39; as the Other, 132, 168n5; racism in depiction of, 128, 131–32, 133–34, 167n3; revisionism regarding, 136–38, 139–45, 168n5, 168n9; Russian appropriation of, 19–20, 122, 130, 148–49. See also Russian Orc(s)
Orki i russkie—brat'ia navek! (Meshalkin), 145
"Orkskaia"/"Orc Song" (Elizarov), 140–41, 143, 144, 146, 148, 149
Ormond, Julia, 154, 156
Orwell, George, 109
Osminkin, Roman, 8
Oushakine, Serguei, 13, 33, 83–84

paleoconservatism, Russian, 129, 167n2
parasite, social: New Russian as, 95; Soviet understanding of, 94
participatory culture, 20–21. See also fandom
"Party Like a Russian" (song), 80–82
Passage (Cronin), 166n3
Pasternak (Elizarov), 140
Pelevin, Victor: *Chapaev and the Void*, 66; *Generation P*, 127; "ork"/"urk" wordplay by, 142, 146; popularity of, 53; on post-Soviet intelligentsia, 51–52, 54, 69; *S.N.U.F.F.*, 141–43, 148
"The People and the Intelligentsia" (Blok), 68
Perumov, Nik, 136
Petrov, Evgeny, 92–93
Philosophical Letters (Chaadaev), 158
Platonov, Andrei, 135
Platt, Kevin, 12–13
politics: Cold War, entanglement with Western mass fantasy, 124–25; fantasy and science fiction compared to, 129
Polyanskaya, Anna, 151
popadantsy genre, 143–45
Poslednii kol'tsenosets (Yeskov), 136–37
posthuman, New Russian as, 104
postmodernism, late- and post-Soviet, 37
postsocialism: built-in limitation of term, 9; definition of, 10–11; end of, eagerness to declare, 12–15; messiness associated with, 14; perspectives on, 9–11; post-Soviet compared to, 11; scholars' discomfort with term, 10–11; as temporal framework, 15; viewed as global condition, 10; virtues of term, 11, 14, 15
post-Soviet: built-in limitation of term, 9; difficulty defining, 33; discursive void left

by, 13–14; end of, eagerness to declare, 12–15, 163n10; end of, joke regarding, 8–9; end of, Putin's declaration of, 11–12; meaning of, 8; postsocialism compared to, 11; virtues of term, 11, 14; weakness associated with, 15
post-Soviet Man, 33
pride: and identity formation, 2–3, 8; reclamation of negative identities as point of, 17, 63, 67; Soviet victory in World War II and, 3, 33, 42–43; transformation of shame into, Russian Orc and, 17, 19, 141, 143; transformation of shame into, *vatniki* and, 75–77
Prilepin, Zakhar, 42, 43
privatization (1990s), 88, 92–93, 94, 97
Prokhorov, Mikhail, 114
The Promised Heavens (film), 55
Pushkin, Alexander: *The Bronze Horseman*, 55; "The Stationmaster," 87
Putin, Vladimir: centralization of state authority under, 109–10; compared to Sauron, 146, 168n12; economic growth under, 114; on end of post-Soviet period, 11–12; historiography under, as state-sponsored affirmational fandom, 160–61; idea of Russophobia under, 62; imaginary world created and sold by, 129; "Nazi" (term) used by, 161–62; and oligarchs, 109–10, 114; paleoconservatism (term) applied to program of, 129; and politics of collective identity reclamation, 7; and *russkii* vs. *rossiiskii*, use of term, 163n12; and salvational myth of New Russia, 15; supporters of, identity labels used for, 67, 73; and war in Ukraine, 159, 161

racial melancholia, 6–7
racism: *Game of Thrones* (TV series) and, 136; *The Lord of the Rings* (Tolkien) and, 128, 130–32, 133–34, 167n3
Radishchev, Alexander, 104
The Rage of the Orc (Kalashnikov and Krupnov), 137–38, 143
Razlogov, Kirill, 126, 169n2
Reagan, Ronald: "evil empire" speech of, 17, 124–25, 126, 127, 128, 137; imaginary world created and sold by, 129
Red Lord (Shkenev), 144
Red Padawan (Dubchek), 145–46
Reitter, Paul, 4, 5
Rhys, Jean, 137
rich Russian(s), 82; *Billionaire* trilogy about, 114–18; New Russian distinguished from, 117, 118, 120; New Russian's transformation into, 110, 112–13, 119–20; origin story of, 119–20; romanticization of, 112–13; self-image of, contradictions inherent in, 119; song about, 80–82
Rich Russians: From Oligarchs to Bourgeoisie (Schimpfössl), 119–20
right-wing circles: crusades against Social Justice Warriors, 136; preoccupation with Middle Ages, 131; and Russian Orc identity, 138–40
The Ring of Darkness (Perumov), 136
robber barons, New Russians compared to, 97
Rodin, Vasily, 75
romance novel, Russian, 82–84, 166n3
Room with a View (Forster), 58
rossiianin: use of term, 14, 86; vatnik as, 72, 74
rossiiskii, use of term, 86, 163n12
Russian Ark (film), 55, 156
Russian Federation: Borat films and, 25; contrast with Soviet Union, 33; Soviet legacy and, 2
Russian Orc(s), 19–20, 130; *bydlo* compared to, 143; and culture, 17; as double projection, 152–53; imagined perceptions of Russians from outside of Russia and, 17, 19, 153; Internet trolls compared to, 151–52; as interpretive strategy, 18, 146; nationalism and, 19–20, 147–49, 153; online, 138–39, 151; pivot from shame to pride in, 17, 19, 141, 143; in revisionist fan fiction, 136–38, 139–45, 168n5; right-wing online circles and, 138–40; roots of, 133–34, 151; self-hatred and, 17, 139, 147–48; song about, 140–41, 143, 144; *sovok* compared to, 139, 146; war in Ukraine and evolution of, 146–47, 148–49
Russian Orc Runet meme, 138, 139
Russian Orthodox Church: Eye of Sauron art installation in Moscow and, 121–22; on Tolkien fans as "foreign sect," 133
The Russians (Smith), 85
The Russians Are Coming! The Russians Are Coming! (film), 125
russkii, use of term, 85–86, 163n12
Russophobia, accusations of: conspiracy theories and, 62, 129, 165n4; Eye of Sauron art installation and, 128–29; history of, 62; image of Vatnik and, 75; in *The Lord of the Rings* (Tolkien), 133–34, 136, 137–38, 139; in Western entertainment, 127
Ryazanov, Eldar: *Irony of Fate* (film), 8–9; *The Promised Heavens* (film), 55
Rykov, Konstantin, 114, 116, 118

Sakharnyi Kreml' (Sorokin), 98
Salt of the earth (band), 148–49
Saturday Night Live (TV show), 25

Saunders, Robert A., 25
Sauron (character): Putin compared to, 146, 168n12. *See also* Eye of Sauron
Schechter, Brandon, 161
Schimpfössl, Elisabeth, 119–20
Schreiber, Liev, 25
science fiction: Cold War dualism and, 123; politics compared to, 129; Russian, "liberpunk" subgenre of, 137
"The Scythians" (Blok), 138, 149
self-hatred: and contemporary Russian identity, 7, 15, 159; depathologization of, 5; and Jewish anxiety, 3–4, 5; libidinal logic of love and hate and, 4; post-Soviet successors to *sovok* and, 62, 63; and racial melancholia, 7; role in conspiracy theories, 62; Russian Orc and, 17, 139; Russia's war on Ukraine as form of, 160, 162
Sergeitsev, Timofei, 162
Shabelnikov, Yuri, 77
Shafarevich, Igor, 62
Shakhnazarov, Yuri, 40
Shakhter (Khort), 145
shame: and contested Russian identities, 3, 8, 16; individual and collective sense of, 5; Soviet and post-Soviet, Borat character exemplifying, 26; after Soviet collapse, 2–3, 18, 26; transformation into pride, Russian Orc and, 17, 19, 141, 143; transformation into pride, *vatniki* and, 75–77
Sharafutdinova, Gulnaz, 7–8, 38, 39
Shkenev, Sergei, 144
Sibirskii tsirul'nik (film). *See The Barber of Siberia* (film)
Sidorov, Aleksei, 112
The Simpsons (TV series), 21–22
Sinyavsky, Andrei, 62, 162
Siutkin, Valery, 61
Skvirskaja, Vera, 75, 77
Sleptsov, Ivan, 133
The Slynx (Tolstaya), 99
Smert' prikhodit po internetu (Tuchkov). *See Death by Internet* (Tuchkov)
Smith, Hendrick: *The New Russians*, 85, 86, 98; *The Russians*, 85
S.N.U.F.F. (Pelevin), 141–43, 148
Soboleva, Maja, 34, 164n5
social asthenia, 6
socialist realist hero, fate of, 110
Social Justice Warriors, right-wing crusades against, 136
socioeconomic class: Marx on, 51; New Russians and, 97; in post-Soviet Russia, stigmatized identities used as proxy for, 79; in Soviet Union, 96; in US, 96
Sokurov, Alexander, 55, 156

Sol' zemli (band), 148–49
Solzhenitsyn, Aleksandr, 40
Sorokin, Vladimir, 37, 98
Souch, Irina, 15
South Ossetia, reconstruction of, 1
Soviet: as nearly empty signifier, 32; *sovok* as slang for, 42–43
Soviet Man: degradation of, 33–38; idea of, 32–33; ideological function of, 39; movement to *sovok* from, 33, 39; New Man compared to, 35; sociological research on, 38–39; supranational nature of, 33; Zinoviev on, 34
The Soviet Novel (Clark), 110
Soviet Union: access in, role of, 96; alleged egalitarianism vs. elitism in, 61, 63; erosion of confidence in, explanations for, 3; as experiment in utopian identity formation, 27; labor as cult in, 93–94; legacy of, pride and shame associated with, 2–3; money in, role of, 95, 96; *sovok* as slang for, 42–43; value of production in, 88
Soviet Union, collapse of: chaos (*bespredel*) after, 109; conspiracy theories regarding, 11; crisis of homelessness following, 16, 64; crisis of naming following, 14; crisis of taste following, 51; identity crisis following, 2–3, 7, 157–58; immigrant experience compared to, 50; *The Lord of the Rings* (Tolkien) as prediction of, 133; loss experienced in, 13; melancholia after, 7; privatization after, 88, 92–93, 94, 97; process leading to, 13; shame after, 2–3, 18, 26; *sovok* after, 50–51; Western fantasy's capture of Russian popular imagination coinciding with, 124–25
"Sovki" (song), 43–44
sovok: ambivalence associated with, 49, 50; Borat character compared to, 26; built-in limit on life span of, 59; *bydlo* compared to, 67–69; catchiness of term, 40; characteristics of, 17; and consumer culture, 17, 45, 49, 50, 51; and culture, 17, 69; as diagnosis, 42; double bind of, 44; in film, 50, 55–59; Homo Sovieticus/Homosos compared to, 34, 37, 40; humor centered on, 45–48; love-hate dynamic associated with, 63; masculine inadequacy of, hint at, 18–19; meaning of, 42–43, 44; as member of late Soviet intelligentsia, 51–53, 57, 69, 108; memetic success of, 42; in MMM ad campaign, 53–54; movement from Soviet Man to, 33, 39; New Russian compared to, 16, 17, 49, 52, 87, 95, 106; oral folklore and, 40, 43; Orc compared to, 139, 146; origins of term, 40–42, 50, 72–73; polyvalence of,

42, 43, 62; post-Soviet successors to, 62–63; as slang for Soviet, 42–43; song about, 43–44; Soviet insecurities projected on, 16; after Soviet Union's collapse, 50–51; and taste, 47, 48, 51, 106; traveling, tropes of, 50, 55–59; Vatnik as successor to, 74, 76; Vatnik compared to, 72–73, 78–79
Sovok of the Week test, 45–48
Spengler, Oswald, 135
Spielberg, Stephen, 25
SpongeBob (cartoon character), Vatnik compared to, 72
Stakhanov, Alexei, 94
Stalin, Joseph: and category of "hereditary proletarian," 61; imaginary world created and sold by, 129; and New Soviet Man, idea of, 28; representation in *The Lord of the Rings* (Tolkien), 134; in Russian revisionist fan fiction, 144, 145; and "Soviet" (term), 32
Star Trek (TV series): political and ideological messages attributed to, 125, 135
Star Wars (film series): Anglo-Saxon values in, 124, 126, 135; Cold War politics and, 124, 126–27; dualistic cosmology of, 130; Russian audiences' response to, 124, 126, 127–28; Russian revisionist fan fiction based on, 145–46
state power, Russian: centralization under Putin, 109–10; merger with wealth, 111
"The Stationmaster" (Pushkin), 87
"Stepnoi barin" (Tuchkov), 100–101, 102
stiliagi, Soviet campaign against, 49
"Stiliagi iz Moskvy" (album), 60–61
"Strashnaia mest'" (Tuchkov), 99–100
Strategic Defense Initiative, 124
styob (ironic overidentification): Chadsky and, 77–78; negative portrayal of Russia in Western media and, 127; Vatnik as, 75
Surkov, Vladislav, 114
Svechenie (art group), 121
Swift, Jonathan, 21

Tal'kov, Igor, 43–44
The Tank Driver of Mordor (Mochalov), 144–45
taste: as cultural capital, 51; New Russian and, 95, 105–7; Soviet collapse and crisis of, 51; *sovok* and, 47, 48, 51, 106
Taxi (film), 25
television, identity constructs associated with, 16, 69–72
Terminal (film), 25
"A Terrible Vengeance" (Tuchkov), 99–100
That '70s Show (TV series), 25
The Three Sisters (Chekhov), 108

Tolkien, J. R. R.: disdain for political interpretations, 141. *See also The Lord of the Rings*
Tolstaya, Tatyana, 99
transformational fandom, 22; liberal nationalism as, 23; *The Lord of the Rings* (Tolkien) and, 131; and Russian Orc, 153
transition to democracy (transitology): notion of, 10; vs. postsocialism, 14
trickster(s): New Russian as, 92, 101; in Russian literature, 92–93
trolls. *See* Internet trolls
Trump, Donald: imaginary world created and sold by, 129; New Russian compared to, 87, 106
Tuchkov, Vladimir, 99–102, 118
The Twelve Chairs (Ilf and Petrov), 92–93
Tycoon (film), 89–93, 102, 112, 114

Ukraine: Chadsky's public art action in, 77–78; imperial attitude of condescension toward, 160, 161, 162; linkage of "orc" to, in revisionist fiction, 142, 146; Russian dismissal of existence of, 78; separatist movement in, 19. *See also* Crimea; Donbas
Ukraine, war in, 12, 159–60; anti-Nazi rhetoric and, 161–62; antisemitism and, 162; ethnic slurs gaining prevalence during, 16, 73; as extreme affirmational fandom, 23; meaning for Russia, 160–62; and Orc identity, evolution of, 146–47, 148–49; Putin and, 159, 161; Russian cultural figures supporting, 76; as self-hatred, 160, 162; Western media on, 121
Ukrainian(s): designation on Soviet internal identity papers, 86; inherent Russianness of, insistence on, 162
ukropy (dills), as ethnic slur, 73, 142, 146
United States: exceptionalism of, and self-proclaimed Russian Orcs, 17, 137; hostility toward, "negative identity" stemming from, 6; identity formation in, 27, 164n3; majority identity in, 3; "middle class" designation in, 96; racial melancholia in, 6–7; Russian interference in elections in, 62, 151–52; slavery in, shame associated with, 5. *See also* Western other
urapatriotizm (hurrah patriotism), Vatnik as mouthpiece of, 72
utopianism: and idea of New Man, 28–29, 35; Marxism and, 27, 28; politics and, 129

Vail', Pyotr, 41
"Varkraft" (song), 148–49
Vasilieva, Natalia, 136

192 INDEX

Vasyas (Vaskas/Vaski), 16; average person indicated by, 61, 165n2; in Bykov's *Living Souls*, 63, 64–67; connection to self-hatred, 62, 63; hint at masculine inadequacy in, 19; origins of term, 60–61; as proxy for socioeconomic class, 79; as successor to *sovok*, 62–63

vatniki, 16, 72–79; American version of, 75, 79; connection to self-hatred, 62; in contemporary Russian fashion, 75; hint at masculine inadequacy in, 19; as proxy for socioeconomic class, 79; reappropriation as positive image, 75–77; *sovok* compared to, 72–74, 76, 78–79; as Ukrainian ethnopolitical slur, 16, 73; visual image of, 72, 75

Vatnik Internet meme, 63, 72, 73, 75, 77

Verdery, Katherine, 10–11

veshchizm, Soviet rejection of, 49

Vesti (TV newscast), 80

Voinovich, Vladimir, 40

Volkov, Shulamit, 4

Volkov, Vadim, 109

Voronezh bombing, meme of, 1–2, 160

Vysotsky, Vladimir, 111

"Warcraft" (song), 148–49

wealth: accumulation of, narratives to sell, 87–88; imaginary post-Soviet identities and, 16–17, 79; merger with state power, 111; New Russians and, 79, 84, 87, 95, 97, 102–3, 117, 166n9

Weininger, Otto, 135

Western (American) other: hatred of, *vatnik* associated with, 74, 75; imagined alienating gaze of, Russian Orc based on, 19, 153; negative identity based on hostility toward, 6; Russian nationalist reinterpretation of *The Lord of the Rings* and, 147–48

Western popular culture: anxieties about, 3, 69; Cold War in, 122–23

Williams, Robbie, 80–82

Window to Paris (film), 50, 55–59

Winters, Joseph R., 6

Woe from Wit (Griboyedov), 77, 101

women (woman): concept of New (Soviet) Man and, 27; in first post-Soviet decade, 18; New Russian, 83–84; nineteenth-century Russian heroines, "terrible perfection" of, 31; Russia represented as, 18; as targets of Internet trolls, 151; and transformational fandom, 22

World War I, 24

World War II: and *The Lord of the Rings* (Tolkien), 128, 134, 141; popularity of superhero comics in run-up to, 123; pride associated with, 3, 33, 42–43; and Soviet storytelling, 122–23; story of Panfilov's guardsmen in, 22

Yang, Gene, 26–27

"Yarovrat" (Vladimir Georgievich Frolkov), 139–40

Yeltsin, Boris, 14, 109

Yeskov, Kirill, 136–37, 139

yokel: Borat character as, 24–26; as common global phenomenon, 26–27; as figure in popular culture, 26; New Russian as, 16; Second World, representations of, 25; Soviet/post-Soviet, 25, 26; *sovok* as, 16

YouTube, and *bydlo*, 69

Zamlelova, Svetlana, 128–29

Zelensky, Volodymyr, 161

ZhD (Bykov), 64, 165n7. *See also Living Souls* (Bykov)

Zhirinovsky, Vladimir Vol'fovich, 145

Zhmurki (film). *See Dead Man's Bluff* (film)

Zhogov, Dmitrii, 77

Zinoviev, Alexander: and Homosos, origins of term, 17, 34, 40; *Homo Sovieticus*, 17, 34–37, 38

Žižek, Slavoj, 125, 151

Znak kachestva (TV program), 69–72

Zubok, Vladislav, 6

Zviagintsev, Andrei, 111

www.ingramcontent.com/pod-product-compliance
Lightning Source LLC
Chambersburg PA
CBHW020237170426

43202CB00008B/112